ROCK & ROLL
Heaven

ROBERT DIMERY &
BRUNO MACDONALD

BARRON'S

A QUINTET BOOK

First edition for the United States and Canada published in 2007 by
Barron's Educational Series, Inc.

All inquiries should be addressed to:
Barron's Educational Series, Inc.
250 Wireless Boulevard
Hauppauge, NY 11788
www.barronseduc.com

Library of Congress Control Number: 2007922522

ISBN-13: 978-0-7641-6090-5
ISBN-10: 0-7641-6090-7

QTT.RRH

Conceived, designed, and produced by
Quintet Publishing ltd
The Old Brewery
6 Blundell Street
London, N7 9BH
UK
                    .

Project editor: Ruth Patrick
Art editor: Dean Martin
Designer: Graham Saville
Publisher: Gaynor Sermon

Manufactured by Pica Digital, Singapore
Printed by SNP Leefung, China

9 8 7 6 5 4 3 2 1

CONTENTS

Introduction	6		
Robert Johnson	8		
Hank Williams	10		
Johnny Ace	12		
Buddy Holly	13		
The day the music died	14		
Eddie Cochran	16		
Sam Cooke	18		
Bill Black	20		
Behind the scenes:			
Dewey Phillips	22		
Otis Redding	23		
Brian Jones	24		
Cursed band			
The Temptations	26		
Jimi Hendrix	28		
Janis Joplin	32		
Jim Morrison	34		
Gene Vincent	36		
Danny Whitten	37		
Cursed band			
New York Dolls	38		
Gram Parsons	42		
Mama Cass Elliot	44		
Nick Drake	46		
Tim Buckley	48		
Florence Ballard	50		
Paul Kossoff	52		
Phil Ochs	53		
Keith Relf	54		
Tommy Bolin	55		
Elvis Presley	56		
Marc Bolan	60		
Cursed band			
Lynyrd Skynryd	62		
Terry Kath	64		
Keith Moon	66		
Donny Hathaway	68		
Sid Vicious	70		
Lowell George	72		
Bon Scott	74		
Ian Curtis	76		
John Bonham	78		
John Lennon	80		
The fatal hand of			
David Bowie	84		
Bob Marley	88		
Randy Rhoads	91		
James Honeyman-Scott	92		
Dennis Wilson	94		
Marvin Gaye	96		
Cursed band			
Mötley Crüe	100		
Ricky Wilson	102		
Ricky Nelson	103		
Phil Lynott	104		
Richard Manuel	106		
Cliff Burton	108		
Peter Tosh	110		
Hillel Slovak	112		
Nico	113		
Roy Orbison	114		
Pete De Freitas	117		
Andrew Wood	118		
Stiv Bators	119		
Stevie Ray Vaughan	120		
Steve Clark	121		
Behind the scenes:			
Martin Hannett	122		
Steve Marriott	123		
Gene Clark	124		
Behind the scenes:			
Bill Graham	125		
Freddie Mercury	126		
Eric Carr	130		
GG Allin	131		
Frank Zappa	132		
Harry Nilsson	136		
Kurt Cobain	138		
Lee Brilleaux	142		
Viv Stanshall	143		
Eazy-E	144		
Selena	146		
Jerry Garcia	148		
Shannon Hoon	150		
Behind the scenes:			
Peter Grant	151		
Tupac Shakur	152		
Randy California	156		
Billy MacKenzie	157		
Brian Connolly	158		
The Notorious BIG	160		
Laura Nyro	163		
Jeff Buckley	164		
John Denver	166		
Michael Hutchence	168		
Carl Wilson	172		
Rob Pilatus	174		
Wendy O. Williams	175		
Dusty Springfield	176		
Rick Danko	178		
Mark Sandman	179		
Curtis Mayfield	180		
Big Pun	182		
Ian Dury	184		
Behind the scenes:			
Jack Nitzsche	186		
Kirsty MacColl	187		
John Phillips	188		
Cursed band			
Ramones	190		
John Lee Hooker	192		
Aaliyah	194		
George Harrison	196		
Stuart Adamson	198		
Zac Foley	199		
Layne Staley	200		
Lisa "Left Eye" Lopes	202		
John Entwistle	204		
Jam Master Jay	206		
Joe Strummer	208		
Mickey Finn	210		
Nina Simone	212		
Warren Zevon	216		
Johnny Cash	218		
Robert Palmer	221		
Elliot Smith	222		
Ray Charles	224		
Rick James	228		
Behind the scenes:			
John Peel	229		
Ol' Dirty Bastard	230		
Dimebag Darrell	232		
Syd Barrett	234		
Arthur Lee	236		
James Brown	238		
Top 50 Death Songs	244		
20 Reaper Cheaters	248		
Dangerous Occupations	252		
Index	254		

INTRODUCTION

The granddaddy of all deceased rockers was probably Orpheus—a prodigiously talented musician from Greek myth whose untimely death came when he was literally ripped apart by women. His head, though, continued to perform his songs as it bobbed along the river Hebrus, with his lyre—much in the way that an enterprising record company might milk a deceased artist's back catalog.

Right from the birth of rock 'n' roll in the 1950s, death has been an unwelcome presence hovering at the sidelines, rather like a tone-deaf backing vocalist. And well before rock 'n' roll, proto-rockers such as bluesman Robert Johnson and country star Hank Williams lived fast, died young, and left the requisite handsome cadaver.

Of course, many rockers have lived to collect their pension, and you'll find a fair few of them too in this book. Their deaths might have been unremarkable but their lives were a different story, and we nod respectfully to them here. However, most of our entrants died well before their allotted three score years and ten. No doubt about it, rock 'n' roll (or reggae 'n' rap, for that matter) can seriously damage your health.

Many of the stars covered in these pages met their unexpected end through sheer bad luck, and not always through their own actions—as Buddy Holly, Peter Tosh, and Marc Bolan would readily attest. The abrupt departure of others was eminently avoidable though, and often not unconnected to the rampant

ego, cocksure arrogance, and recreational substances generally associated with success in the field of popular music. Untimely demise is always sad, but rarely boring.

We can't hope to encompass all the residents of rock 'n' roll heaven within this slim volume, but we trust it offers an insight into some extraordinary lives—and, indeed, some extraordinary deaths. It also provides a dark treasure trove for trivia fans. Who was rock 'n' roll's first big-name casualty? Who bought the plane he died in from Jerry Lee Lewis? And which guitarist took the ultimate showbiz last bow by being shot on stage? By the time you finish this book, you'll know the grim truth.

In the meantime, may we finish up this introduction—and whet your appetite for the funerary fare to come—with some heartfelt advice? If you want a long, prosperous career in rock 'n' roll—and are not already a member of The Rolling Stones—try not to:

— engage in bi-coastal rap tiffs
— use heroin
— use airplanes
— join seminal U.S. punk bands
— indulge in drunken gunplay
— sell your soul to the Devil

Rock In Peace.

ROBERT JOHNSON
(ROBERT LEROY JOHNSON)
POISONING

Born: May 8, 1911
Died: August 16, 1938

Born in Hazlehurst, Mississippi, Robert Johnson's early years were characterized by regular jaunts from farm to farm with his mother, a field worker. Once settled in Robinsonville, Mississippi, the young boy soon became fascinated by the blues, learning Jew's harp and harmonica and pestering guitarists such as Charlie Patton and Son House, whom he heard at local clubs, to teach him their tricks.

By his teens, Johnson was a blues performer himself, and left Robinsonville, first to return to his hometown of Hazlehurst (where bluesman Ike Zinnerman became a musical mentor), then to gig intensely in the South (and even north to Canada). Blues songs are often laments or complaints, but many of Johnson's most memorable compositions—"Me And The Devil Blues," "Hell Hound On My Trail"—had a strikingly unusual dread at their heart, underlined by his high, rather unsettling vocals.

That darkness that worries away at the listener is, of course, part and parcel of the most famous myth about Robert Johnson, one that he spun himself. To explain his transformation from blues ingénue to master of the form, Johnson told the story that he had met the Devil at a Mississippi crossroads and had exchanged his soul for the ability to play the blues like no one before him (or since). The truth was doubtless more prosaic: former associates such as Son House might have been taken aback by Johnson's scintillating guitarwork, but natural ability and eagerness to learn probably account for his startling progress. He was a naturally gifted musician, and was as comfortable in other genres, such as contemporary popular songs and ballads, as he was in the blues.

No single version of the events that led to the end of Robert Johnson's life has ever been proved. Johnson had been a serial womanizer, and it's likely that he died—wracked in agony—having drunk whiskey mixed with rat poison by a husband he had cuckolded. (John Hammond had made efforts to trace Johnson for his famous *From Spirituals To Swing* concert in December 1938, without realizing he was already of the spirit world.) His grave site remains unknown.

The paucity of photographs of Johnson (only two confirmed) and his limited recordings—made in a San Antonio hotel room in 1936 and the back room of an office in Dallas the following year—only added to the mystery surrounding the man. His records sold poorly during his lifetime, but a 1961 compilation of his work, *Robert Johnson: King Of The Delta Blues Singers*, sparked the interest of a whole new generation of acolytes, mainly in the UK. Jimi Hendrix and Eric Clapton's Cream covered "Crossroads" (in 2004 Clapton released an entire album of Johnson covers, *Me And Mr. Johnson*), The Rolling Stones covered "Stop Breaking Down" and "Love In Vain," and Led Zeppelin reworked "Traveling Riverside Blues."

He was ahead of the game in other respects, too. Like Brian Jones, Janis Joplin, Jimi Hendrix, and Jim Morrison—all of whom produced music that owed a debt to him—Robert Johnson died at the age of twenty-seven.

RIGHT Robert Johnson with his famous Gibson guitar, in Memphis, 1935. Devil not shown.

HANK WILLIAMS
(HIRAM KING WILLIAMS)
HEART ATTACK BROUGHT ON BY DRUG AND ALCOHOL ABUSE

Born: September 17, 1923

Died: January 1, 1953

Country music made him its first superstar, but Hank Williams was a rock 'n' roller in all but name.

He spent much of his life in pain—literally; he suffered from the spinal column disorder *spina bifida*, and also claimed to have incurred serious injuries after two horse-riding accidents when young. Williams had his share of emotional pain, too, from a young age: his father died in a psychiatric ward and young Hank started his lifelong relationship with booze at the age of eleven.

Like Elvis and Jerry Lee Lewis after him, Williams had a strong religious upbringing. His mother was an organist in their Baptist church, and even after he'd made it as a country star, Williams continued to release moralistic songs under the moniker "Luke The Drifter." He left school young, in favor of guitar lessons from a black street entertainer called Rufe "Tee-Tot" Payne—hence the strong blues element in many of his songs—and formed his first band, The Drifting Cowboys, at the age of fourteen. Williams spent years playing honky-tonk dives in the South, and it wasn't until 1946 that he moved to Nashville, urged on by his wife Audrey.

He started off there as a songwriter for music publishers Acuff-Rose ("I pick up the pen and God moves it," he once said), but after racking up hits with "Move It On Over" and a cover of "Lovesick Blues" (a country No. 1 for sixteen straight weeks in 1949), he'd attracted enough attention to garner a spot on the *Louisiana Hayride* radio show. Country-music institution the Grand Ole Opry soon came calling, Williams got a show on radio station WSM, and by 1950 he was a country giant. Tracks such as "I'm So Lonesome I Could Cry," "Cold, Cold Heart," and "Hey, Good Lookin'" became instant country classics—Williams scored twenty-seven country Top Ten hits from 1949 to 1953. But they garnered even greater success when reworked as pop songs by the likes of Frankie Laine and Tony Bennett (whom Williams once called to ask, tongue-in-cheek, "What's the idea of ruining my song?").

Booze and prescription painkillers for his bad back undermined that success, however; even as his star was rising, Williams was earning a reputation as an unreliable performer—and husband. Like Elvis after him, he brought a new sex appeal to his genre, but his womanizing ways brought an end to his first marriage in 1952.

Hank Williams' untimely demise came on the way to a couple of New Year's Day shows at the Canton Memorial Auditorium in Ohio. Williams was in the back seat of a 1952 Cadillac convertible, driven by seventeen-year-old Charles Carr; in Williams himself were two shots of morphine, prescription tablets, and alcohol. En route in Virginia, Carr was pulled over by a policeman for speeding; the cop noted that his passenger "looked dead." So it proved: Williams' heart had given out. (Nashville frowned on scandal; the pathologist's autopsy report cited heart and neck hemorrhages and the cause of death simply as "acute right ventricular dilation." Some booze; no drugs.) His burial on January 4 drew the biggest crowd seen in the country for a century.

Hank Williams and Robert Johnson (see page 8): take them together and you've got the DNA of rock 'n' roll.

RIGHT Hank Williams just before his marriage to Audrey May Sheppard, December 1944.

JOHNNY ACE
(JOHN MARSHALL ALEXANDER, JR.)
RUSSIAN ROULETTE

Born: June 9, 1929

Died: December 25, 1954

He was rock 'n' roll's first-ever martyr, the prototype good-looking corpse.

John Marshall Alexander, Jr. joined the Teen-Town Singers on Memphis' black radio station WDIA in the early 1950s. A meeting with B. B. King saw Alexander become singer and pianist with B. B.'s group The Beale Streeters, then—rechristened Johnny Ace—strike out solo. With his plaintive voice, he soon established himself as a successful R&B ballad singer, racking up hits with debut release "My Song," "Cross My Heart," "The Clock," "Saving My Love For You," and (posthumously) "Pledging My Love," which topped *Billboard*'s R&B charts for ten straight weeks.

In common with many premature exits you'll read about in these pages, Johnny Ace's death was eminently avoidable. Following a Christmas Day performance at the City Auditorium in Houston, Ace was drinking backstage with some of the other acts, including Big Mama Thornton. With his girlfriend on his knee, firearm-loving Ace produced a .22-caliber "Saturday Night Special," pointed it at a couple of those present, and pulled the trigger; both times the chamber was empty. Not so when Ace pointed the gun at himself; after allegedly announcing "I'll show you that it won't shoot," he shot himself in the head and died instantly. Five thousand people attended his funeral at the Clayborn Temple AME church in Memphis.

A slew of tribute records marked rock's first casualty, including The Rovers' "Salute To Johnny Ace" and The Five Wings' "Johnny's Still Singing." Nearly thirty years later, the event inspired Paul Simon's "The Late Great Johnny Ace," a song that also served as tribute to another John who had died by the gun: Lennon.

BELOW Johnny Ace (left), blues guitarist B. B. King (third from left), saxophonist Bill Harvey(third from right), and singer Big Mama Thornton (second from right) pose with other performers at a 1953 concert.

BUDDY HOLLY
(CHARLES HARDIN HOLLEY)
PLANE CRASH

Born: September 7, 1936

Died: February 3, 1959

Along with Chuck Berry, Buddy Holly was the most influential songwriter/performer of the first flush of rock 'n' roll. He'd started out country, but after seeing Elvis Presley perform in his hometown of Lubbock in 1955, Holly switched to rockabilly—with dramatic results.

Starting with "That'll Be The Day" (a *Billboard* No. 1 in September 1957), he penned an unimpeachable run of gilt-edged pop songs, from up-tempo rockers ("Oh Boy!," "Rave On") to laid-back ballads ("Words Of Love," "Raining In My Heart"). Holly's command of the form was absolute, and his songcraft inspired a host of musicians, including the songwriting nuclei of both The Beatles and The Rolling Stones. Both groups covered Holly songs—the Stones memorably with their kinetic cover of "Not Fade Away"—while Paul McCartney later bought the rights to Holly's catalog. Indeed, The Beatles' insect-derived name had been in part inspired by that of Holly's backing group, The Crickets.

His songs were only the most obvious part of Holly's legacy, however. His famous Fender Stratocaster was the first used by a major star and inspired English guitar legend Hank B. Marvin to get his own. And Holly's bespectacled, unprepossessing appearance anticipated the rise of "geek chic" pop stars, including John Lennon, Elvis Costello, Jarvis Cocker, and E of Eels.

Holly's career was on the slide by 1959, though—he had split with The Crickets in October of the previous year—and it was his rocky financial state that prompted him to sign up for what would prove to be his final tour. Turn over for details on The Day The Music Died.

ABOVE Buddy Holly and the Crickets performing on *The Ed Sullivan Show* in New York, December 1, 1957.

THE DEPARTED

BUDDY HOLLY
(Charles Hardin Holley)
Born: September 7, 1936

THE BIG BOPPER
(Jiles Perry Richardson, Jr.)
Born: October 24, 1930

RITCHIE VALENS
(Richard Steven Valenzuela)
Born: May 31, 1941

ABOVE A poster for one of the last dates of the Winter Dance Party tour. Four days later, three of the main stars died in a plane crash.

Rock 'n' roll was still in its infancy when it experienced its first real taste of tragedy. And the impact of the event has held a unique place in rock history ever since.

On January 23, 1959, a strapped-for-cash Buddy Holly began a potentially lucrative twenty-four-date "Winter Dance Party" tour of the American Midwest which he was headlining. His costars were Ritchie Valens (then riding high with the double-sided classic "Donna"/"La Bamba"), The Big Bopper (who'd had a No. 6 hit in 1958 with "Chantilly Lace"), Dion And The Belmonts (about to make their big break with "A Teenager In Love"), and Frankie Sardo (enjoying success with "Fake Out"). The previous year Holly had parted company with The Crickets to concentrate on producing and songwriting, and for the tour he had a new backing band that included future country star Waylon Jennings on bass.

Bad weather saw the cancellation of a show in Green Bay, Wisconsin, on February 1, but a date the next day at the Surf Ballroom in Clear Lake, Iowa, went ahead. It was fearsomely cold; during the Surf Ballroom gig, Belmonts bassist Carlo Mastrangelo sat in for Holly's drummer Carl Bunch, whose feet were frostbitten. The tour bus had broken down once already and at one point, when its heater stopped working, they had burned newspapers in the aisle to keep warm.

Understandably frustrated, some of the party decided to charter a four-seater, single-engine Beechcraft Bonanza plane to fly to the next venue in Moorhead, Minnesota, at a cost of U.S. $36 each. Valens flipped a coin with Holly's

guitarist Tommy Allsup for a place on the plane with Holly, while Waylon Jennings exchanged his seat with The Big Bopper (who was feverish) at the last minute. On hearing this, Holly quipped to the bassist, "Well, I hope your old bus freezes up." In a phrase that was to haunt him for years to come, Jennings replied, "Well, I hope your plane crashes."

Shortly after its 1 A.M. take-off from Mason City Municipal Airport on February 3, 1959, Beechcraft Bonanza N 3794N encountered a blinding snowstorm. In the atrocious conditions, it seems that the pilot, Roger Peterson, began to misread the plane's gyroscope. The plane had only been airborne for a few minutes before it crashed—at about

170 mph—in a cornfield around five miles northwest of the airport; all on board were killed. So violent was the impact that the bodies of the three stars were thrown from the plane; guards were later posted to keep away sightseers.

"It Doesn't Matter Anymore," written by Paul Anka and released a month before the accident, gave Holly a posthumous UK No. 1, and Eddie Cochran paid emotional tribute to the lost rockers in his single "Three Stars" (Holly had been a friend, and Cochran's voice broke after the verse about him). But the most lasting tribute has been Don McLean's perennial "American Pie," a poignant reflection on rock 'n' roll and "the day the music died."

EDDIE COCHRAN
(EDWARD RAY COCHRANE)
HEAD INJURIES SUSTAINED
IN A CAR CRASH

Born: October 3, 1938

Died: April 17, 1960

Elvis was an icon, but he was no songwriter. In his wake, however, a host of A-list rockers proved that they could look good *and* pen timeless hits—and one of the best was Eddie Cochran.

Like fellow rocker Buddy Holly, Cochran had started off performing country hits of the day in a duo (first with bassist Connie "Guybo" Smith, then with the unrelated Hank Cochran as The Cochran Brothers), but made the switch to rockabilly, then to rock 'n' roll proper, inspired by Presley.

His first solo Top Twenty hit came with a cover of John D. Loudermilk's "Sittin' In The Balcony," but more typical of Cochran's style was the rousing "Twenty Flight Rock" as heard in rock 'n' roll cash-in movie *The Girl Can't Help It* (1956)—the girl in question being pneumatic blonde Jayne Mansfield. (In July of the following year, Paul McCartney used the song in his audition for John Lennon's Quarrymen.)

In the late 1950s, Cochran released a clutch of classic singles that became part of the lifeblood of adolescents everywhere. Any teenager could identify with the sassy, sharply observed lyrics of "Summertime Blues" (*Billboard* No. 8, 1958), "C'mon Everybody" (UK No. 6, 1959), and "Somethin' Else" (1959), each driven by Cochran's urgent strumming. There's a timeless quality to those songs—Blue Cheer and (more famously) The Who laid down supercharged versions of "Summertime Blues" for the hippie era, while the Sex Pistols (with Sid Vicious on vocals) scored two UK

No. 3 hits a decade later with surprisingly faithful versions of "C'mon Everybody" and "Somethin' Else."

Reaction to a Cochran/Gene Vincent tour of the UK in 1960 was feverish—years later, legendary DJ John Peel described the thrill of seeing Cochran at the Liverpool Empire as a lifetime high—and a new tour was immediately penciled in. First, though, Cochran was due to return to the United States for a two-week break. On April 17, 1960, following a concert at the Bristol Hippodrome, Cochran, Vincent, and Cochran's fiancée Sharon Sheeley (cowriter of "Somethin' Else") were heading towards London in a taxi. Near Chippenham, it blew a tire at high speed, sending the Ford Consul saloon skidding into a concrete lamppost. Sheeley suffered a broken pelvis; Vincent had his collarbone broken. Cochran, who was thrown against the cab's roof, then out onto the road, was less lucky: he died of brain lacerations at 4 P.M. on Easter Sunday, in St. Martin's Hospital, Bath. One of the first to the scene was sixteen-year-old police cadet David Harman, later to become Dave Dee of Dave Dee, Dozy, Beaky, Mick, and Tich. Legend has it that Harman rescued Cochran's trademark Gretsch guitar from the wreckage and played it at the police station for a while before returning it to Cochran's mother.

Eddie Cochran was buried on April 25 at Forest Lawn Cemetery, Cypress, California, but scored a posthumous UK No. 1 in June 1960. The song? "Three Steps To Heaven."

RIGHT Eddie Cochran with fiancée Sharon Sheeley, who survived the accident that claimed his life, in 1960.

SAM COOKE
(SAMUEL COOK)
GUNSHOT

Born: January 22, 1931
Died: December 11, 1964

Strikingly good-looking. Velvet of voice. Songwriting class in spades. A sharp business brain. Sam Cooke truly had it all, and before his untimely death he had established himself as one of the most inspirational black figures in the United States.

Cooke began his career as a six-year-old chorister in gospel trio The Singing Children at his father's Baptist church, and the emotional fervor of gospel singing was to remain an enduring influence on his vocal style; at high school he joined gospel troupe The Highway QCs and first made his name with gospel legends The Soul Stirrers, whose ranks he joined in 1950. The charismatic Cooke attracted droves of women to concerts with his looks and soulful voice, and became a giant in the gospel field by mid-decade, but before long he decided to strike out for better money in the secular world.

After a false start (as Dale Cooke) at Specialty Records, he moved to Keen Records, where "You Send Me" became his first hit. He set up his own SAR Records in 1959 (for both gospel and pop acts), racking up major smashes in the early 1960s with "Chain Gang," "Cupid," "Twistin' The Night Away," and "Bring It On Home To Me"—all Cooke compositions. RCA took on the rising star in January 1960, but after noticing discrepancies in their royalty statements, Cooke employed the services of Allen Klein, known for his terrier-like tenacity in matters financial (and later, for his role in the break-up of The Beatles).

Cooke's musical achievements weren't restricted to the world of transient pop songs. He loved—and covered—Bob Dylan's "Blowin' In The Wind," and took the song as something of a challenge: after all, Cooke was a member of the race whose persecution had prompted the birth of the civil rights movement.

LEFT Sam Cooke performing on *The Ed Sullivan Show*, 1957.

He penned his own anthem—"A Change Is Gonna Come"— a passionately delivered plea for racial harmony that more than matched Dylan's. It was a hit—posthumously.

Sam Cooke's demise was abrupt, unexpected, and shrouded in mystery. Back in L.A. in 1964 for the Christmas break, Cooke checked into the Hacienda Motel at 9131 Figueroa Street in Watts with a young lady—Elisa Boyer—whom he had met that evening at a restaurant, and with whom he had later visited a bar. Boyer was in her early twenties and may have been a "working girl." Shortly after they signed in, Boyer ran from their room, with Cooke's clothes, pursued by a semi-naked (and drunk) Cooke. Believing that the manager (Bertha Franklin) was in cahoots with Boyer, the singer shoulder-barged her office door open and demanded Franklin tell him where she was. Franklin told him to call the police, but Cooke was in no mood to argue, and after searching the kitchen area of Franklin's apartment, he returned and shook her by the shoulders. There was a struggle, but then Franklin grabbed her .22 revolver and fired. The first shot hit the ceiling. Two more followed, the second of which sent a bullet through both of Sam Cooke's lungs, his heart, and his shoulder blade. According to Franklin, however, he still came at her, so she swung a stick at him, breaking it in two over his head. And that was that.

Did Cooke try to rape Boyer, as she later claimed? Was she robbing him? Was he murdered (soul singer Etta James, who saw Cooke's body at the funeral home, attested that he was also exceptionally badly beaten)? As there were no other witnesses, we'll never know; indeed, the seedier details of his death were kept even from his immediate family for years.

Certainly, Sam Cooke's premature demise was deeply felt within the black community, and beyond. Around six thousand fans (including Muhammad Ali and Smokey Robinson) turned up, in freezing weather, to pay their final respects to an icon.

BILL BLACK
(WILLIAM PATTON BLACK, JR.)
SLIPPED INTO A COMA AFTER AN OPERATION TO REMOVE A BRAIN TUMOR

Born: September 17, 1926

Died: October 21, 1965

In the early 1950s, Tennessean Bill Black was playing bass with guitarist Scotty Moore in The Starlight Wranglers when Sam Phillips, owner of Memphis' Sun Records label, decided they would be perfect to back a new discovery of his: Elvis Presley. Black's initial impressions of the youngster were lukewarm—"Well, he didn't impress me too damn much. Snotty-nosed kid coming in here with those wild clothes and everything." Little did he know that they

> ## "Well, he didn't impress me too damn much. Snotty-nosed kid coming in here with those wild clothes and everything."

would join forces to create the most influential trio in rock 'n' roll. But in the Sun studio on the evening of July 5, 1954, the threesome created magic with their rockabilly take on Arthur Crudup's blues number "That's All Right (Mama)." They followed it up with a high-tempo cut of country standard "Blue Moon Of Kentucky"—two sides of the single that would launch Elvis and rock 'n' roll.

Bill and Scotty toured with Elvis at the very start of his meteoric rise, Black's spirited horseplay, such as straddling his stand-up bass like a rodeo rider, becoming a comic counterpoint to Elvis' suggestive stage moves. "Elvis was such an oddity, if you will, when people first saw him, they were practically in shock," Scotty Moore later reflected. "But Bill's antics loosened them up." Elvis' manager, Colonel Tom Parker, kept their fees pitifully low, however (perhaps irked that Black's onstage showmanship might outshine Elvis), prompting the two to quit in 1958. Thereafter, the bass player formed The Bill Black Combo, recording fourteen albums (five million units sold) in six years.

Tragically, Black was diagnosed with a brain tumor in 1965. After handing over his band to guitarist Bob Tucker, he underwent three operations; he fell into a coma after the last, on October 8, 1965, and passed away two weeks later at Memphis' Baptist Memorial Hospital. Elvis' autopsy was to take place there twelve years later.

RIGHT Onstage with The Bill Black Combo in 1962.

20

Behind the Scenes

DEWEY PHILLIPS
HEART ATTACK

Born: May 13, 1926

Died: September 28, 1968

ABOVE DJ Dewey Phillips photographed with Elvis and Natalie Wood after one of his shows in 1956.

During the early 1950s, DJ Dewey "Daddy-O" Phillips was responsible for introducing many white listeners to the hottest sounds of contemporary black music on his Memphis WHBQ show *Red, Hot, And Blue*. Phillips' off-beat humor, enthusiasm, and unpredictable behavior endeared him to his listeners. At its peak, his three-hour, six-nights-a-week show received around 3,000 letters weekly.

He was a close friend of Sun Records owner Sam Phillips (no relation), and it was to Dewey that Sam took the first single by a new Sun artist, Elvis Presley. Dewey played "That's All Right (Mama)" at around 9:30 P.M. on July 10, 1954. Deluged by calls from listeners, he played it again. And again. Eventually he got Elvis' parents to drag him in to WHBQ for his first-ever interview that same night. The

two remained good friends for years, until Dewey visited Elvis in Hollywood, purloined a copy of the King's forthcoming single "Teddy Bear," and played it on his show. RCA, Elvis' label, and Elvis himself were furious, and relations cooled.

Phillips' on-air eccentricities started spilling over into his everyday life, exacerbated by pills (amphetamines, and painkillers for injuries sustained in two car crashes) and booze. He was fired in 1958 and his final DJ stint, in Millington, Tennessee, ended when his amphetamine-fueled rap simply became too garbled for his audience.

Dewey Phillips died of a heart attack aged just forty-two. The funeral was held in the Memphis Funeral Home. Although the two had been distant for a while, Elvis came to pay his last respects to the man who had first played him on the radio.

OTIS REDDING
(OTIS RAY REDDING)
PLANE CRASH

`Born: September 9, 1941`

`Died: December 10, 1967`

Of rock's posthumous hits, few are less representative than "(Sittin' On) The Dock Of The Bay"—a wistful departure from the R&B for which Otis Redding was known. Its whistling (improvised to fill a missing last verse) provides a counterpoint to grim images of the singer's body being dragged from Lake Monona in Wisconsin.

Redding created an extraordinary legacy. He wrote "Respect"—immortalized by Aretha Franklin—and ended Elvis' reign as Best Vocalist in music paper *Melody Maker*'s readers' poll. He inspired acts from Peter Gabriel to the Stones. He put a show-stopping stamp on "Try A Little Tenderness" and wrote "Hard To Handle," a cover of which kick-started The Black Crowes' success.

In June 1967, The Beatles' kaleidoscopic *Sgt. Pepper…* entranced Redding, inspiring him to write "Dock Of The Bay" with guitarist Steve Cropper. In December, Redding and his band boarded a plane for Wisconsin. Its crash—cause undetermined—killed all on board except for trumpeter Ben Cauley, who was thrown clear while the icy water of Lake Monona claimed the others. Redding's body was recovered when the lake was dragged the following day. He was twenty-six years old.

The funeral was held in his hometown Macon, and Redding was laid to rest in Round Oak, Georgia.

"(Sittin' On) The Dock Of The Bay" became Redding's biggest hit and the first posthumous chart-topper in the United States. Acts from Talking Heads to Christina Aguilera have since cited his influence.

"He was a pure man," said Steve Cropper. "Anything you say about him has to be good."

RIGHT A surprise appearance by Otis Redding at Hunter College, New York, in January 1967.

BRIAN JONES
(LEWIS BRIAN HOPKIN-JONES)
DROWNED

IVA002 Brian JONES

Born: February 28, 1942
Died: July 3, 1969

Brian Jones cofounded The Rolling Stones, secured their early bookings, and supplied their name (from a Muddy Waters track) along with his scintillating guitar and harmonica work. With his air of innocence and luxurious blond locks—*the* mid-1960s male 'do, as copied by The Byrds among others—the ex-Cheltenham Grammar School boy also provided much of the Stones' early sex appeal ("The most charismatic member of the band [in 1964]," recalled Stones photographer Gered Mankowitz, "the star."). And, indeed, their bad-boy reputation. He had a taste for petty thievery (the striped jumper that became an early Jones trademark had been purloined from the wardrobe of another Brian—Pendleton, of The Pretty Things—with whom Jones was then rooming). By the age of seventeen—before leaving his hometown for London—he had already fathered two children; at the time of his untimely death, the number of known Jones offspring had reached five.

Jones was an extravagantly gifted musician, adorning early Stones releases with devastating slide guitar (stinging on "I Wanna Be Your Man," lazily seductive on "Little Red Rooster"), marimba ("Under My Thumb"), dainty dulcimer ("Lady Jane," "I Am Waiting"), and exotic sitar ("Paint It, Black") among other instruments. As the songwriting partnership of Mick Jagger and Keith Richards took off, however, he was forced to cede leadership and this, coupled with his relentless drug abuse (and several damaging drug busts) saw his fragile self-confidence—and musical abilities—badly shaken. His self-esteem was severely damaged when his girlfriend, Anita Pallenberg, ran off with Richards—though Jones' repeated abuse of Pallenberg hadn't helped his case.

The Stones underwent an artistic renaissance with their 1968 album *Beggars Banquet*, but Jones' presence on the record is negligible. At one point in the studio he had asked Mick Jagger, "What can I play?" "I don't know, Brian," came the waspish response, "what *can* you play?" Now an unreliable, spent power, he was ousted from the Stones in 1969.

As befits one of the best-known faces of his generation, Brian Jones' death inspired a wealth of conspiracy theories. He drowned in the swimming pool of his Sussex home, Cotchford Farm (once owned by A. A. Milne, creator of *Winnie the Pooh*) on July 3, 1969, after taking a dip around midnight; his girlfriend, Anna Wohlin, discovered him face down at the deep end of the pool, though she maintained he was alive when taken from the water. True, Jones was an asthmatic and traces of drugs and alcohol were found in his system—hence the coroner's verdict of "death by misadventure." But he was also a very strong swimmer...

In 1993, a builder named Frank Thorogood, who had been at the house that night, allegedly confessed on his deathbed that he had killed Jones (whom he disliked, and who had criticized his work earlier that same day) by holding him underwater. But that hasn't stopped the speculation. As Keith Richards commented, years later: "It's the same feeling with who killed Kennedy. You can't get to the bottom of it."

RIGHT Brian Jones performing at Alexandra Palace, London, wearing a trademark striped sweater.

THE TEMPTATIONS

PAUL WILLIAMS
Suicide
Born: July 2, 1939
Died: August 17, 1973

ELBRIDGE BRYANT
Cirrhosis of the liver due to
alcohol abuse
Born: September 28, 1939
Died: October 26, 1975

DAVID RUFFIN
(Davis Eli Ruffin)
Drug overdose
Born: January 18, 1941
Died: June 1, 1991

EDDIE KENDRICKS
(Edward James Kendrick;
later also Eddie Kendrick)
Lung cancer
Born: December 17, 1939
Died: October 5, 1992

They produced some of Motown's finest moments. But singers seeking to enjoy their old age should avoid The Temptations…

With the help of Motown's in-house songwriting genius Smokey Robinson, the five-piece Temptations racked up a string of classic singles from the mid-1960s on, including *Billboard* No. 1 "My Girl" (1965), "Ain't Too Proud To Beg," and "(I Know) I'm Losing You" (both 1966). Thereafter, under the wing of producer Norman Whitfield, they underwent a Sly Stone-style change of direction and produced a rack of psychedelic-soul gems, notably "Cloud Nine" and an incendiary snapshot of

LEFT Portrait of The Temptations taken in the mid-1960s. From left, Melvin Franklin, Paul Williams, Eddie Kendricks, David Ruffin, and Otis Williams.

RIGHT The Temptations performing during their induction into the fourth Rock And Roll Hall Of Fame.

contemporary society, "Ball Of Confusion (That's What The World Is Today)" (both 1969); Whitfield's epic production "Papa Was A Rollin' Stone" gave them another U.S. chart-topper in December 1972.

Baritone vocalist and choreographer Paul Williams had quit the Temps in 1971, suffering from sickle cell anemia and a liver problem, which was compounded by his abuse of both alcohol and drugs. Two years later, he was discovered dead in his car, in a parking lot near Motown's offices. Distressed by his ill health, personal problems, and owing U.S. $80,000 in taxes, he had apparently shot himself in the head. However, his family dispute this: the bullet entered the left side of Williams' head, but Williams was right-handed.

Elbridge Bryant's tenor was featured on a number of The Temptations' early non-hits in

the 1960s, but his booze-fueled mood swings swiftly made him a liability. In 1963, he smashed a bottle across Williams' face—narrowly missing his eye—and launched his own exit from the group (he was replaced by David Ruffin). Persistent alcohol abuse over the following years brought about Bryant's death, through cirrhosis of the liver, in October 1975.

David Ruffin had quit the Temps 1968, seeking a more soul-oriented direction and frustrated at Motown's treatment of its artists. His solo career faltered, however, and in 1982 he was back touring with The Temptations. In 1989, he was arrested for possessing crack cocaine; two years

later, he overdosed in a crack house; his comatose body was dropped off, by limousine, at University of Pennsylvania Hospital, where he later died. Forty thousand dollars in checks and cash, which Ruffin had with him in a briefcase on entering hospital, mysteriously vanished, and his friend Michael Jackson wound up paying for the funeral at Detroit's New Bethel Baptist Church.

Troubled tenor Eddie Kendricks was arrested at Ruffin's funeral, where he was a pallbearer, charged with owing U.S. $26,000 in child support to his ex-wife Patricia. Later in the year, he underwent surgery to remove his right lung, which had become cancerous

(Kendricks had been a chain smoker for thirty years), but the operation only postponed the inevitable. On October 5, 1992, he died of lung cancer at the Baptist Medical Center in Birmingham, Alabama.

Augmented by new vocalists, various versions of The Temptations continue to reap the rewards of the nostalgia tours to this day, though original members are now seriously thin on the ground. (From their inception in 1961, there had been 18 Temptations by 1997.) When Melvin Franklin (bass vocals) died from heart failure at L.A.'s Cedars-Sinai Medical Center on February 23, 1995, Otis Williams became the only original Temptation left alive.

JIMI HENDRIX
(JOHNNY ALLEN HENDRIX; RENAMED
JAMES MARSHALL HENDRIX, 1945)
ASPHYXIATION

Born: November 27, 1942

Died: September 18, 1970

Born in Seattle, the young Hendrix mastered the ukelele and harmonica before acquiring his first guitar—a U.S. $5 acoustic. (Starting with this first ax, the left-handed Hendrix always chose right-handed instruments, which he then restrung and played upside down.) By the late 1950s he had gravitated to electric guitar as a member of The Rocking Kings, but in 1960, an underage Hendrix abandoned music to join the 101st Airborne Division in Fort Campbell, Kentucky. His military stint didn't last long—he was released after injuring his ankle and back in a parachute jump.

In the early 1960s, Hendrix learned his craft backing a host of established stars, including The Isley Brothers and Little Richard (who resented the young guitarist's showmanship, and fired him). After a brief stint with Curtis Knight's R&B combo, Hendrix formed Jimmy James And The Blue Flames, and it was while playing with this outfit at Greenwich Village's Café Wha? that he attracted the attention of ex-Animals bassist Chas Chandler, who immediately offered to manage him. They flew to London on September 23, 1966; en route, Jimmy became Jimi.

With the addition of bassist Noel Redding (who had mostly played guitar in previous bands but switched to bass to play with Hendrix) and jazz-influenced drummer Mitch Mitchell, The Jimi Hendrix Experience was born, and promptly began slaying London's pop royalty. As an incentive to get Hendrix to London, Chandler had offered to introduce him to guitarist Eric Clapton ("God," according to a famous graffito of the time), but after Chandler got Clapton's group Cream to allow the unknown Hendrix onstage for a jam at the Polytechnic of Central London, "God"'s days appeared numbered. "He [played the guitar]

with his teeth, laying the guitar on the floor, playing behind his head, did the splits, it was incredible," Clapton recalled. After an Experience appearance at scenesters' club the Bag O'Nails— before a crowd that included various Beatles, Small Faces, Rolling Stones, The Who's Pete Townshend, and Clapton—singer Terry Reid met Brian Jones outside the men's room. "It's all wet down in the front," Jones announced, "wet from all the guitar players crying!" Some of Hendrix's stage moves—crotch thrusts, "humping" the amp with his guitar—were audaciously sexual for the time, and his personal magnetism ("The way he moved—he was like a cat crossed with a spider," reflected Motörhead frontman and former Hendrix roadie Lemmy) attracted women by the score.

Hendrix's debut single, a slow-and-sexy take on the murder ballad "Hey Joe," released January 16, 1966, stormed into the UK Top Ten; his next release, "Purple Haze," was psychedelia *in excelsis*, clattering drums, doomy backing vocals, and a jagged solo; third single "The Wind Cries Mary" dropped the pace, Hendrix almost crooning the vocal. Debut album *Are You Experienced* (1967) offered the exhilarating rush of "Manic Depression," the trippy title track, and slow-burning blues "Red House"; it made UK No. 2. A matter of months after arriving, Hendrix had turned the English pop scene on its head. America beckoned.

It's a measure of the impact Hendrix had already made that Paul McCartney urged the organizers of the Monterey International Pop Festival, staged in June 1967, to book him, and that Brian Jones introduced his set. Hendrix played a stunner, pulling out all his tricks (and famously burning his guitar at the end), stunning the crowd. It proved the perfect springboard for a U.S.

RIGHT Jimi Hendrix wields a Fender Stratocaster in Waikiki, Hawaii, May 30, 1969.

assault; sophomore album *Axis Bold As Love* (1967) made *Billboard* No. 3, and the following year his audacious reworking of Bob Dylan's "All Along The Watchtower," from Hendrix's 1968 magnum opus *Electric Ladyland* (UK No. 6; *Billboard* No. 1), gave him a *Billboard* No. 20 hit.

But success bred discontent. Audiences still clamored for the early showmanship that had helped Hendrix grab attention, but by now the guitarist was impatient to be appreciated for the quality of his music. ("I don't want to be a clown anymore," he told *Rolling Stone* in November 1969.) Moreover, Hendrix had eagerly embraced LSD early on, but as his drug intake increased through 1968 and '69, he strayed into cocaine and worse (in May 1969, he was arrested for possession of heroin in Canada). He also got very drunk very publicly and crashed a string of cars. Frustrated by the guitarist's increasing unreliability, and by the swelling numbers of hangers-on he now attracted, Chas Chandler quit as manager, shortly before Noel Redding's departure from, and ensuing break-up of the Experience.

"The way he moved—he was like a cat crossed with a spider."

Hendrix was the highest-paid act (U.S. $125,000) at the biggest gig of the 1960s—Woodstock. Backed by pick-up band Gypsy Sun And Rainbows that included ex-Army pal Billy Cox and Experience drummer Mitch Mitchell, on August 18, 1969 he delivered a jaw-dropping reworking of "The Star Spangled Banner," in which he mimicked the sound of sirens, screams, and bombs, referencing both the civil tensions then rife in America and the distant Vietnam War. It was his final triumph.

His last performance was a small-scale jam with Eric Burdon's band War in Ronnie Scott's jazz club in Soho, London, on September 16, 1970. Two days later, he spent the evening at a party in London held by ex-Monkee Mike Nesmith (in one of pop's great mismatches, the Experience had supported teenybopper favorites The Monkees, post-Monterey). Afterwards, he made his way back to the Samarkand Hotel—where he was staying with his current squeeze, Monika Danneman—for a tuna sandwich and a chat. He also took nine tablets of Vesperax, a sedative (half a tablet would be a normal dose), before falling asleep. The next morning, Danneman awoke and noticed that Hendrix had vomited during the night. Unconcerned, she went out for some cigarettes, returned, and noticed that he had now stopped breathing. After a frantic call to Eric Burdon, she finally summoned an ambulance, but Jimi Hendrix was pronounced dead on arrival at St. Mary Abbot's Hospital—from "inhalation of vomit due to barbiturate intoxication," according to the coroner's report.

Unsurprisingly, Hendrix's death attracted rumors and speculation. Danneman initially claimed that the paramedics who attended the scene had mishandled Hendrix, causing him to choke on his own vomit. Subsequently, evidence came to light that suggested Danneman herself may have been to blame for not calling an ambulance quickly enough, and many of her claims were challenged or discredited. The truth went with Danneman to her grave when she committed suicide in 1996.

He had asked to be buried in England—scene of his meteoric rise to stardom—but Jimi Hendrix was finally laid to rest in Greenwood Memorial Park, a cemetery in Renton, Washington.

RIGHT Not long to go: Jimi Hendrix in California, 1970.

JANIS JOPLIN
(JANIS LYN JOPLIN)
DRUG OVERDOSE

Born: January 19, 1943

Died: October 4, 1970

Like many of rock's mavericks, Janis Joplin grew up a misfit, seeking solace in painting and poetry as a teenager before music took over. She bounced between clubs in Austin, Houston, and the West coast in the early 1960s, spending time in the fledgling folk scenes of both San Francisco and New York, and acquiring an amphetamine addiction that nearly killed her.

Joplin's no-nonsense vocals owed much to blues goddess Bessie Smith; with passion as her watchword, the young Texan could whip from a fragile whimper into a frenzied wail, her sheer passion setting her aside from her female peers. At one point she was even asked to join fellow Texas outcasts The 13th Floor Elevators, but opted instead to return to San Francisco and college pal Chet Helms, who was now managing a band called Big Brother And The Holding Company, which she was invited to join. Initially signed to minor label Mainstream Records, the group delivered a storming set at the Monterey International Pop Festival in June 1967 (at one point in D. A. Pennebaker's movie of the event, *Monterey Pop*, "Mama" Cass Elliott is caught open-mouthed in astonishment). To capitalize on their success, Mainstream quickly released an album, the uneven *Big Brother And The Holding Company* (1967).

With Dylan's manager Albert Grossman now in charge of the band, they signed a new contract with Columbia Records, and produced the much-loved *Cheap Thrills* (1968, originally titled "Dope, Sex, And Cheap Thrills"), highlighted by Joplin's vocal tour de force "Ball And Chain" and featuring memorable covers of "Piece Of My Heart" and "Summertime," and an era-defining

cartoon cover by Robert Crumb. The album topped the U.S. charts for two months straight, but already there were tensions in the camp. Grossman advised Joplin to find a more accomplished backing group, and follow-up album *I Got Dem Ol' Kozmic Blues Again Mama!* (1969, *Billboard* No. 5) saw the debut of The Kozmic Blues Band. By this time, however, the insecure Joplin—already a renowned boozer—had begun to take refuge in heroin.

Another backing group—The Full Tilt Boogie Band—was formed for *Pearl* (1971, the title a reference to Joplin's nickname), which proved to be her most consistent set, and featured the song for which she is best remembered, Kris Kristofferson's "Me And Bobby McGee." Both album and single made No. 1, though Joplin died before either was released.

After a hard day in the studio with Doors producer Paul Rothchild, the singer headed back to Room 105 of the Landmark Hotel in Hollywood, to shoot up. Unfortunately, the heroin she'd bought was not from her usual dealer; doctors later estimated that it was around 40 per cent pure, whereas the purity of street dope would be only 1–2 per cent. She had previously overdosed five times non-fatally. Not this time. Her body was found the following day by her roadie, John Cooke. Joplin had died before completing vocals for the track "Buried Alive In The Blues," which was left as an instrumental for *Pearl*.

Hendrix and Joplin, gone within weeks of each other. And after Joplin's departure, our next entrant on the following page was prophetically heard to announce to bar buddies, "You're drinking with number three… "

RIGHT Hot Joplin: Janis Joplin performing in August 1969.

JIM MORRISON
(JAMES DOUGLAS MORRISON)
HEART ATTACK?

Born: December 8, 1943

Died: July 3, 1971

Sex and death: few subjects have attracted creative minds more consistently. In rock music, The Doors pretty much made them their own. They were helped, of course, by having a live-wire lead singer who seemed to straddle both those exotic worlds.

Jim Morrison developed an aversion to authority early on, bringing him repeatedly into conflict with his father (at one point the youngest admiral in the U.S. Navy). At Florida State University, Morrison studied Rousseau, Sartre, and Nietzsche, and began to formulate the radical ideas of freedom that would later characterize his lyrics. Later, as a UCLA film student, he discovered a like-minded soul in keyboardist Ray Manzarek, to whom he recited the lyrics of what would become "Moonlight Drive" on Venice Beach in 1965. Impressed, Manzarek suggested they form a rock band and make a million dollars. This—with the addition of Manzarek's friends guitarist Robby Krieger and drummer John Densmore—they proceeded to do. Their name—The Doors—came from the title of Aldous Huxley's classic work on hallucinogenic drug-taking, *The Doors Of Perception*, itself a quote from poet William Blake.

Debut single "Break On Through (To The Other Side)" flopped, but an abridged version of "Light My Fire" from their eponymous 1967 debut album shot to the top of the U.S. charts. Morrison swiftly became rock's psychedelic poster boy, a role that initially tickled him but one that he swiftly came to find onerous.

The Doors eschewed the sunny optimism characteristic of many of their West Coast peers. They were a dark band, Morrison's lyrics running to Oedipal musings ("The End"), apocalyptic visions ("When The Music's Over"), and angry calls to arms ("Five To One"). And his personal life was no less controversial. He performed drunk or stoned (live and in the studio), goading his audience, pushing the limits of what could be done on stage.

Things came to a head at a 1969 concert in Miami, at which a hammered, weighty, and bearded Morrison reportedly exposed himself. Promoters canceled future gigs and a lengthy trial ensued. The stress hit Morrison hard. In March 1971, eager for a break, the beleaguered singer headed for Paris with his partner Pamela Courson.

The events of July 2, 1971 still remain vague. After dinner with Courson, Morrison may have headed for a bar by the Seine called the Rock 'n' Roll Circus; he may have caught a Robert Mitchum film at the cinema; he may have simply returned to their apartment. According to Courson, the singer complained of feeling unwell, so she ran a bath for him. When she awoke the next morning, he was still in it—dead.

Or was he? Had the coffin been sealed before an effective postmortem could take place? Had Morrison faked his own death to escape the circus his life had become, and simply vanished? Had Courson given Morrison a fatal shot of heroin that night, as she later reportedly told Doors biographer Danny Sugerman? Or had Jim Morrison's much-abused body simply given up the ghost?

Whatever the truth, Jim Morrison's allure remains undiminished over time, and his grave in Paris' Père Lachaise cemetery has become one of the city's most visited attractions.

RIGHT A bearded Morrison onstage with The Doors.

GENE VINCENT
(EUGENE VINCENT CRADDOCK)
CHRONIC ILL HEALTH BROUGHT ON BY DRUG AND ALCOHOL ABUSE

Born: February 11, 1935

Died: October 12, 1971

While convalescing from the motorcycle injury that gave him his infamous gammy leg, Eugene Vincent Craddock taught himself to play guitar. He also struck up a friendship with fellow hospital patient Don Graves, paying him the grand sum of U.S. $25 for the rights to Graves' song "Be-Bop-A-Lula."

Still wearing a leg cast, Craddock played a number of gigs in his native Virginia and was spotted by DJ Bill "Sheriff Tex" Davis, who helped him to demo some material. Capitol jumped at the chance of having a rival to RCA's Elvis Presley, and "Be-Bop-A-Lula" was soon a smash. Vincent and backing band The Blue Caps provided a memorable performance of the song in early rock movie *The Girl Can Help It* (1956) and went on to score a number of hits. Vincent's black leather outfit (anticipating a look later sported by fan Jim Morrison—who later became a drinking buddy—and Elvis), greasy drooping forelock of hair, and impassioned delivery made him a favorite with rockers; he toured the UK with Eddie Cochran to great acclaim in 1960 and survived the same car accident that killed Cochran (see page 16).

Vincent continued to tour England and France throughout the 1960s, but his leg continued to trouble him, exacerbating his already moody nature. Rather than have it amputated, as advised, he killed the pain with booze and aspirin; his weight ballooned and his health declined drastically. In 1971, during a visit from his parents, he tripped, ruptured some of the ulcers with which he was afflicted, and began vomiting up blood. This most troubled of rock pioneers finally gave up the ghost at Inter-valley Community Hospital, Newhall, California.

RIGHT Sweet Gene Vincent performing at Calais Harbour, France, in 1960.

DANNY WHITTEN
(DANNY RAY WHITTEN)
DRUG OVERDOSE

Born: May 8, 1943
Died: November 18, 1972

When Neil Young was scouting around for a band to back him on his sophomore album, *Everybody Knows This Is Nowhere* (1969), he settled on The Rockets (soon to become Crazy Horse), a three-piece who shared a squalid home (and a love of drugs) in Laurel Canyon, California, and played dirty, no-nonsense rock 'n' roll. Guitar duties were shared between Young and the talented but troubled Danny Whitten.

Within the year, Whitten's escalating heroin addiction was giving cause for concern. Joel Bernstein, a photographer who snapped Crazy Horse in July 1970, noted, "By this time Neil had already had guitars ripped off and sold by Danny without Neil even *knowing* it." Whitten played on Young's breakthrough *After The Gold Rush* (1970), though he had a minder to make sure he didn't stray to the bathroom too often. The follow-up, *Harvest* (1972), featured "The Needle And The Damage Done," a harrowing and moving reflection on Whitten's addiction.

For Crazy Horse's 1970 debut album, Whitten had written the memorable "I Don't Want To Talk About It," but by 1972—when Young was looking to build a kick-ass rock band for a tour to blow away the singer/songwriter mellowness of his previous two LPs—Whitten was fading fast and proved useless in rehearsals at Young's ranch (he'd forsaken the heroin, but was boozing heavily). On November 18, Young gave him U.S. $50 and packed him off on a flight back to L.A. That same night, Whitten overdosed—on pure heroin, according to most sources, though some have argued for a fatal cocktail of diazepam and alcohol. In addition to his other problems, the recent death of his mother had devastated the guitarist.

"Don't Be Denied," featured on *Time Fades Away* (1973), was Young's response to the tragedy, and remains one of his standout compositions.

LEFT Crazy Horse in January 1970, from left to right: Danny Whitten, Jack Nitzsche, Billy Talbot, and Ralph Molina.

CURSED BAND
NEW YORK DOLLS

THE DEPARTED

BILLY MURCIA
Born: January 1, 1951
Died: November 6, 1972

JOHNNY THUNDERS
(John Anthony Genzale Jr.)
Born: July 15, 1952
Died: April 23, 1991

JERRY NOLAN
Born: May 7, 1946
Died: January 14, 1992

ARTHUR "KILLER" KANE
(Arthur Harold Kane, Jr.)
Born: February 3, 1949
Died: July 13, 2004

RIGHT New York Dolls performing in the 1970s.

FAR RIGHT David Johansen performing at Little Steven's International Underground Garage Festival, Randall's Island, New York, in August 2004.

38

Brian Eno remarked that only a few people bought the first Velvet Underground album, but all of them went on to form bands. Only a few people bought the first New York Dolls album, too, but a good portion of them went on to form bands, wear makeup, and/or take drugs. The Dolls themselves crashed, burned and, periodically, died.

Guitarists Johnny Thunders and Sil "Sylvain Sylvain" Mizrahi united with drummer Billy Murcia in high school. With bassist Arthur "Killer" Kane, and singer David Johansen, they became the New York Dolls in 1971.

Their somewhat shambolic music might have gone unnoticed had they not worn shiny stretch pants, platform heels, and more makeup than Alice Cooper. In much the same way as David Bowie was dumbfounding British audiences at the time, so the Dolls were enthralling the 1970s New York music scene.

One admirer was Rod Stewart, at whose behest they toured the UK. But at a party on December 6, 1972, Murcia passed out due to barbituates and alcohol. Endeavoring to revive him, partygoers poured coffee down his throat and put him in a bath, where he drowned. He was twenty-one.

Yet to release a record, the Dolls were already notorious. "I saw a picture," said Keith Richards. "They looked pretty. One of 'em died, didn't he?"

The drum stool went to Jerry Nolan and the band landed a deal. From "Personality Crisis" to "Jet Boy," *New York Dolls* (1973) was the most uproarious debut until *Never Mind The Bollocks* (1977). Shunned at home, where the album crawled to No. 116, the Dolls were embraced in Europe—and the seeds of punk were sown.

George "Shadow" Morton, producer of the Dolls' beloved Shangri-Las, helmed the prophetically titled *Too Much Too Soon* (1974). Sales were again catastrophic, partly because of the band's less than assiduous approach to touring in the United States. Thunders in particular was reluctant to stray too far from his hometown drug dealers. "He was this lovable loser," recalled Johansen, "Like a young Pacino character. He'd decided he was going to make a career of being a junkie."

Malcolm McLaren, the Dolls' new manager (later to manage the Sex Pistols), attempted to salvage their career— by portraying the band as Communists. The effort backfired, and Thunders and Nolan quit. The Dolls imploded in 1977.

Johansen reemerged as lounge singer Buster Poindexter. Sylvain and Kane sank beneath the radar. Thunders formed The

began a parallel solo career, yet classics like "You Can't Put Your Arms Around A Memory" were overshadowed by his addictions. Nolan, who got into heroin on joining The Heartbreakers, said in 1982: "Johnny—he's done much better when we were younger. We got a lot more accomplished without drugs than we have with drugs… I think he just needs a little bit more of a chance… "

Nolan also played with Sid Vicious of The Sex Pistols, who was living with the drummer at the time of his death in 1979.

Nolan himself died of a stroke on January 14, 1992. He was being treated for meningitis and pneumonia, just months after performing at a tribute concert for Thunders, who died on April 23, 1991, in a New Orleans motel room. Though authorities dismissed the death as a heroin overdose, Thunders had been on methadone, and it is speculated that dealers killed him. He and Nolan are buried at Mount St. Mary's Cemetery, New York.

Morrissey—a champion of the Dolls—asked Johansen, Sylvain, and Kane to appear at London's Meltdown festival in 2004. Kane was delighted to accept, despite his conversion to Mormonism (akin in shock value, said Blondie's Clem Burke, to "Donny Osmond joining the New

But within weeks of the show, Kane was dead. On July 13, the leukemia he'd been battling finally claimed him. The bassist, said Johansen, "felt that there was unfinished business, and he was so focused on that that I think it kept his disease at bay." The heartbreaking story is told in the 2005 movie *New York Doll*. Kane was replaced by Sami Yaffa of Hanoi Rocks—one of innumerable bands, from Kiss and The Clash to The Sex Pistols and the Libertines, to bear the influence of the Dolls. The band's twenty-first century incarnation, astonishingly enough, delivered a splendid comeback album, 2006's *One Day It Will Please Us To Remember Even This*.

"You can't bring back Johnny Thunders," said Sylvain, "You can't bring back Billy Murcia; you can't bring back Arthur Kane or Jerry Nolan. But you can certainly bring back that spirit."

GRAM PARSONS
(CECIL INGRAM CONNOR III)
DRUG OVERDOSE

Born: November 5, 1946

Died: September 19, 1973

Gram Parsons' family could have walked straight from the pages of a William Faulkner novel. When he was twelve years old, his father—songwriter and ranch hand Cecil "Coon Dog" Connor—shot himself. His wealthy mother remarried, but died of alcoholism on the day of Parsons' graduation from high school. His trust fund afforded him the luxury of devoting himself to his biggest passion: music. After a brief jaunt to study divinity at Harvard, Parsons dropped out and formed The International Submarine Band with some high-school friends; their 1968 album *Safe At Home* is today regarded as a landmark country-rock recording. His next band was rather better known.

Chris Hillman of The Byrds met Parsons one day in a Beverly Hills bank and invited him to join the band in early 1968. Parsons' presence bolstered the country accents in The Byrds' music, which peaked with *Sweetheart Of The Rodeo* (1968), the first out-and-out country album by a major rock group. Parsons was only a Byrd for three months, though, quitting rather than touring apartheid South Africa with the band.

Soon after, Hillman quit, too, and he and Parsons formed The Flying Burrito Brothers, enlisting the support of Chris Ethridge and "Sneaky" Pete Kleinow, with a view to creating music that joined all the dots between folk, country, soul, and rock 'n' roll —"Cosmic American music," in Parsons' famous phrase. *The Gilded Palace Of Sin* (1969) remains a country-rock landmark, its bittersweet songs highlighted by Parsons' tender, rather high vocals. With an arresting debut album, Parsons' pretty-boy good looks, and the band's flash Nudie suits (pitched somewhere between Hank Williams and Elvis' Vegas attire), they had the makings of stars. Instead, a string of under-rehearsed shows and Parsons' increasingly wayward behavior (plus the distraction of his growing friendship with Keith Richards) saw the Burritos' early promise fizzle away in 1970.

Parsons' solo career got off to a promising start: after an initial unproductive relationship with A&M Records, he signed with Reprise and his first solo album, *GP*, was released in 1973, to a favorable critical (but poor commercial) reception. His posthumously released album *Grievous Angel* (1974)— on which he was beautifully partnered by future country queen Emmylou Harris— remains highly regarded. He never lived to deliver on that potential, though.

Parsons' friend, the gifted country-rock guitarist (and fellow ex-Byrd) Clarence White, had been run over on July 14, 1973. Visibly upset by the rites at the funeral, Parsons later told his road manager, Phil Kaufman, that when his time came he wanted to be cremated. A couple of months later, Parsons and three friends checked into the Joshua Tree Inn. Parsons never checked out—he overdosed in Room Eight of the inn in the late hours of September 18. Morphine, cocaine, amphetamine, and alcohol were found in his system. ("He was so full of poison I about died myself," commented Al Barbary, son of the inn's manager.) But that wasn't the end of the drama.

Mindful of Parsons' words to him, Phil Kaufman and roadie Michael Martin intercepted the body en route to New Orleans at Van Nuys airport, California—cockily signing the release papers "Jeremy Nobody"—loaded it into a hearse, and set off for the Joshua Tree monument, near L.A. There, they poured gasoline on the deceased singer and set fire to his body, granting his final wish. (They were later arrested on a misdemeanor charge—"Gram Theft Parsons," in Kaufman's words.) Parsons' remains were subsequently interred in the Garden of Memories cemetery in Metairie, Louisiana. The headstone above reads "God's Own Singer."

RIGHT The Grievous Angel, 1970.

MAMA CASS ELLIOT
(ELLEN NAOMI COHEN)
HEART ATTACK

Born: September 19, 1941

Died: July 29, 1974

Ozzy Osbourne never bit the head off a bat, The White Stripes were not born of the same womb, and Mama Cass did not choke to death on a ham sandwich. She did, however, guest in *Scooby-Doo*, which makes her at least as cool as Jack White and company.

Though best remembered as one quarter of The Mamas And The Papas, Cass Elliot (born Ellen Naomi Cohen) was a much-loved star in her own right. The group's final major hit—after classics like "California Dreamin'" and "Dedicated To The One I Love"—was Elliot's take on "Dream A Little Dream Of Me." It showcased the soprano skills that were a pivotal element of the group's harmonies, and which she allegedly acquired after being concussed. "It's true," she insisted to *Rolling Stone*. "I did get hit on the head by a pipe that fell down and my range increased by three notes."

Elliot also had solo hits, appeared in the 1970 movie *Pufnstuf*, collaborated with Traffic's Dave Mason, and became a U.S. chat show regular, even guest-hosting *The Tonight Show Starring Johnny Carson*. She made fruitless attempts to distance herself from the "Mama" moniker too. "I hated it," she told *Rolling Stone*. "Everybody'd say, Hey, Mama, what's happening? Then came the Mamas and Papas and I was stuck with it. And now people call me Mama Cass because of the baby." (Elliot's daughter Owen now runs a website about her mother.)

In 1974, she visited Britain for sold-out engagements at the London Palladium. After the rapturously received sets, she called fellow "Mama" Michelle Phillips. Through tears and champagne, she expressed her elation at becoming a star in her own right. The next day she was dead of a heart attack. She was thirty-two.

A newspaper report that a half-eaten sandwich was found at her Mayfair apartment triggered the myth that trivialized her reputation for decades. Elliot's death on July 29, 1974, was due to obesity that had loomed throughout her life. "What Streisand did for Jewish girls in Brooklyn," *Esquire* ventured, "Cass Elliot was doing for fat girls everywhere."

Yet her "larger than life" persona came to mean more than physical size. Charismatic, opinionated ("I think everybody who has a brain should get involved in politics."), and cheerful ("I could have been a pharmacist. I'd make a good one. I'm jolly."), she was a welcome contrast to the era's other 1960s survivors.

Her body was flown back to the United States and cremated. Her ashes are at Mount Sinai Memorial Park Cemetery in The Mamas And The Papas' spiritual home, Los Angeles (Elliot herself was from Baltimore), where her neighbors include Red Hot Chili Peppers' guitarist Hillel Slovak (see page 112).

Asked what she would be doing when her daughter grew up, Elliot said, "I hope they don't ask me to sing. But if that's what they want me to do, I'll do it."

LEFT Mama Cass posing for a promotional shoot for her television special *Don't Call Me Mama Anymore*, September, 1973.

NICK DRAKE
(NICHOLAS RODNEY DRAKE)
SUICIDE BY DRUG OVERDOSE?

Born: June 19, 1948

Died: November 25, 1974

"I don't think he wanted to be a star," Nick Drake's mother said in 1979, "and I don't honestly think he was the least interested in money. But I think he had this feeling that he'd got something to say to the people of his own generation. He desperately wanted to communicate with them—feeling that he could make them happier, that he could make things better for them—and he didn't feel that he did that."

Of all the artists in this book, few have left so unimpeachable a legacy as Nick Drake. The albums issued in his lifetime—1969's *Five Leaves Left*, 1970's *Bryter Layter*, and 1972's *Pink Moon*—are almost unbearably beautiful. And so lovely are songs like "Northern Sky," it is easy to forget the warm-voiced singer was the most ill-suited person to enter the industry until Kurt Cobain.

Like Cobain—and Syd Barrett, with whom he is often compared—Drake desired success, yet abhorred the conventions of his profession. However, unlike Cobain and Barrett, Drake experienced scant success in his lifetime. His albums sold negligibly and he was so dissatisfied with playing live that, after a few British dates, he gave it up. Depressed at what he regarded as his own failure, Drake recorded *Pink Moon* in just two days, then retreated to the family home in Tanworth-in-Arden, in England's Warwickshire.

Antidepressants finally propelled him back to the studio in 1974, and he even left the shires for a barge in France (making an abortive attempt to work with chanteuse Françoise Hardy). Newly optimistic, Drake returned home to England—only to die on November 25, 1974, of an overdose of antidepressants. He was twenty-six years old.

Though the coroner ruled it a suicide, it is plausible he mistook the tablets for sleeping pills. *NME*'s Nick Kent certainly thought so, Drake having left no suicide note, "no grand flourish which so often tends to typify the self-imposed taking of one's life." Drake himself dismissed suicide as a cowardly act for which he nonetheless lacked the courage.

However, the artist's sister Gabrielle (a British television actress) declared: "I personally prefer to think Nick committed suicide. I'd rather he died because he wanted to end it than it to be the result of a tragic mistake."

Ignored in his lifetime, Drake has since been rediscovered, via retrospectives such as 1979's *Fruit Tree*, soundtracks (most recently, "One Of These Things First" on *Garden State*, 2004) and artists such as Blur's Graham Coxon ("I wish I could bring Nick Drake back to life," he sang on the *Sky Is Too High* album, 1998). There was a marked increase in Drake's record sales in the United States following the use of "Pink Moon" in a Volkswagen television commercial, and he now has a cult following.

Drake is buried in Tanworth-in-Arden. "Inside the church next to the cemetery is a magnificent pipe organ" wrote T. J. McGrath in a 1992 article for U.S. magazine *Dirty Linen*. "Once a year the church organist plans a special recital of Nick Drake's songs. They say you can hear the singing for miles around, and I know Nick would have liked that."

RIGHT Nick Drake, for many the archetypal English singer-songwriter, in reflective mood.

TIM BUCKLEY
(TIMOTHY CHARLES BUCKLEY III)
DRUG OVERDOSE

Born: February 14, 1947

Died: June 29, 1975

After working his way around California's folk-club circuit, Buckley delivered an eponymous debut album (charming, if a bit stilted) for Elektra Records in 1966. From then on, the singer charted a path unique in contemporary music. Sophomore release *Goodbye And Hello* (1967) saw more intricate, baroque arrangements framing a voice alternately fragile and intimate ("Once I Was"), biting ("Pleasant Street"), and eye-poppingly explosive ("I Never Asked To Be Your Mountain"). Buckley's influences were wide-ranging—as a teenager he subscribed to fabled folk mag *Sing Out!* while lapping up Sinatra, Hank Williams, and Johnny Cash; he also used his five-octave range to indulge in the free-flowing curlicues of traditional Turkish music.

During the course of his prolific output (nine albums in nine years), Buckley never repeated himself. *Happy Sad* (1969—his bestseller, making No. 81 in the *Billboard* album charts) had a relaxed, sometimes melancholic jazziness to it (witness the mesmerizing vocal swoops of "Buzzin' Fly"). The intense *Lorca* (1970) threw up dark reflections on the storms of love, its music heading toward the avant-garde experimentation of *Starsailor* (1970), by which time Buckley was sacrificing melody in favor of fierce atonal expressionism more readily associated with the likes of Captain Beefheart. But at the calm eye of that tempest lay "Song To The Siren," a spellbinding reflection on love inspired by Homer's *Odyssey*, probably his finest song. A revival in Buckley's popularity during the 1980s was partly due to a sublime cover of "Song To The Siren" by This Mortal Coil. Guest singer Elizabeth Fraser—who was singer with the Cocteau Twins—was later to have an affair with Tim's son Jeff. (Oddly enough, though Tim wrote the

song, the first recorded version was by 1950s white-bread crooner Pat Boone in 1969.)

Needless to say, at a time when laid-back West Coast navel-gazers ruled the roost, Tim Buckley was triumphantly out of step. Disillusioned, at one point the singer briefly abandoned music to become chauffeur to Sly Stone, whose own musical output may have inspired Buckley's next move. The funked-up *Greetings From L.A.* (1972) found the one-time tender troubadour horny as a dog, delivering paeans to down-'n'-dirty sex in the city, vocals whipped up with moans and ecstatic whoops. Not an easy listen, but perversely captivating.

Perhaps unsurprisingly, given the willful career trajectory he carved, Tim Buckley rarely troubled the charts. Token efforts to temper his talents toward more mainstream success (1973's *Sefronia*, 1974's *Look At The Fool*) sounded unconvincing—and still died commercial deaths.

Tim Buckley was no stranger to drugs, though by 1975 he had taken steps to clean up his act. Nevertheless, he celebrated the end of a tour by imbibing heroin and alcohol at a friend's house; perhaps, as some have speculated, he'd mistaken the heroin for cocaine. The toxic cocktail rapidly took effect, and a clearly unwell Buckley was taken to his wife's house and put to bed. When she looked in on him later, he had turned blue, dead of "acute heroin-morphine and ethanol intoxication" (i.e. an overdose) in the words of an L.A. medical examiner.

Only one other singer/songwriter has a claim to equaling the panoramic glory of Tim Buckley's voice. And funnily enough, he was his son…

LEFT Yawning glory: Tim Buckley on stage at Knebworth, England, in 1974.

FLORENCE BALLARD
(FLORENCE GLENDA BALLARD)
CORONARY THROMBOSIS

Born: June 30, 1943
Died: February 22, 1976

When Jennifer Hudson won a Golden Globe for her role in *Dreamgirls*, she dedicated the award to Florence Ballard. It was overdue acknowledgment for a woman who founded one of pop's most successful acts, yet died—ousted, overshadowed, and broke—at thirty-two.

Ballard recruited Mary Wilson and Diana Ross for The Primettes, protégées of The Primes (later The Temptations). Dogged persistence found them signed to Motown, where their in-house nickname was the "no-hit Supremes," Ballard having chosen the name from a list provided by Motown boss Berry Gordy. After three years of negligible success, the trio hit in 1964 with "Where Did Our Love Go?". It triggered a record-breaking run that made them the most successful girl group until Destiny's Child and the Spice Girls.

But Ballard's position was constantly threatened. Considering his girlfriend Ross' vocals more palatable to white America, Gordy made her the figurehead. Mary Wilson admitted that Ballard—possessor of the strongest voice—stood 17 feet from studio microphones, while the other two stayed close. Ballard was even robbed of her onstage showcase when the blockbuster "People" was assigned to Ross instead.

Resentful, she turned to drink. Then, increasingly unreliable and ill-suited to the figure-hugging costumes for which the band was famed, Ballard was ousted in July 1967. She would later unsuccessfully sue Motown for her "subversively and maliciously plotted" dismissal, and the "meager" settlement.

Mismanaged and contractually forbidden from trading on the Motown or Supremes names, her career faltered. By 1974, she

was forced to apply for welfare. Ironically, this returned her to the spotlight—the contrast with Diana Ross' fortunes could not have been greater.

Rebuilding her life with the settlement from an accident, Ballard appeared to be recovering. But—just one day after entering hospital complaining of numbness—she died on February 22, 1976, killed by a coronary blood clot. A misleading police report said she had "ingested an unknown amount of pills and consumed alcohol." (The pills were, doctors confirmed, to combat weight and blood pressure.)

To the derision of Ballard's fans, Diana Ross sent a wreath inscribed, "I love you Blondie [Ballard's nickname]" and attended a memorial service led by Aretha Franklin's father, Reverend C. L. Franklin. Thousands lined the street, obliging police to ward them off with floral arrangements. Ballard's pallbearers included Stevie Wonder, the irony of whose role was eclipsed when the organist played "Someday We'll Be Together," a Supremes song on which session musicians filled Ballard and Mary Wilson's places.

Ballard was laid to rest in her hometown, Detroit. Her headstone describes her as a "beloved wife and mother," with just two musical notes representing her pivotal role in pop history.

And so she lay, doomed to ancillary status in the legend of The Supremes, until the *Dreamgirls* movie, thirty years after her death. Based on the band's story, it starred Beyoncé, yet supporting actress Jennifer Hudson won the awards. Let's hope Ballard is finally smiling in satisfaction.

RIGHT One of Ballard's final performances with The Supremes in 1967. From left to right: Diana Ross, Florence Ballard, and Mary Wilson.

PAUL KOSSOFF
CEREBRAL AND PULMONARY EDEMA

Born: September 14, 1950

Died: March 19, 1976

"Paul Kossoff is alive," reported UK music paper *Sounds* in November 1975, "and as well as anyone could be after being at death's door only a few weeks ago." Less than five months later, the same writer had to write an obituary: "What can you do but grieve. No one should have hurt like that for the sake of playing great guitar licks." Paul Kossoff was twenty-five years old.

He was turned on to electric blues when he saw Eric Clapton in concert and, working in a London music shop, met Jimi Hendrix. With Simon Kirke, Paul Rodgers, and Andy Fraser, he formed Free—one of the most fondly remembered rock acts of the early 1970s. "The music should come from the soul and be simple and straightforward so everyone can enjoy it," said Kossoff, "and this is why we're going down well."

Still in his teens, he was good enough to audition for the Stones and Jethro Tull, and even asked to demonstrate his distinctive *vibrato* by Clapton. Meanwhile, Free's live following translated into mainstream success with 1970's transatlantic smash "All Right Now." "We were hell-bent on what we did," said Rodgers. "I didn't care if I lived or died but for the band."

With success came pressure. Musical differences were exacerbated by Kossoff's fondness for Quaaludes and his depression after the death of Hendrix. Free splintered into solo projects (hence Kossoff's 1973 album *Back Street Crawler*) before reconvening in 1972. "That year, when the band was apart, was when Koss really got into a lot of dope," manager John Glover told interviewer Dave McNarie. "It really screwed him up from then onwards. From what his father [actor David Kossoff] said, he was doing dope from the age of ten or twelve."

Free eked out two more albums, and another classic single, "Wishing Well." But on 1973's *Heartbreaker*, Rodgers and session musician Snuffy Walden had to fill in on guitar and, on a final U.S. tour, Wendell Richardson of Osibisa replaced Kossoff.

While Rodgers and Kirke won stratospheric success with Bad Company, Kossoff's career dwindled. His band, also called Back Street Crawler, managed two albums but, in rehab in London in 1975, his heart stopped for half an hour. Then, on a flight from L.A. to New York on March 19, 1976, he was killed by a build-up of fluid in the brain and lungs, induced by his damaged heart. "I don't think it was a genuine OD," said manager Glover. "Paul could take a lot of dope and it wouldn't make a lot of difference. It was just one of those things. He'd abused his system badly."

Back Street Crawler struggled on, finding coffins left outside their dressing rooms. Among the band's support acts were AC/DC, making their UK debut—a bittersweet honor for Kossoff-loving guitarist Angus Young.

Still remembered with awe as a guitarist, Kossoff helped create—in "All Right Now"—an anthem that will outlive us all.

LEFT The re-formed Free performing at the Fairfield Hall on September 10, 1972, Croydon, London.

PHIL OCHS
(PHILIP DAVID OCHS)
SUICIDE BY HANGING

Born: December 19, 1940

Died: April 9, 1976

Phil Ochs worked the same Greenwich Village folk-club circuit as Bob Dylan in the early 1960s, but politics remained a cornerstone of Ochs' oeuvre long after Dylan set sail for broader—and more commercial—waters.

After dropping out of Ohio State University, Ochs relocated to New York's Greenwich Village. There, his songwriting talents—fired by fervent left-wing beliefs—soon established him as a mainstay of the folk scene. Songs about civil rights, the Vietnam War, and social justice purveyed *All The News That's Fit To Sing* (1964) and *I Ain't Marching Anymore* (1965, highlighted by the wryly witty "Draft Dodger Rag").

Unsurprisingly, such confrontational songs garnered little airplay (though they did attract the attentions of the FBI, who compiled a dossier on the singer). Ochs sardonically referenced his commercial failings with the ironically titled, rock-oriented 1970 album *Greatest Hits*; on the cover, he sported a gold lamé suit—echoing the cover of *50,000,000 Elvis Fans Can't Be Wrong* (1959)—which he subsequently donned for a concert at New York's Carnegie Hall. His increasingly erratic behavior (the cover of his 1969 album *Rehearsals For Retirement* had featured Ochs' mock tombstone) was rapidly alienating his modest fan base, and during the 1970s, the singer abandoned the music industry for journalism and to travel to Australia, South America, and Africa. While visiting the latter he was violently mugged and his vocal cords irreparably damaged.

Ochs was a chronic depressive, and this—along with musical writer's block and alcohol abuse—reduced him to a pitiful figure. In early April 1976, he had refused to start taking antidepressants he had been prescribed. One week later, he hanged himself at his sister's house in Far Rockaway, New York.

ABOVE Phil Ochs performing onstage at the Naumburg Bandshell in Central Park, New York, as part of a peace march in April 1969.

53

KEITH RELF
(WILLIAM KEITH RELF)
ELECTROCUTION

Born: March 22, 1943

Died: May 14, 1976

It's fair to say that Keith Relf's talents as a singer and songwriter have been overlooked over the years. Relf had the misfortune to be the lead singer of one of the 1960s' most famous groups—The Yardbirds—whose ranks at various times included three rock guitar gods: Eric Clapton (a friend from Kingston art college whom Relf had brought into the band), Jeff Beck, and Jimmy Page.

The Yardbirds emerged in the early 1960s as one of Britain's foremost blues acts, taking over The Rolling Stones' residency at London's Crawdaddy Club and supporting Sonny Boy Williamson in late 1963. However, they made their name with a string of memorable pop hits in the mid-1960s, including "For Your Love" (1964), "Heart Full Of Soul" (1965), and "Shapes Of Things" (1966). Relf was a star by the age of twenty—some achievement, given the poor health he had endured from a young age. He suffered from chronic asthma, aggravated by playing smoky clubs, that nearly killed him on three occasions and made his success as a singer and harmonica player all the more impressive. On the eve of The Yardbirds' commercial breakthrough in 1964, Relf suffered a collapsed lung during the band's first American tour. And he was afflicted with emphysema.

Following The Yardbirds' split in July 1968, Relf moved through a string of bands, including Renaissance, Armageddon, and Medicine Head, without ever coming close to recapturing former glories. He died in his home basement studio, electrocuted while standing over a concealed gas line, playing a badly grounded guitar; his emphysema had turned a relatively mild electric shock into a fatal one.

RIGHT The blond 'bird: Keith Relf performing in August 1965.

TOMMY BOLIN
(THOMAS RICHARD BOLIN)
DRUG OVERDOSE

Born: August 1, 1951

Died: December 4, 1976

Deep Purple often appear aristocratically aloof from rock 'n' roll cliché. Tommy Bolin, recruited to replace Ritchie Blackmore, was the renegade in their ranks.

Born in 1951, he was inducted into rock by an Elvis concert and dropped out of school rather than cut his hair. After three albums with Zephyr, he toured with Albert King, then replaced Joe Walsh in Ohio rockers the James Gang.

He made the classic cock rock album *Teaser* (1975) and joined future Whitesnake leader David Coverdale in Deep Purple, whose *Come Taste The Band* (1975) was a funky anomaly in their thumperiffic discography.

By this point he was using heroin, reportedly paralyzing his arm on tour in Japan. His unreliability contributed to Purple's undignified end in 1976, although there have been numerous reunion projects and tours since with various lineups.

Bolin continued gigging, claiming his biggest problem was "trying to find a fuckin' house"; *Exorcist* star Linda Blair put him up in the meantime. On December 3, 1976, he opened for Jeff Beck—whose jazz-rock was partly inspired by Bolin's work on Billy Cobham's *Spectrum* (1973). The next day, he was dead in his Miami hotel room—overdosed on morphine, cocaine, lidocaine, and alcohol. The coroner found needle marks, but not the tracks indicative of a junkie.

Bolin was buried in his native Sioux City, Iowa, wearing the ring Hendrix wore the day he died (a present from Purple's manager). "Don't worry about me," he told a reporter before his final show. "I'm going to be around for a long time."

RIGHT Tommy Bolin in action.

ELVIS PRESLEY
(ELVIS ARON PRESLEY)
CARDIAC ARRYTHMIA?
CARDIOVASCULAR DISEASE?
DRUG OVERDOSE?

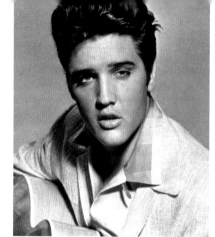

Born: January 8, 1935

Died: August 16, 1977

In the summer of 1953, Elvis entered Sam Phillips' Sun Studios in Memphis to cut a double-sided demo acetate—possibly for his mother, to whom he was exceptionally close. His talent as yet unproven, the youngster already had attitude in spades, telling Sun receptionist Marion Keisker, "I don't sound like nobody." Presley returned to Phillips' studio the following January to record another double-sided demo acetate, and that June, Phillips contacted him about recording formally for Sun.

Presley, guitarist Scotty Moore, and bassist Bill Black assembled at Sun on July 5, 1954, but seemed to be getting nowhere until— for light relief—Elvis launched into a country-style spoof on a blues song by Arthur "Big Boy" Crudup, "That's All Right (Mama)." A few nights later, they repeated the magic with an up-tempo rockabilly version of Bill Monroe's "Blue Moon Of Kentucky." Phillips whipped the single across town to legendary DJ Dewey Phillips (no relation) on radio station WHBQ. He dropped this new hybrid sound on Memphis and was promptly rewarded with an avalanche of calls and telegrams. By the following year, Elvis had left Sun (for the then unprecedented sum of U.S. $35,000) for RCA and had acquired a ruthlessly ambitious manager—Colonel Tom Parker.

Sam disliked Elvis' first RCA single—"Heartbreak Hotel"—calling it a "morbid mess," but it sold a million copies, giving the Memphis Flash his first *Billboard* No. 1, in May 1956. For the next two years, Elvis ruled the charts with a string of rock 'n' roll gems, including "Don't Be Cruel," "All Shook Up," and "Jailhouse Rock."

Elvis' raunchy onstage gyrations provoked the wrath of moral guardians everywhere. Their objections increased after an appearance on *The Milton Berle Show* in 1957, when he performed burlesque bumps and grinds to a suggestively slowed-down "Hound Dog."

Many pop stars employed crafty tactics to avoid being drafted. Not Elvis, who began a two-year military stint (inaugurated by rock's most famous trip to the barber) on March 24, 1958. Already shaken by her son's tumultuous success, his mother now feared for his life. Her own health worsened after he left for basic training, and she died of a heart attack five months later. Elvis was devastated: "Everything I have is gone," he lamented at her funeral.

With a gift for PR that bordered on genius, the Colonel had kept Elvis' name in the public eye during his army years (spent in Germany, where he met the girl who would become his wife, Priscilla Beaulieu), and the star was able to pick up where he left off, with an ambitious album (the imaginatively titled *Elvis Is Back!*, 1960) and more chart-toppers in "Stuck On You" and "It's Now Or Never," the latter showcasing his maturing vocal skills. Yet as the 1960s wore on, Elvis' momentum stalled. In the wake of the "British Invasion" of bands heralded by The Beatles, the King seemed decidedly old hat, his image problem not helped by a series of increasingly uninspired Hollywood films and lame soundtrack albums.

The beginnings of Elvis' artistic renaissance stem from his 1966 gospel album *How Great Thou Art*, featuring his first truly heartfelt performances for years. Better still was his performance on an NBC television show at the end of 1968, the '68 *Comeback Special*.

RIGHT Ripping it up onstage at the Olympia Theater, Miami, Florida in August 1956.

Slimmed down and sporting a tight-fitting black leather outfit, Elvis was mesmerizing. His vocals, now deeper and more soulful, sounded committed and inspirational once more. He cemented the artistic turnaround with *From Elvis In Memphis* (1969), one of his finest albums; "In The Ghetto," an atypical social-conscience stirrer, was extracted from it and soared to No. 3. Later in the year, "Suspicious Minds" gave him his first No. 1 hit in the United States since 1962. But could he still cut it live? The answer came on July 31, 1969, when the King took the stage at the International Hotel in Las Vegas to storm through a set of 1950s hits and contemporary numbers with newfound vigor. Elvis was back—again.

Alas, a slow decline ensued. True, there were occasional highs—he sold out four nights at Madison Square Garden in June 1972, while 1973's *Elvis: Aloha From Hawaii* show attracted an audience of a billion via satellite. But as the 1970s wore on, the stage shows became increasingly predictable, the arrangements more overblown, Elvis' performances more eccentric, more tired.

His personal life was unraveling, too. Elvis had become increasingly moody over the previous few years, a trait influenced partly by the prescription pills he'd been popping. (He had started taking amphetamines on maneuvers during his army days.) This,

and his inveterate womanizing, cost him his marriage: Priscilla left him—for his karate teacher—in December 1971. His spontaneous generosity and high-rolling lifestyle brought on financial crises. His weight began to increase—partly due to comfort-food binges (deep-fried peanut-butter-and-banana sandwich, anyone?), partly due to a faulty colon—making the once-beautiful King of Rock 'n' Roll a roly-poly figure of fun, corseted to squeeze into his stage jumpsuits.

His divorce from Priscilla was finalized on October 11, 1973. Days later, he collapsed into a semi-comatose state with suspected heart failure—probably brought on by a doctor's unwise prescriptions, which may have left him with a permanent dependency on opiates. (Sound engineer Bill Porter once asked his doctor, George Nichopoulous, what it would take to stop Elvis' drug addiction. "Six feet of dirt," came the reply.) By now he was taking steroids to combat constipation and an adrenal gland deficiency; these led to weight gain, so he also popped diet pills. And year after year, he kept on touring.

At around 2 P.M. on August 16, 1977, Elvis' fiancée, Ginger Alden, discovered his dead body in his bathroom at Graceland; he had apparently pitched forward onto the floor from the toilet. A post-mortem revealed that fourteen separate drugs were in his system at the time, and it is likely that years of prescription drug abuse had weakened Elvis' heart and other vital organs, bringing about his death. He weighed around 350 pounds at the time, his heart was abnormally enlarged, and, according to one hospital worker, "Elvis had the arteries of an eighty-year-old man."

When he died, Elvis' career had stalled. Thirty years later, his achievements seem, if anything, all the more remarkable, and have inspired a host of "sightings" by those who cling to the idea that he staged his own death to start another, less stressful life. And even in death, Elvis leads the competition: with annual earnings of U.S. $52 million in 2006, he is the world's highest-earning dead rock star.

FAR LEFT Still a big star—and getting bigger all the time. Live at Nassau Coliseum, Long Island, New York, in July 1975.

LEFT The Hollywood years, mid-1960s.

MARC BOLAN
(MARK FELD)
CAR CRASH

Born: September 30, 1947
Died: September 16, 1977

Mark Feld's quest for fame—and his penchant for pseudonyms—started early. In 1962, a magazine feature on Mods included an interview with Feld the dandy. By the time he was seventeen, he was a folk singer called Toby Tyler. It proved a false start, and soon *Marc* Feld had moved to France. Back in time for Swinging London's high-water mark, Feld secured a recording contract with Decca; his 1965 single, "The Wizard," marked the debut of Marc *Bolan*. Another false start. Even a six-month tenure with infamous psychedelic shockers John's Children couldn't ignite his career.

Better luck came when Bolan teamed up with percussionist Steve Peregrine-Took in Tyrannosaurus Rex, purveyors of whimsical hippie acoustic fare and album titles such as *My People Were Fair And Had Sky In Their Hair… But Now They're Content To Wear Stars On Their Brows* (1968). But paydirt was finally hit when Bolan hitched that whimsy to an electric band (T-Rex, a punchier version of its predecessor) for 1970 single "Ride A White Swan." It hit No. 2 in the UK; at last, Marc Bolan was off.

"I think I'd like to die in a car crash just like [James] Dean, only I'm so small it would have to be a Mini."

His serious songwriting skills, elfin good looks, and playful androgyny made Bolan glam-rock royalty in early 1970s Britain. T-Rex racked up 11 Top Ten UK singles from 1970 to '73 (including four chart-toppers). The best—"Hot Love," "Get It On," "Jeepster," "Telegram Sam," "Metal Guru," "Children Of The Revolution," and the earth-shaking "20th Century

Boy"—were timeless singalong teen anthems rooted in Bolan's gutsy guitar riffs, which harked back to early rock 'n' roll. (As a teenager, Bolan had seen Eddie Cochran at London's Hackney Empire; legend has it that he carried the star's guitar to his car afterwards.) "Get It On" was released as "Bang A Gong (Get It On)," and became their only substantial U.S. hit, making the Top Ten in 1972, one of the handful of British glam-rock tracks to make it in the United States.

But success bred arrogance in the pint-sized pop star. Bolan belittled rival David Bowie in *Creem* magazine ("I don't consider David to be even remotely near big enough to give me any competition"), along with Slade ("I don't think anyone can seriously compare them to what I do"). In fact, by the time of that interview—1973—T-Rex was fading. To Bowie, image reinvention seemed almost an obsession in the 1970s; by contrast, when glam waned, so did Bolan. A tax-exile stint in Monaco saw his weight balloon and his appetite for cocaine soar. One heart attack later, he was back in the UK to try again.

Some time after 5 A.M. on September 16, 1977, Bolan and girlfriend Gloria Jones (of "Tainted Love" fame) were returning home from a London nightclub. Jones was at the wheel of their purple Mini GT when it swerved off the road, and into a tree, at an accident black spot on Queen's Ride, Barnes. Jones, though injured, survived; Bolan was crushed, thrown onto the back seat of the car, and died immediately. (The tree is now a Bolan shrine.)

Spookily, he'd once told former manager Simon Napier-Bell "I think I'd like to die in a car crash just like [James] Dean, only I'm so small it would have to be a Mini."

RIGHT The glam guru performing in London in 1973.

CURSED BAND
LYNYRD SKYNYRD

THE DEPARTED

RONNIE VAN ZANT
(Ronald Wayne Van Zant)
Born: January 15, 1948
Died: October 20, 1977

STEVE GAINES
(Steven Earl Gaines)
Born: September 14, 1949
Died: October 20, 1977

CASSIE GAINES
Born: January 9, 1948
Died: October 20, 1977

DEAN KILPATRICK
Died: October 20, 1977

- -

RIGHT The original cover of Lynyrd Skynyrd's *Street Survivors* (1976).

CENTER Lynyrd Skynyrd performing in 1974, from left to right: Allen Collins, Ronnie Van Zant, Gary Rossington, Ed King, and Leon Wilkeson.

FAR RIGHT The band photographed in the 1970s.

When it came to deciding which aircraft to hire for their 1977 tour, Aerosmith decided against hiring a Corvair plane. They'd heard that the pilots weren't averse to chugging Jack Daniels or smoking the odd joint. Not all rock bands of the time were so picky, though.

Lynyrd Skynyrd's roots lay in My Backyard, a high-school group featuring singer Ronnie Van Zant, guitarists Allen Collins and Gary Rossington, bassist Larry Jungstrom, and drummer Bob Burns. Line-up changes and name switches followed (short-lived monikers included The Noble Five, The Wildcats, Sons Of Satan, and One Percent), before they settled on Lynyrd Skynyrd (a twist on the name of a gym teacher, Leonard Skinner, who had persecuted Bob and Gary for their long hair).

By the early 1970s, Skynyrd were gaining a reputation as a kick-ass Southern rock band, their fiery sound perhaps best captured on the anthemic guitar-fest "Freebird" (a lament for the then recently departed rocker Duane Allman and now a perennial FM radio fave), from 1973's *Pronounced Leh-Nerd Skin-Nerd*. Follow-up *Second Helping* (1974) provided a No. 8 hit on the *Billboard* charts with "Sweet Home Alabama," a tongue-in-cheek riposte to Neil Young's Dixie-bating "Southern Man." Over the next few years, Skynyrd built up a towering live reputation, regularly breaking box-office records, while bad boy singer Van Zant racked up an impressive record of his own, for bar fights. By the end of 1976, they'd amassed four gold albums and scored a platinum disc for that year's double live set *One More For The Road*. Expectations were high for the tour to promote their strong forthcoming album, *Street Survivors*, which initially sported a cover showing the band standing in flames. For understandable reasons, that was later changed.

On October 19, 1977, a fire broke out in the engine of the

1948 Corvair 240 plane that Skynyrd had chartered for the tour. Shaken, backing singer Cassie Gaines announced that she wouldn't use that Corvair again, and booked herself a ticket on a commercial airline to the next gig at Louisiana University; her fellow bandmates eventually teased her into staying with them.

Gaines, and Steve Gaines all perished, along with both pilots and roadie Dean Kilpatrick; twenty other passengers were injured. In a particularly gruesome postscript, the scene was raided by numerous scavengers that night, who picked the crash site (and the survivors) clean of valuables.

"Our co-pilot, John Gray, had been drinking the night before," reflected surviving keyboard player Billy Powell later, "and, for all I know, may still have been drunk."

"Our co-pilot... had been drinking the night before... "

The following afternoon, at around 4 P.M., a distress call came into Houston air traffic control from the plane, which was dangerously low on fuel (it has been speculated that the pilots had accidentally jettisoned it). Shortly thereafter, both of the Corvair's engines died and it crash landed in woods near Gillburg, Mississippi, at around 90 miles per hour, breaking apart on impact. Ronnie Van Zant, Cassie

TERRY KATH
(TERRY ALAN KATH)
SELF-INFLICTED GUNSHOT WOUND

Born: January 31, 1946

Died: January 23, 1978

Hard to believe now, but 1970s soft-rock giants Chicago started out life as an altogether more radical proposition. Originally dubbed Chicago Transit Authority by manager James Guercio, the group developed a tantalizing line in jazz rock, heard to sparkling effect on their eponymous 1969 debut album, which featured a hit cover of The Spencer Davis Group's funky classic "I'm A Man." Key elements in CTA's early sound were the vocals and imaginative guitar work of Terry Kath (admired by Jimi Hendrix, for one), whose lengthy solos became a trademark, and who was effectively the leader of the fledgling outfit.

Legal threats from Chicago's bus company—that city's *genuine* transit authority—necessitated a name change, and it was as Chicago that the group released their sophomore effort, the Top 10 *Chicago II* (1970).

This album contained the hit singles "Make Me Smile" and "25 Or 6 To 4," the latter featuring a memorable Kath solo; its title, meanwhile, spawned an uninterrupted—indeed, unimaginative—series of album titles right up to 1999's *Chicago 26*. As the decade progressed, however, and commercial nirvana beckoned, the hard edges were gradually knocked off the Chicago sound. Hits such as "Feelin' Stronger Everyday" (1973) and "Old Days" (1975) saw the band clean up; "If You Leave Me Now" (1976) topped the UK charts, too, though Chicago's success was always greatest

Stateside. Kath's final album with the group was 1977's *Chicago XI*, by which time he was allegedly laying plans for a solo album. They were to remain unfulfilled.

"Don't worry—it's not loaded, see?"

A week before his thirty-third birthday, Kath and his wife Camelia turned up at a party in Woodland Hills, Los Angeles, held by Chicago band technician Donnie Johnson. As proceedings died down toward the end of the day, an inebriated Kath took it upon himself to start cleaning a .38 revolver that belonged to Johnson. (He was an enthusiastic firearms collector, often traveling armed.) The booze had left Kath in a somewhat fuzzy and unpredictable state of mind, though, and Johnson became increasingly worried by him, not least when Kath placed the gun to his own head and pulled the trigger. The chamber was empty, and Johnson breathed a sigh of relief. But Kath wasn't finished.

From his pocket, he now produced a 9 mm semi-automatic pistol that he carried, prompting Johnson to shout out a warning. Kath unclipped the magazine—forgetting that some semi-automatics retain the bullet when a magazine is removed from the gun—and raised the pistol to his head. Uttering the infamous line, "Don't worry—it's not loaded, see?" Terry Kath then pulled the trigger—and blew his brains out.

RIGHT Terry Kath puts his personalized Fender Telecaster through its paces.

KEITH MOON
(KEITH JOHN MOON)
DRUG OVERDOSE

Born: August 23, 1946

Died: September 7, 1978

"I survived all the major earthquakes," says Keith Moon in The Who's movie *The Kids Are Alright* (1979), "and the *Titanic*, and several air crashes."

For over a decade, Moon possessed cartoon-like indestructibility. He flushed cherry bombs down hotel plumbing, drank brandy like water, drove a Rolls Royce into a stagnant pond (immortalized in the press as "Rock Star Drives Roller Into Swimming Pool"), and revolutionized rock 'n' roll drumming—inspiring Animal from *The Muppets*.

In 1964, at the age of seventeen, Moon joined The Who after declaring himself better than the drummer with whom he had seen them play. One trashed kit later, he was in. Though best appreciated live, Moon's drumming was integral to classics such as "I Can See For Miles," "Bargain," "Won't Get Fooled Again," and "The Real Me." He blasted around a double-bass drum kit, straining to steal the limelight from singer Roger Daltrey and guitarist Pete Townshend. In a bid to upstage them on TV's *The Smothers Brothers Comedy Hour*, he loaded his kit with explosives. The resultant blast at the climax of "My Generation" caused fellow guest Bette Davis to faint and initiated Townshend's tinnitus.

At home, violent arguments with his partners were punctuated by blasts of his beloved Beach Boys. On a night out in 1970, he saved himself and friends from an unruly group of pub-goers, only to inadvertently run over and kill his friend and driver Neil Boland. Though absolved of any crime, Moon was haunted by the incident.

He remained a charismatic raconteur, his friends including Ringo Starr (whose son drummed for The Who decades later) and right-hand man Dougal Butler (whose *Moon The Loon* is essential reading). But he was frustrated by the grandiosity of Townshend's music; 1974's solo album *Two Sides Of The Moon* was a spirited, albeit hopeless, bid to recapture his roots. He lost his good looks to drink, and countered depression with frightening quantities of drugs. After he nose-dived into his drum kit during one show, an investigation found his system swimming in animal tranquilizers.

On September 7, 1978, after attending a preview of the movie *The Buddy Holly Story* with Paul and Linda McCartney, he returned to an apartment in Mayfair. Owned by Harry Nilsson (with whom Moon and John Lennon had enjoyed many a loony night on the latter's "lost weekend" in 1973 and '74), it was where Mama Cass had died four years previously. Moon watched the Vincent Price movie *The Abominable Dr. Phibes*, consumed thirty-two pills prescribed to combat alcoholism (coincidentally, he was thirty-two years old)—and never awoke. The death was ruled by the coroner as accidental.

Mourners at his funeral included Roger Daltrey, whose wreath depicted a champagne bottle smashed in a TV, and Eric Clapton. Moon's ashes were scattered at Golders Green Crematorium in North London.

On the sleeve of *Who Are You* (1978), his final album with the band, Moon sits astride a chair stenciled "Not to be taken away." The Who would spend the ensuing decades in his shadow.

LEFT Moon the Loon onstage in the late 1970s.

DONNY HATHAWAY
(DONNY EDWARD HATHAWAY)
SUICIDE BY JUMPING FROM A WINDOW

Born: October 1, 1945

Died: January 13, 1979

Singer/songwriter/producer Donny Hathaway was one of the hottest talents in R&B at the beginning of the 1970s. He brought his gospel-inflected croon to secular material, giving it a palpable depth, and has been namechecked as an influence on—or mentioned in the material of—artists as diverse as The Whispers, George Benson, and Justin Timberlake.

Hathaway's musical career got off to an early start. With his grandmother, gospel singer Martha Cromwell, he took to the road as "Donny Pitts, the Nation's Youngest Gospel Singer," at the age of three, and the twin loves of music and religion stayed with Hathaway throughout his life. During the mid-1960s, he considered devoting his life to the church, but after completing a scholarship at Howard University in Washington, D.C. (where he majored in music theory), he opted instead to become keyboardist in the jazz-influenced Ric Powell Trio.

Back in his hometown of Chicago, Hathaway produced a number of prominent artists, including The Impressions and Pops Staples, and was subsequently signed up as a solo artist/songwriter/producer by Atlantic Records. Following his debut album, the smooth and soulful *Everything Is Everything* (1970), he attracted the help and encouragement of producer Jerry Wexler (who considered him "the most brilliant musical theorist I ever encountered"). Hathaway fared better with the follow-up, *Donny Hathaway* (1971), featuring a Top Ten hit with a cover of James Taylor's "You've Got A Friend," on which he duetted with Roberta Flack. The two had been classmates at Howard University, and went on to enjoy further success in the 1970s with the album *Roberta Flack And Donny Hathaway* (1972) and the million-selling

Top Ten hit "Where Is The Love?" (1972). Hathaway moved to the producer's seat later in the decade, but shared the mic with Flack again for the 1978 smash hit "The Closer I Get To You." Their intimate duets gave rise to speculation that the two might be romantically involved, but if Hathaway had feelings for Flack, they were unrequited: she was happily married.

An air of mystery still surrounds his demise. Donny Hathaway died after a fall from a fifteenth-floor window of New York's Essex House Hotel (he landed on a window ledge at the second floor), apparently having jumped after carefully removing the windowpane. The official verdict was suicide ("No adult ever fell from a waist-high window," maintained the coroner), but there was no note; moreover, as the Reverend Jesse Jackson later pointed out in Hathaway's eulogy, suicides don't generally get dressed up in a hat, scarf, and coat to kill themselves. True, Hathaway suffered from bouts of depression, but earlier on the day of his death he'd seemed chipper to associates: Hathaway and Flack had met up in New York for some fresh recordings, working on another album of duets—two tracks of which appeared on her next album, *Roberta Flack Featuring Donnie Hathaway* (1980)—and he was reportedly upbeat at the time.

Perhaps his faith held the key to the riddle all along. Back home in Chicago, Hathaway frequently preached and broke into song from the seventeenth-floor window of his apartment—much to the annoyance of his neighbors; indeed, a number of hotels had evicted him for such behavior. Could his untimely death have simply been the accidental outcome of an overly enthusiastic sermon?

RIGHT Justin Timberlake's favorite artist, Donny Hathaway.

SID VICIOUS
(SIMON JOHN RITCHIE, LATER SIMON JOHN BEVERLEY)
DRUG OVERDOSE

Born: May 10, 1957
Died: February 2, 1979

Hanging around Malcolm McLaren's King's Road boutique, Sex, would never satisfy Simon John Beverley (born Simon John Ritchie, soon to become Sid Vicious)—especially after McLaren invited Beverley's friend John Lydon to become lead singer in a new band, The Sex Pistols, in late 1975. The following year, Vicious formed the short-lived Flowers of Romance; in September 1976, he drummed for a nascent Siouxsie And The Banshees at the 100 Club. Then in March 1977, Lydon (aka Johnny Rotten) asked him to become the new bassist in The Sex Pistols.

"There's nothing glorious in dying," sniffed John Lydon in his autobiography. "Anyone can do it."

Petty acts of violence aside, "Up to that time, Sid was absolutely childlike," Lydon recalled in his autobiography years later. Many speak of his natural intelligence and off-kilter wit, too. But now spiky of hair and attitude, Vicious certainly looked the part of a Pistol and quickly started to live up to the anti-star image. However, it was only after meeting Nancy Spungen—of whom few people have a good word to say—that matters really began to get out of hand. Sid fell hook, line, and sinker for the blond New Yorker, and for heroin shortly thereafter. Things came to a head with the Pistols' ill-fated American tour in 1978. In Dallas, Vicious took to the stage with "Gimme a Fix"

cut into his bare chest. Their final gig—Winterland Ballroom, San Francisco—ended with Rotten's famous kiss-off "Ever get the feeling you've been cheated?" And that should have been that, but after Rotten quit, Sid took the mic, recorded his memorable take on "My Way" (with an all-star supporting cast)—a highlight of the group's film—*The Great Rock 'n' Roll Swindle*, and scored two posthumous UK hits with cover versions of Eddie Cochran's "Somethin' Else" and "C'mon Everybody."

On October 12, Vicious phoned the New York police from the room he and Nancy shared at the Chelsea Hotel to report that someone had stabbed her. Spungen was found dead under the bathroom sink in blood-soaked underwear; Vicious was charged with second degree murder and sent to the hospital wing of the infamous Riker's Island Penitentiary. Pistols manager McLaren bailed him with U.S. $25,000 (£50,000) from the group's label, Virgin.

On February 2, 1979, Vicious died at a party in Greenwich Village, from an accumulation of fluid on his lungs as a result of a heroin overdose; the drug was paid for by his mother. Spungen's mother refused to have Vicious interred next to her daughter, as had been his wish, though his ashes may secretly have been scattered on her grave. Then again, other rumors have it that the urn containing his ashes was accidentally smashed (or dumped in a garbage bin) in an airport.

A chaotic end to a chaotic life. Punk had its first martyr, but Lydon, for one, has no time for myth making: "There's nothing glorious in dying," he wrote in *Rotten*, "Anyone can do it."

RIGHT Sid and Nancy photographed in London in January 1977.

LOWELL GEORGE
(LOWELL THOMAS GEORGE)
HEART ATTACK

Born: April 13, 1945
Died: June 29, 1979

They were Jimmy Page's "favorite American group." Jackson Browne called their founder "the Orson Welles of rock 'n' roll." Pink Floyd soundchecked with their "Lafayette Railroad." When they toured Europe in 1975—stealing the show from the headlining Doobie Brothers—The Rolling Stones made their first appearance as a group in years to see them.

They were Little Feat, and their leader was Lowell George. "A charming, great bear-like man," remembered a *Mojo* magazine writer, "Rumpled and a little worse for wear, and far too stoned to negotiate the spiral staircase in his hotel suite."

A multi-talented musician from childhood, George was instrumental in bringing the slide guitar from the blues into rock. He joined his first band, The Factory, in 1965, and endured a brief stint in garage rockers The Standells (best known for "Dirty Water"). "I replaced Dicky Dodd, the lead singer… " he told *ZigZag*. "He quit because he couldn't stand it. And I finally quit because I couldn't stand it either." Then he landed in Frank Zappa's Mothers Of Invention. "I was initially hired to be the singer… " George recalled, "but I really ended up playing more guitar."

Having graced a clutch of Zappa albums—including uncredited playing on 1969's classic *Hot Rats*—George was bounced from the Mothers of Invention, allegedly for suggesting they record his song "Willin'" (apparently the abstemious Zappa objected to its druggy references).

Encouraged by the response to his demos—"Willin'" was snapped up by Linda Ronstadt—George assembled Little Feat

(from Mothers drummer Jimmy Carl Black's observation about Lowell's size eights). Having hatched classics such as "Dixie Chicken" and "Feats Don't Fail Me Now," they peaked with 1978's live album *Waiting For Columbus*.

On June 28, 1979, touring his long-awaited solo album *Thanks, I'll Eat It Here*, George played in Washington, D.C., a Little Feat stronghold. The next day, in the Twin Bridges Marriott Hotel, Arlington, Virginia, he was dead at thirty-four years old.

The official cause was a heart attack. "George had grown extremely fat," reported music paper *NME*. "Partially as a result of the debilitating hepatitis that laid him low for much of last year, he probably weighed close to 300 lbs…One fan said that he seemed to have a dangerous amount of energy for a man of his size and health record."

However, according to observers, the body was "white-lipped, and the bluishness around the eyes… consistent with post mortem symptoms of a drug overdose." *NME* also quoted a hotel employee who claimed to have seen a "large phial of white powder about one half the size of a tennis ball canister, which was practically empty." George was cremated in Washington on July 2, 1979. The ashes, at his request, were scattered into the Pacific Ocean by his family. Little Feat subsequently re-formed and enjoyed considerable success in the 1980s and early '90s after recruiting singer/songwriter Craig Fuller.

"What is the future of rock music as we head toward the '80s?" asked *Chic* magazine in 1978. Answered George: "It'll be the same old crap warmed over."

RIGHT Lowell George performing with Little Feat in New York, 1978.

BON SCOTT
(RONALD BELFORD SCOTT)
ACUTE ALCOHOL POISONING

Born: July 9, 1946
Died: February 19, 1980

"Bon is a very individual person," said AC/DC's Angus Young in 1979. "He's a lunatic, but he's great." Scott said simply: "I am the poet with this band."

There is certainly something poetic about the most exhilarating epitaph any rocker has written for himself: "Hey Satan! Paid my dues / Playin' in a rockin' band / ... I'm on my way to the promised land... I'm on the highway to hell!"

Ronald Belford Scott traveled a rocky road before AC/DC. Born in Scotland in 1946, he moved to Australia as a child. "My new schoolmates threatened to kick the shit out of me when they heard my Scottish accent. I had one week to learn to speak like them if I wanted to remain intact. 'Course, I didn't take any notice. No one railroads me."

He served time in Australian bands, notably the bubblegummy band The Valentines and hippified Fraternity. "The dollar sign is not the ultimate," he told an interviewer of the latter. "We want to try and help each other develop and live."

A serious motorcycle accident ended Scott's time with Fraternity, and by 1974 he was working as an occasional chauffeur for the fledgling AC/DC. More impressed by his singing than his driving, the band soon installed him as front man.

"I've never had a message for anyone in my entire life," declared Scott, "except maybe to give out my room number." This bourbon-powered roguishness fueled increasingly popular albums, including Keith Richards' favorite *Powerage* (1978) and the multi-platinum *Highway To Hell* (1979).

Scott-stamped classics included the lascivious "Whole Lotta Rosie," self-mythologizing "Live Wire," and atypically reflective "Ride On." On February 15, 1980, Scott recut the latter with French band Trust. It is his last known recording.

On February 19, he went to a London club, leaving at 3 A.M. with friend Alisdair Kinnear. Unable to drag the inebriated vocalist from his car, Kinnear left him to sleep it off. He awoke the next day to find Scott asphyxiated by his own vomit. "Death by misadventure," ruled the coroner. "Acute alcoholic poisoning." His body was cremated at Fremantle Cemetery in Western Australia.

AC/DC carried on with 1980's *Back In Black*, whose stark sleeve and introductory tolling bell paid tribute to Scott. The singer had drummed on a jam that became the title track, and even recommended his own replacement—he had been impressed by Brian Johnson's screaming with the band Geordie, not knowing the impassioned performance was due to Johnson's appendicitis.

Scott's music was celebrated in AC/DC's 1997 box set *Bonfire*. But it is likely he would find other legacies more amusing. In 2007, Alex O'Loughlin, of cop show *The Shield*, was rumored to be his son. Meanwhile, in 2006, a plaque erected at his grave site was stolen on what would have been his sixtieth birthday.

RIGHT Bon Scott in London, 1979.

IAN CURTIS
(IAN KEVIN CURTIS)
SUICIDE BY HANGING

Born: July 15, 1956

Died: May 18, 1980

Who is the laziest in the group, Peter Hook is asked in the 1993 documentary *NewOrder Story*. "Ian Curtis," the bassist replies. "I haven't seen him do anything for years."

In 1976, Curtis united with Hook and guitarist Bernard Dicken (later Sumner), inspired by the Sex Pistols to create a band of their own. With Stephen Morris on drums, they became Joy Division in 1977. Though associated with sepulchral synthesizers, the band was at that time more violent; they even scrapped their debut album when the producer overdubbed it with synths. Early classics included "Transmission" (covered by The Smashing Pumpkins) and "Dead Souls" (covered by Nine Inch Nails).

The sound evolved with 1979's bleak *Unknown Pleasures*, produced by Martin Hannett. Among his other clients were U2, who visited when Joy Division recorded "Love Will Tear Us Apart" and were bemused to find them listening to Wagner and Frank Sinatra. Neither is much in evidence on 1980's *Closer*, as terrifying as it is somber. "It would be hard to find a darker place in music than Joy Division," remembers Bono. "Their name, their lyrics, and their singer were as big a black cloud as you could find."

Meanwhile, Joy Division prepared for their first U.S. tour. Just before the flight, on May 18, 1980, Ian Curtis hanged himself in his kitchen. He was twenty-three years old.

The reason for his death will never be known. A letter left for his wife, Deborah, was, she said, not a suicide note. It instructed her not to get in touch for a while as it was hard for him to talk to her.

Curtis was, in fact, conducting an affair with a Belgian woman Annik Honoré, which added to the intrigue.

The most plausible reason is Curtis' epilepsy, which had already caused him to attempt suicide. "Everyone's got their theories..." said Lindsay Reade, wife of Joy Division's label head Tony Wilson, and coauthor of a book on Curtis, "...but doing the research did bring to mind...the epilepsy and how debilitating it was and how gloomy he felt about the future." The letter to Deborah declared, "At this very moment, I wish I were dead. I just can't cope anymore."

Closer—whose artwork, designed before Curtis' death, features a shrouded body in a tomb—became an enduring classic. "Love Will Tear Us Apart"—the title of which is inscribed on Curtis' headstone in Cheshire's Macclesfield Cemetery—became one of music's best-loved songs.

The story has inspired several books, notably Deborah Curtis' *Touching From A Distance*. A film based on it, *Control*, released in September 2007 and directed by Joy Division photographer Anton Corbijn, features music by Iggy Pop, whose *The Idiot* was found on Curtis' turntable.

Joy Division's remaining trio regrouped as New Order. "Somewhere on the southern outskirts of Manchester there is a graveyard," reported *The Face* in 1983. "Next to the graveyard is a rehearsal room where the four members of New Order come to practise their spells. The joke is not lost on them."

LEFT Here is the young man: the singer's grave in England's Cheshire.

JOHN BONHAM
(JOHN HENRY BONHAM)
ASPHYXIATION

Born: May 31, 1948
Died: September 25, 1980

From Frankie Goes To Hollywood to Dr. Dre, Depeche Mode to Massive Attack, one drumbeat has—thanks to sampling—thundered through four decades. It comes from "When The Levee Breaks" on Led Zeppelin's untitled fourth album, and its architect was John Henry Bonham.

"Bonzo" fought his way into the world in 1948. Born after his mother was in labor for twenty-six hours, his heartbeat stopped, beginning again only after a doctor was able to revive him. "It was," a nurse said, "a miracle."

A drummer by age ten, Bonham wound up in Band Of Joy, with singer Robert Plant. Onstage, he set up his kit at the front, to share the limelight. "You *are* good," he once told Plant, "but you are half as good as a singer as I am a drummer." Jimmy Page asked

"The man who broke every window in Room 1019 last night..."

both to join a refashioned version of the Yardbirds after that band's split. The band was initially called The New Yardbirds, soon to become Led Zeppelin (for whom Bonzo turned down offers from Joe Cocker and Chris Farlowe). With bassist John Paul Jones, one of history's greatest bands was born. Bonham, said Page, was the reason they had to buy bigger amps.

His drumming was key to many Zeppelin classics. Thrashing out Little Richard's "Good Golly Miss Molly," he kick-started "Rock And Roll." For "When The Levee Breaks," his kit was placed in a stairwell, the sound echoing skywards to microphones three stories up. Of "Kashmir," Plant said, "It was what he didn't do that made it work."

The hacking cough on "Sick Again," the exultant "That's gotta be the one" after "In My Time Of Dying," and the inspiration for "Out On The Tiles" were also Bonzo.

Onstage, he dressed like a droog from A *Clockwork Orange*, and soloed at length in "Moby Dick" (originally "Pat's Delight," for his wife). Offstage, he raced motorbikes along hotel corridors and partook in the carnage for which Zeppelin were renowned. "The man who broke every window in Room 1019 last night," Plant introduced him one night. "The man who smashed wardrobes, the man who set fire to his own bed... Mr. Quaalude—John Bonham!" But by the late 1970s, Page and Bonham were using heroin. In 1977, Bonham broke three ribs in a car accident, and was arrested for beating a security guard. During a 1980 show, he fell off his stool after three songs.

On September 24, 1980, he slept at Page's home in Windsor, England, after a vodka-fueled day of rehearsals. The next morning John Paul Jones found him dead, asphyxiated by his own vomit. Bonham was thirty-two. He is buried at a churchyard in Rushock, in his home county of Worcestershire.

The band split on December 4, 1980: "The loss of our dear friend, and the deep respect we have for his family, together with the sense of undivided harmony felt by ourselves... have led us to decide that we could not continue as we were." Bonham's legend lives on as new generations discover Zeppelin, and standard-bearers like Dave Grohl pay tribute.

"He never really had an idea of how important he was," said Plant. "It really was an exasperating loss."

RIGHT The New Yardbirds' first show at Copenhagen's Gladsaxe Teen Club, September 14, 1968. "Bonham," said photographer Jorgen Angel, "was what you'd call 'aggressive' on drums." The band became Led Zeppelin one month later.

JOHN LENNON
(JOHN WINSTON LENNON)
SHOT BY FANATIC

Born: October 9, 1940

Died: December 8, 1980

As one half of perhaps the world's greatest songwriting partnership, John Lennon's pop immortality is gilt-edged guaranteed; simply put, along with Paul McCartney he is responsible for more out-and-out pop classics than any other songsmith, and in *Sgt. Pepper's Lonely Hearts Club Band* (1967), rock's greatest album. (Probably.)

Received wisdom pairs Lennon the wordsmith with McCartney the melody genius, and while such generalizations fail to capture the nuances of each man's strengths, Lennon's verbal inventiveness inspired many of McCartney's more ambitious lyrics (witness "Eleanor Rigby"). Lennon's way with words also resulted in two books of absurdist humor—*In His Own Write* and *A Spaniard In The Works*. The former won him the Foyle's Literary Prize in 1964—no mean feat for a "mere" pop star.

In the exhilarating first rush of Beatlemania, John Lennon emerged as the Fab with the sharpest wit, charming press and public alike with his quips—which, like his books, owed much to the humor of Victorian English eccentrics Edward Lear and Lewis Carroll, and the zany 1950s radio program *The Goon Show*. At press conferences, his lines were generally the funniest and the fastest ("Question: 'Are The Beatles disinterested in politics?' Lennon: 'No. We just think politicians are disinteresting.'")

To top it off, Lennon possessed one of rock's finest voices. He could scream with the best of them—his intense readings of "Twist And Shout" (1963), "Money (That's What I Want)" (1963), "Revolution" (1968), and "I Want You (She's So Heavy)" (1969) all prefigure the throat-shredding vocals on his debut solo *John Lennon/Plastic Ono Band* (1970), famously influenced by Dr. Arthur Janov's "primal scream" therapy. He did quiet too,

though, injecting songs as diverse as "If I Fell" (1964), "Across The Universe" (1969), and "Love" (1970) with an arresting vulnerability.

In The Beatles' formative years, Lennon's intense charisma marked him as the band's leading force. That intensity spilled over into violence on occasion, though—at Paul McCartney's twenty-first birthday party in June 1963, Lennon beat up Liverpool DJ Bob Wooler, giving him a black eye and bruised ribs.

Lennon also displayed a voracious sexual appetite (although divorced by his wife Cynthia in 1969 for adultery with Yoko Ono, he had been promiscuous throughout the 1960s). But his appetite for life, for drugs (pills in Hamburg; later, marijuana, LSD in copious amounts, and heroin), for sex, also epitomized that of the Sixties generation famously described as "Swinging." And those early experiences did much to produce the pacifist who staged a "bed-in" on his honeymoon with Yoko in Amsterdam, to promote peace. "That is why I am always on about peace," he told *Playboy* in 1980. "It is the most violent people who go for love and peace."

Lennon's solo career started strongly, with the bare-bones confessional *John Lennon/Plastic Ono Band* and its more polished, melodic follow-up, *Imagine* (1971), a worldwide best-seller. However, as the decade wore on, his output became less consistent, and other concerns (the fight for his Green Card to stay in the United States; the birth of Sean, his son with Yoko) took over. Mid-decade, he abandoned music altogether, to become a house husband and bring Sean up. It was only in 1980 that he felt inspired to make music again.

John Lennon knew all about untimely death. His mother Julia had been run over and killed by an off-duty policeman when Lennon was sixteen, a traumatic event that haunted him for years,

RIGHT John Lennon and Yoko Ono in the Presidential Suite of the Hilton Hotel in Amsterdam during their seven-day bed-in for peace.

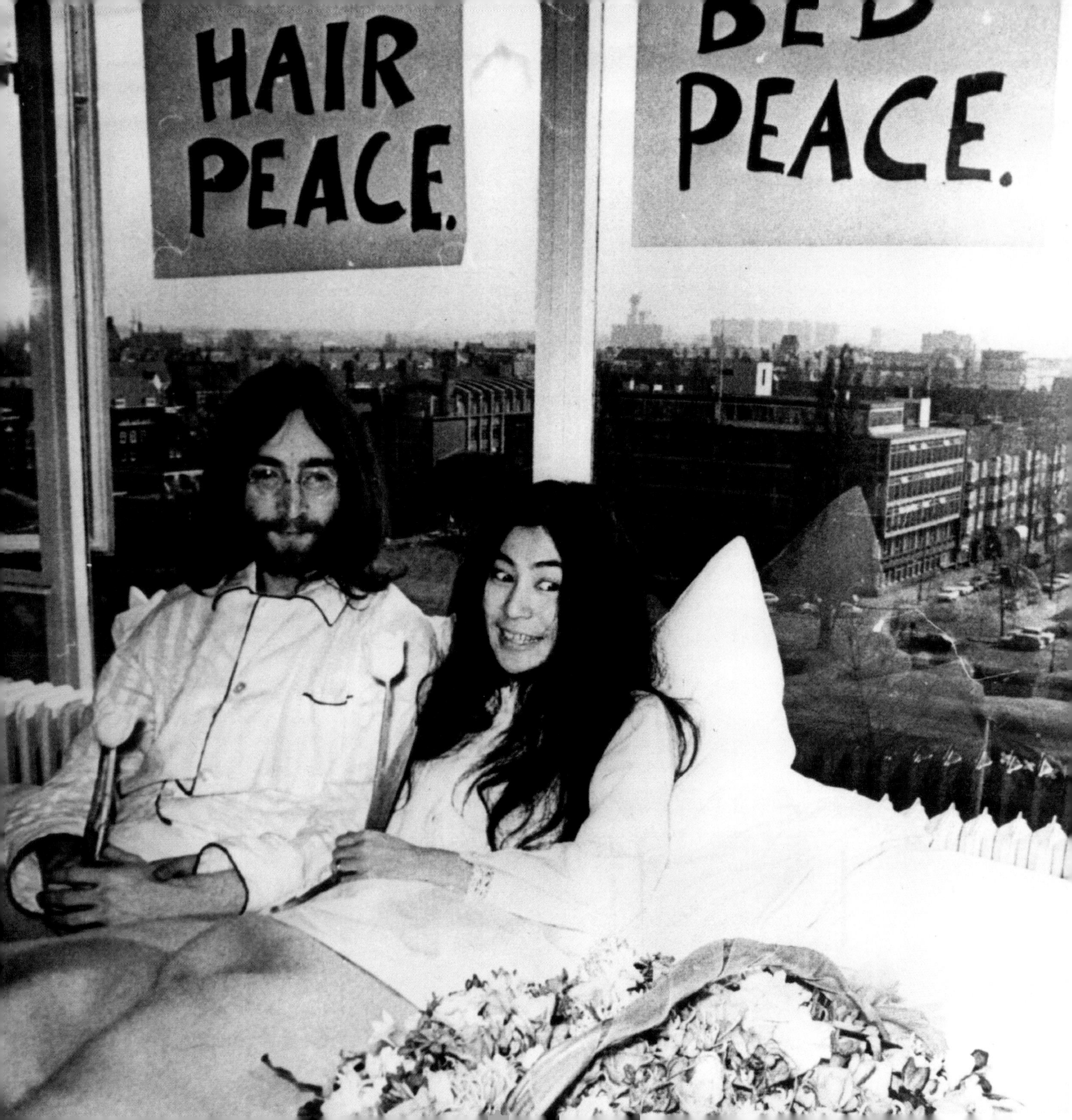
HAIR
PEACE.
PEACE.

encouraged the growth of his sarcastic and violent sides ("I thought, I've got no responsibility to anyone now"), and informed two of his most personal songs—"Julia" (1968) and "Mother" (1970). Lennon's closest college friend had been gifted artist Stuart Sutcliffe, later bassist in the five-man Beatles who traveled to Hamburg. But Sutcliffe died of a brain hemorrhage in Hamburg at the age of twenty-one, in 1962. Beatles manager Brian Epstein died from an overdose in 1967, and without his presence the Fabs' days were numbered—"I knew that we were in trouble then," Lennon reflected in 1970. "I thought, 'We've fuckin' had it.'" In 1976, Mal Evans, roadie and stalwart throughout The Beatles' career, was gunned down by Los Angeles police. Lennon's own end was as unexpected as any of them.

On December 8, 1980, Mark David Chapman succeeded in getting Lennon to sign a copy of his new album, *Double Fantasy*, outside the Dakota building, where the Ono-Lennons had an apartment. At 10:49 P.M., Lennon and Ono returned to the Dakota from the Record Plant studio, but as Lennon stepped from their car and headed toward the entrance, Chapman appeared once more, this time with a .38 revolver, and called out "Mr. Lennon?" As Lennon turned, Chapman shot him five times, hitting his arm and back. In the ensuing chaos, Ono screamed for an ambulance and Lennon managed to crawl up the six steps to the concierge's office, gasping, "I'm shot, I'm shot." Within two minutes a police car had arrived and sped him to Roosevelt Hospital, where they attempted heart massage. But by then, Lennon—having suffered massive blood loss—was dead.

The brutal murder prompted worldwide scenes of grief. As with the death of another 1960s icon, JFK, many can remember exactly where they were when they heard that John Lennon had been killed; Lennon records were soon soaring up the charts again.

It's bitterly ironic that after nearly twenty years of living with the pressures of superstardom (including death threats in 1966, following his infamous comment that The Beatles were more popular than Jesus Christ), Lennon felt he had finally found peace in New York. "I mean, people come and ask for autographs or say, 'Hi,'" he told BBC DJ Andy Peebles just two days before his death, "but they don't *bug* you, you know?"

RIGHT Onstage at Madison Square Garden, New York, 1975. Lennon's last concert.

THE FATAL HAND OF
DAVID BOWIE

THE UNLUCKY ASSOCIATES
Ziggy Stardust (1971–1973)
Marc Bolan (1947–1977)
Bing Crosby (1903–1977)
Sid Vicious (1957–1979)
Major Tom (1969–1980)
John Lennon (1940–1980)
Terry Burns (c.1938–1985)
Stevie Ray Vaughan (1954–1990)
Vince Taylor (1939–1991)
Freddie Mercury (1946–1991)
Mick Ronson (1946–1993)
Kurt Cobain (1967–1994)
Princess Diana (1961–1997)
George Harrison (1943–2001)
Luther Vandross (1951–2005)
Syd Barrett (1946–2006)

RIGHT Hello Earthlings! Onstage, around 1996.

FAR RIGHT "Our Father...only kidding!"—around 1999.

Rarely has a star strolled more nonchalantly through the Valley of Death. While his career rolls unstoppably on, passengers aboard the Bowie bandwagon keep hitting dead ends. His catalog is littered with teases: "My Death," "Rock 'N' Roll Suicide," "We Are The Dead," "Dead Man Walking," and, tellingly, "Somebody Up There Likes Me."

At the heart of this morbid musing is family. "Everyone," explained Bowie, "says, 'Oh yes, my family is quite mad.' Mine really is. No fucking about. Most of them are nutty—in, just out of, or going into an institution. Or dead." The specter of his schizophrenic stepbrother Terry—who died on railroad tracks in 1985—hangs over 1970's "All The Madmen" ("Written for my brother"), 1971's unsettling "The Bewlay Brothers," and 1993's "Jump They Say."

After 1969's hit "Space Oddity"—the tale of doomed astronaut Major Tom—Bowie waited until 1972 for major success. *The Rise And Fall Of Ziggy Stardust And The Spiders From Mars* told the tale of an androgynous star from the glitter galaxy, based in part on eccentric rocker Vince Taylor. "The guy was not playing with a full deck at all" remembered Bowie. "I remember him opening a map outside Charing Cross tube station, putting it on the pavement and kneeling down with a magnifying glass. He pointed out all the sites where UFOs were going to land." In the month *Ziggy Stardust* was released, Taylor issued the rather less celebrated *Vince Is Alive, Well And Rocking In Paris*. After spells in prisons and asylums, he died of cancer in 1991. "The weird and rather scary thing," Bowie said incredulously, "is that poor Vince died... near to where I lived when I was living in Switzerland... He was an aircraft maintenance guy at Geneva Airport. Can you believe that? Ziggy was a maintenance guy!"

Bowie killed the Ziggy persona in 1973—"Anything he did now would just be repetition, carrying it on to the death"—and, slimmed to skeletal proportions by cocaine, became the Thin White Duke. While other rock stars sold their souls to the devil, Bowie was more circumspect: believing Satan was living in his L.A. swimming pool, he had it exorcised.

By the late 1970s, he was backing Iggy Pop, with whom he met The Sex Pistols. "Sid [Vicious] was near catatonic and I felt very bad for him," he recalled. "He was so young and in such need of help." Vicious duly died due to a drug overdose in 1979. In September 1977, Bowie lent a helping hand to Marc Bolan, duetting with his old hippy-cum-glam rival on a TV show. Precisely one week later, the bopping elf was bopping no more, owing to a fatal car crash. In the intervening days, Bowie had duetted with Bing Crosby for *his* TV show. Three days later, Bing, too, had been struck down after a heart attack. "It seemed like everyone I worked with was dropping dead," marveled Bowie.

In 1980, his success soared again, thanks to "Ashes To Ashes," in which he killed off Major Tom from "Space Oddity." John Lennon—with whom Bowie cowrote "Fame" in 1975—had a rather less fortunate year, getting gunned down by a deranged fan in December. Lennon's fellow Beatle, George Harrison, lost his battle with cancer in 2001, prompting a cover of his "Try Some, Buy Some" on Bowie's *Reality* (2003).

Stevie Ray Vaughan was virtually unknown when Bowie talent-spotted the guitarist for *Let's Dance* (1983) and fruitlessly tried to enlist him for live work. Vaughan was killed in a helicopter crash in 1990, just as Bowie was filling stadia on his *Sound+Vision* tour. Another guitarist, Mick Ronson—featured on Bowie's breakthrough 1970s albums, and his visual foil in the Ziggy

shows—returned to the Bowie bosom to collaborate on Cream's "I Feel Free." The cover appeared on *Black Tie White Noise* in April 1993, by the end of which Ronson had died from cancer.

Freddie Mercury lasted a decade after collaborating with Bowie on "Under Pressure," until dying of AIDS-related complications in 1991. At a 1992 tribute concert, Bowie made millions watching cringe by dropping to his knees and reciting The Lord's Prayer. Luther Vandross survived a whole three decades after touring with Bowie and cowriting "Fascination" on *Young Americans* (1975), but breathed his last in 2005 after a stroke.

Kurt Cobain performed Bowie's "The Man Who Sold The World" on *MTV Unplugged* in November 1993. Within five months, Cobain had committed suicide. Bowie promptly restored the song to his live set, only to be accused of covering Nirvana.

Earning even more columns than Cobain, Princess Diana died in a car crash in 1997. Bowie was the only artist she had specifically asked to

meet at Live Aid, photos from which show him sitting near her at Wembley Stadium. However, he declared he had no interest in the royal family, had only met her "at two or three functions," described her death as "just more proof of the consequences of drinking and driving" and, within weeks, added *Low*'s "Always Crashing In The Same Car" to his setlists.

In 2004, a panting Grim Reaper finally got close enough to tap Bowie on the shoulder, in the form of a lollipop stick in the eye (courtesy of a Norwegian audience member), then a minor heart attack in June. In 2006, he made a rapturously received return with David Gilmour at London's Royal Albert Hall, performing "Arnold Layne"—written by one of his formative influences, Syd Barrett. Two months later, Barrett was beamed up to the Great Beyond after a battle with cancer.

The moral: unless you have the constitution of Iggy Pop, avoid working with the dangerously immortal Mr B. "Tombstone!" he scoffed, when asked what he would like on his. "I'd like a memorial. I'd never be content with a tombstone."

RIGHT Still going strong in the twenty-first century, the indestructible Mr. Jones.

BOB MARLEY
(ROBERT NESTA MARLEY)
BRAIN, LUNG, AND STOMACH CANCER

Born: February 6, 1945

Died: May 11, 1981

He was the first and greatest musical superstar of the developing world, a man whose face is as instantly recognizable as that of Elvis or Jimi Hendrix, whose protest songs were as hard-hitting and eloquent as those of Bob Dylan. He was a Rastafarian rebel whose unprecedented achievements saw him awarded Jamaica's Order of Merit and who secured international mainstream success with a distinctively and defiantly Jamaican genre. (His *Redemption Songs* compilation remains the best-selling CD box set of all time.) For millions of people worldwide, the soul of reggae is Bob Marley.

As The Wailers, Marley, Peter Tosh, and Bunny Livingston scored a slew of hits in their native Jamaica during the 1960s. However, their ska and rocksteady underwent a sea change after the three converted to Rastafarianism—a faith native to Jamaica since the 1930s but which received a huge boost with the visit of Ethiopia's Emperor Haile Selassie to the island in April 1966.

It was while attending a Rasta "grounation" (a chant-and-drum jam) that Marley met American singer Johnny Nash. On hearing Marley's songs, Nash was blown away, later telling business partner (and future Marley music publisher) Danny Sims, "I've just met this guy with long dreadlocked hair, and man, every song this guy played was a smash hit!" It was only when The Wailers teamed with bonkers-but-brilliant producer Lee "Scratch" Perry, though, that magic was born, and the trio's smooth, sweet harmonies were underpinned with a gutsier sound, the prototype for 1970s reggae.

Nash had scored a UK Top Five hit with Marley's "Stir It Up" in April 1972, but The Wailers' first taste of recognition outside their homeland came with the 1973 album *Catch A Fire*, their debut for Island Records. Island boss Chris Blackwell overdubbed synthesizers and bluesy guitar licks to make the sound more palatable to Western rock-oriented ears, but Nash's reggae-lite hits and success of the Jimmy Cliff's cult ghetto movie *The Harder They Come* (1972) had also helped prepare the ground. The new direction may have upset purists (Tosh disparagingly dubbed Blackwell "Whiteworst"), but it had the desired effect. By the time of grittier follow-up *Burnin'* (1973), featuring strident call to action "Get Up, Stand Up," The Wailers were winning over a new audience; Eric Clapton turned *Burnin'*'s "I Shot The Sheriff" into a U.S. chart topper in 1974.

A set at L.A.'s Roxy Theater on July 9, 1975, attracted rock royalty in droves, including The Rolling Stones, George Harrison, and The Grateful Dead. The U.S. tour that it kicked off saw *The New York Times* crown the dreadlocked singer the "Black Prince of Reggae," and by October The Wailers were supporting (and regularly upstaging) Sly And The Family Stone. By that time, though, Tosh and Livingston were long gone: they'd quit in December 1973, balking at evolutions in the group's sound and the way that Marley's fiery anthems of black empowerment were giving way to messages of universal love.

Gradually, the regular tours and high quality of Marley's recorded output started to reap dividends. Released as *Live!*, a storming set at London's Lyceum in July 1975 provided a UK Top Forty hit (and a UK No. 8 with the gorgeous "No Woman No Cry"), while 1976's *Rastaman Vibration* reached No. 8 in the United States. On December 3 of that year, however, a group of gunmen piled out of two white Datsuns outside Marley's home on Hope Road, Kingstown, and blanketed the place with bullets; several

RIGHT Marley onstage at London's Rainbow Theatre, on June 3, 1977, on the first night of the *Exodus* tour.

members of the band were hit (including Marley, though non-fatally). The Wailers had been rehearsing for a free concert—Smile Jamaica—at the time, and as then prime minister Michael Manley had announced a general election for two weeks later, it's likely that some had interpreted Marley's concert as a sign of support for Manley's People's National Party.

To escape the violence and tension, Marley moved to London, where domestic contentment (and the influence of the UK-originated "lover's rock," a softer, more melodic take on reggae) inspired some of his best-loved songs, including "Jamming," "Waiting In Vain," "Three Little Birds," and "One Love/People Get Ready" (all from 1977's *Exodus*). Indeed, the end of the decade proved an exceptionally fruitful one for the Jamaican legend. At the One Love Peace Concert on April 22, 1978, he managed to get bitter political rivals Michael Manley and Edward Seaga (of the Jamaica Labor Party) up on stage to shake hands, where he embraced them both—proof positive of Bob Marley's seismic influence. By decade's end, Marley and The Wailers were on a commercial high: in 1980, they played to a crowd of 100,000 in Milan (their largest audience), while *Uprising* (1980) provided a huge hit in "Could You Be Loved" and one of Marley's most stirring pieces, "Redemption Song."

After the triumph, though, came an unexpected and dramatic decline. During a European tour for *Exodus* in May 1977, Marley injured a big toe playing soccer with some French journalists in Paris. The injury wouldn't heal, and when he went to a doctor back in England, a dismayed Marley learned that this was because he had developed cancer. As amputation was counter to Rastafarian beliefs, he opted to complete the tour. In July, he underwent an operation in Miami that appeared to have saved his toe and removed the disease, but it proved to be a false dawn. The cancer returned, and spread to his brain. In September 1980, Marley collapsed while jogging in New York's Central Park. He died in Miami's Cedar Lees Hospital the following May.

Bob Marley was buried at a full Jamaican state funeral on May 21, 1981, holding a bible, open at the 23rd Psalm, in one hand and his blond Gibson guitar in the other.

RIGHT
Onstage at the Rainbow Theatre,
London, in June 1977.

RANDY RHOADS
(RANDALL WILLIAM RHOADS)
PLANE CRASH

Born: December 6, 1956

Died: March 19, 1982

"Everyone says there's nothing new that can be done with a guitar," said AC/DC's Angus Young. "But when people like Randy come along, they realize they're wrong."

Classical guitar enthusiast and modest Catholic boy from Santa Monica, California (who had previous minor U.S. success in Quiet Riot), Randall William Rhoads was bemused to audition for Ozzy Osbourne in 1980. "I wasn't," he understated, "a big Black Sabbath fan."

Nonetheless, he helped turn the madman into metal's biggest star. "Randy Rhoads," said Ozzy, "was the first guy who ever sat down with me and listened to my humming and worked with it."

Rhoads cowrote classics like "Crazy Train" and forged a unique rapport with the singer. Sharon Osbourne, who confessed to a pre-nuptial night with the guitarist, said Ozzy "was just as in love with Randy as I was."

On March 19, 1982, in Leesburg, Florida, Rhoads was persuaded onto a private plane for a short ride. The plane clipped the band's tour bus and crashed into a mansion—killing all aboard. "The plane ripped the bus into a million pieces," said Ozzy. "If I ever hear anybody say it was one of my practical jokes that went wrong, I'll strangle the bastard. It was an accident, a horrible accident." Rhoads was twenty-five years old.

His tomb—visited by Ozzy and legions of fans—is at Mountain View Cemetery in San Bernardino, California. His legacy is celebrated on 1987's album *Tribute*, compiled by Ozzy and Rhoads' mother.

"He was an angel," said Ozzy, "and too good for this world. His death's always on my mind."

ABOVE Randy Rhoads recording *Blizzard Of Oz* with Ozzy Osbourne at Ridge Farm Studios, in Surrey, England, May 1980.

JAMES
HONEYMAN-SCOTT

HEART FAILURE

Born: November 4, 1956

Died: June 16, 1982

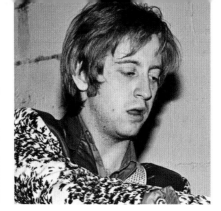

The Pretenders became known as the band you couldn't leave when two of the original members died within a year. Most fondly remembered is guitarist James Honeyman-Scott, who was killing time as a vegetable gardener in England's Hereford when friend and bassist Pete Farndon invited him to an audition.

The audition was actually an attempt to lure drummer Phil Taylor from Motörhead, for a band that Farndon and singer Chrissie Hynde were putting together. Taylor was unconvinced and Honeyman-Scott was wary, but he agreed to play on demos for "£100 [U.S. $200] and a load of speed."

"Jimmy Scott was already a burned-out speed freak when I met him," said Hynde in the documentary *No Turn Left Unstoned*, "and he was only a kid." Nonetheless, she admitted, "He brought out all the melody in me."

Enlisting drummer Martin Chambers (with whom Honeyman-Scott had played in the band Cheeks), the group became the Pretenders, who conquered the world with "Brass In Pocket," 1980's *Pretenders* (featuring what Lemmy called "the ultimate guitar solo" on "Tattooed Love Boys," in which Honeyman-Scott emulates his heroes in seconds), and 1981's *Pretenders II*. "One way or another I was going to get heard...," said Honeyman-Scott. "You've got to make a fight for it."

Farndon—"starstruck by Johnny Thunders," said Hynde—was fired in 1982 for alcohol and drug abuse. "Two days later," recalled the singer, "I get a phone call from Dave [Hill, the band's manager]. He said, 'I've got some really strange news. Jimmy's dead.' And that was the end of the Pretenders as we knew it."

"He'd played a few dates with The Beach Boys," said Chambers, "and that was one of the highlights of his life." Honeyman-Scott had also planned dates with ex-Rolling Stones guitarist Mick Taylor when cocaine-induced heart failure killed him in London on June 16, 1982. He was twenty-five years old.

"It was a total surprise," said Hynde, "coz he wasn't strung out. He wasn't a junkie. He was just a common drug abuser." He was laid to rest in Pipe Cum Lyde, Herefordshire.

With Honeyman-Scott's idol Billy Bremner of Rockpile on guitar, Hynde and Chambers recorded "Back On The Chain

"One way or another, I was going to get heard..."

Gang"—dedicated to their comrade. The song heralded the band's greatest period of success (Honeyman-Scott inspired 1983's plaintive hit "2000 Miles"), but the bittersweet triumph was dampened again when, on April 14, 1983, Farndon injected heroin while in his bath, passed out, and drowned. He was thirty years old.

The Pretenders' ongoing success, Chambers told *Trouser Press*, "is all thanks to Jimmy. If he's looking down upon us, I'll bet he's awaiting our first gig with as much excitement and anticipation as I am... Anybody you've been close to, you can feel their presence, or at least you think you do. Funny things have been moving around my flat, and his sister, who was very close to him, has had various experiences. Jimmy always was a tease. He had a funny sense of humor."

RIGHT The Pretenders perform onstage during their first U.S. concert tour stop in 1980 in Nashville, Tennessee. From left to right: Pete Farndon, Chrissie Hynde, and James Honeyman-Scott.

DENNIS WILSON
(DENNIS CARL WILSON)
DROWNED

Born: December 4, 1944

Died: December 28, 1983

With his good looks, blond hair, and athletic physique, Dennis Wilson epitomized the sunny optimism of brother Brian's early songs. It was Dennis who first suggested Brian write a surfing song to capitalize on the craze that had swept the West Coast since the late 1950s. Dennis was the only Beach Boy who surfed. And the first Beach Boy to die.

A run of pop jewels ("I Get Around," "Fun, Fun, Fun," "Help Me, Rhonda," "California Girls")—graced by trademark sun-kissed harmonies—saw The Beach Boys become America's answer to The Beatles in the early 1960s. Drummer Dennis was not ostentatiously gifted ("I'm not an artist; I'm a clubber") and rarely sang live, but as fellow Beach Boy Al Jardine recalled, "Onstage, all he had to do was stand up to stretch and the crowd would go nuts… He was a star without even trying."

Even at the height of his success, however, Dennis Wilson's appetite for self-destruction was palpable: "I could probably never be happier in my life… yet I know I'm gonna fuck it up," he told one friend. "It's just too perfect."

That foible brought him some strange bedfellows. In the late 1960s, Dennis befriended Charles Manson and his Family—including young nubiles from whom he contracted the clap. Soon, Manson and company were ensconced in the drummer's Sunset Boulevard home, and around U.S. $100,000 of The Beach Boys' cash was lining Manson's pockets.

Although Dennis left Manson's circle before the notorious murder of actress Sharon Tate in 1969 ("At least all I lost was my money," he told the district attorney), he had been instrumental in getting The Beach Boys to cover a Manson song, "Cease To Exist" (retitled "Never Learn Not To Love"), as a 1968 B-side.

As Brian's talents and energy began to wane in the early 1970s, Dennis investigated new avenues. He pulled off an impressive acting debut alongside James Taylor in *Two Lane Blacktop* (1971) and produced a more-than-credible solo album with 1977's *Pacific Ocean Blue*—featuring the mighty gospel-rock "River Song"—which sold 250,000 copies. The cracks and weariness in his voice were telling, though. Fueled by cocaine binges, a heroin habit, and alcohol, Dennis was an unpredictable handful who once burned down girlfriend Christine McVie's pool house. (Her response, to his buddy Gregg Jackobson: "A bit excessive, your friend Dennis, isn't he?") He was also a serial womanizer; one of his five wives—teenager Shawn Love—was the illegitimate daughter of fellow Beach Boy Mike.

By the early 1980s he was broke, occasionally living on the streets, and had been checked into St. John's Medical Center in Santa Monica, California, for drug and alcohol problems. It was a depressed Dennis Wilson who spent much of December 28, 1983, diving off his friend Bob Oster's yawl *Emerald* into ten feet of cold water at Marina del Ray, Los Angeles. Wilson had once moored his beloved yacht *Harmony* there, and now repeatedly dived to the sea bed to retrieve items he had thrown there years before. Returning from one underwater trip, he hit his head on the bottom of the boat, passed out, and drowned. Somewhat bizarrely, he was later afforded an official Coast Guard funeral and sea burial.

The remaining Beach Boys were left to reflect on an overlooked talent: "He was not only under-appreciated in the rock world," Al Jardine told *Mojo* in 2002, "he was under-appreciated in our band. We didn't know what we had."

RIGHT Carl and Dennis Wilson of The Beach Boys performing in harmony, New Year's Day 1970.

MARVIN GAYE
(MARVIN PENTZ GAY, JR.)
SHOT BY HIS FATHER

Born: April 2, 1939

Died: April 1, 1984

The parallels with his idol Sam Cooke are myriad. Both soul stars were blessed with charm, good looks, and honeyed larynxes. Both started their musical careers singing gospel. Both rose to become black icons. And both died violently, well before their time.

Marvin Gay (the "e" was added later, in tribute to Cooke), first sang publicly in the choir of an Apostolic church in his native Washington, D.C.; his father, an ordained minister, was a strict disciplinarian and Marvin harbored accumulating resentment toward him from an early age. After a spell in the U.S. Air Force, Gaye returned to his hometown, falling in with doo-wop ensemble The Marquees in 1957 (much to his father's disapproval). The group had a lucky break when singer/songwriter/producer Harvey Fuqua decided to substitute them for his regular backing band, The Moonglows, at a gig in Washington's Howard Theater. When Fuqua moved to Chicago to record for Chess Records, he took the group with him, and it was there that Gaye delivered his debut vocal, in 1959, on "Mama Loccie."

The group soon split, but Gaye stuck with Fuqua, relocating with him once more, to Detroit, where Fuqua set up a couple of record labels, employing Gaye as a session musician. When Fuqua's labels were snapped up by Motown boss Berry Gordy, Gaye followed them, performing backing vocals for The Marvelettes and drumming for The Miracles with Smokey Robinson. (Further entrenching himself in the Motown fold, Gaye married Berry's sister Anna—seventeen years his senior—in 1961.) It was Robinson who first encouraged Gaye to try his hand at songwriting. Gaye's first solo album—*The Soulful Moods of Marvin Gaye* (1961)—was not a great success, but he cowrote a hit for The Marvelettes, "Beechwood 4-5789," in 1962.

Abandoning his hitherto smooth, supper-club style, Gaye now hitched a ride on the soul bandwagon and soon racked up a string of hits, including "Hitch Hike" and "Ain't That Peculiar." "I Heard It Through The Grapevine" gave Gaye his biggest hit in 1968 (quite an achievement—Gladys Knight And The Pips had scored big with it just a year earlier), but he proved a successful duettist, too, scoring hits with Kim Weston, Mary Wells, Diana Ross, and Tammi Terrell. Gaye and Terrell were close friends as well as singing partners, and when she died in 1970—having collapsed onstage in his arms in the summer of 1967—he was so devastated that he temporarily retreated from the music business.

His triumphant return marked the emergence of Gaye the maverick talent. Grown weary of Motown's production-line pop, and desperate to produce a piece of work that chimed with the times, he created *What's Going On* (1971), an album that served as a snapshot of the new decade, taking in civil rights, the Vietnam War, and the ecology of the planet. It was a stunning suite of songs, built around Gaye's glorious informal multi-tracked vocals (smooth now, devoid of the rasp in many

LEFT Gaye performing onstage at the Montreux Jazz Festival in July 1980.

RIGHT Gaye's funeral casket.

of his soul hits); standouts included the breezily jazzy title track (a *Billboard* No. 2) and the darkly mesmerizing closer "Inner City Blues (Make Me Wanna Holler)." Concerned that the album was too uncommercial, Berry Gordy initially balked at releasing it, though the healthy sales and critical hosannahs did much to mollify him.

The follow-up was two years coming, and represented another change of direction: inspired by his new love and soon-to-be second wife, Janis Hunter (seventeen years his junior), the sizzling *Let's Get It On* (1973) introduced Marvin the Loverman. Gaye subsequently signed a new and highly profitable Motown contract, but the remainder of the decade was not kind to him. His marriage to Anna Gordy was on the rocks, and despite scoring a *Billboard* No. 1 hit with "Got To Give It Up" (1977), the following year he declared bankruptcy—legal fees, maintenance payments, and his prodigious appetite for cocaine all playing their part. In response, he produced the extraordinary *Here, My Dear* (1979) a record that picked through the debris of his marriage.

Hounded by the IRS, Gaye escaped—to London, then Ostend in Belgium. There he dieted, exercised, played darts (badly), and worked up a set of songs that would make up the album *Midnight Love* (1982), produced by old friend Harvey Fuqua. Its highlight was the seductively crooned "Sexual Healing," a minimalist masterpiece and transatlantic smash.

Any euphoria was short-lived. Having had his house repossessed, Gaye was forced to move back into the parental home, and it wasn't long before the old tensions between Marvin and Gay Sr. escalated. On April 1, 1984, an overweight, tired Marvin Gaye entered into a violent argument with his father, during which he physically struck the older man. His father responded by shooting his son in the chest, from close range, with Marvin's own .38-calibre revolver; as he fell to the floor, his father shot him again.

You might read it as a form of suicide—a desperate man under such pressure that he engineers a situation that can only have one outcome. Gay Sr. certainly saw his son as the aggravating party, flaunting his bruises to the cameras later. In a sad footnote, Gaye died intestate—none of his offspring received a share of his estate, which was used to pay off debts. A tragic end to a revolutionary talent—"our John Lennon," as Janet Jackson called him.

RIGHT Marvin Gaye performing onstage, September 29, 1976.

THE BAND

VINCE NEIL
(Vincent Neil Wharton)
Born: February 8, 1961

MICK MARS
(Robert Alan Deal)
Born: April 4, 1955

TOMMY LEE
(Thomas Lee Bass)
Born: October 3, 1962

NIKKI SIXX
(Frank Carlton Serafino Feranna)
Born: December 11, 1958

- -

THE UNLUCKY ASSOCIATES

Nicholas "Razzle" Dingley
Robbin Crosby
Randy Castillo
Skylar Neil
Daniel Karven-Veres
Michael Koda

RIGHT Promotional shot of
Mötley Crüe.

FAR RIGHT Mötley Crüe performing
in concert, January 1, 1980.

The most gleefully despicable
band in the world, Mötley Crüe
mixed the violent nihilism of
punk, Satanic destruction of
Led Zeppelin, and narcotic
excess of Aerosmith.

Incredibly, the four originals—
Vince Neil, Mick Mars, Tommy
Lee, and Nikki Sixx—are still alive.
Others snared in their craziness
have been less fortunate.

On December 9, 1984,
Nicholas "Razzle" Dingley—
drummer for glam metallers
Hanoi Rocks—went on a beer-
run with Neil in his new Pantera.

Just blocks from his home in
California, Neil lost control
and smashed into an
oncoming vehicle. Razzle
died of head injuries.

A depressed Mick Mars had
earlier set off to drown himself,
but passed out en route.
Returning to Neil's house after
Razzle's death, he assumed
crying partygoers were
mourning his own demise
and that he must therefore
be a ghost. Trying to walk
through a glass door
persuaded him otherwise.

Mötley's next album,
originally titled *Entertainment
Or Death*, was released as
Theater Of Pain. Liner notes
warned fans not to drive drunk.
Notoriously unsentimental, they
revived *Entertainment Or Death*
for a 1999 retrospective, and
titled a 2003 collection *Music To
Crash Your Car To*.

Sixx dealt with the tragedy as
he dealt with everything else—
heroin. A near-fatal overdose in
February 1986 (in the company
of Hanoi guitarist Andy McCoy)
inspired lyrics on *Girls, Girls, Girls*,
but Sixx ignored the omens. On
December 22, 1987, at an L.A.
hotel with Robbin Crosby of
Ratt and Slash of Guns N' Roses,
he was injected with heroin by
Crosby's dealer, turned blue

and died—only to be revived by paramedics armed with adrenalin. Discharging himself from hospital, Sixx changed his answering machine message to "Hey, it's Nikki. I'm not home because I'm dead," shot

> ## "Hey, it's Nikki. I'm not home because I'm dead."

up, and passed out again. Crosby died in 2002 of a heroin overdose. The same year, Randy Castillo—who replaced Lee in 1999—died of cancer. Neil's daughter Skylar also died of cancer, in 1995, at the age° of four (movingly detailed in Mötley's otherwise horrifying biography *The Dirt*).

In 2001, Daniel Karven-Veres, a four-year-old, attending a party for Lee's son, died in the drummer's swimming pool, and kidney failure killed Michael Koda of Brownsville Station, writer of the Crüe's hit "Smokin' In The Boys Room."

Mötley's maddest moment came courtesy of Matthew Trippe, who claimed he had been secretly hired to replace Sixx when the latter sustained severe injuries in a 1983 car crash. After arguing his case for five years, helming a band called Sixx Pakk, and inspiring the Crüe's "Say Yeah," he dropped his lawsuit in 1993.

RICKY WILSON
(RICKY HELTON WILSON)
COMPLICATIONS FROM AIDS

Born: March 19, 1953

Died: October 12, 1985

Ricky Wilson is most famous for his innovative guitar techniques, developed to compensate for the fact that the B-52's did not have a bass player. His methods certainly made an impression on John Lennon. "I was at a dance club one night in Bermuda... " he told *Rolling Stone* in 1980. "I suddenly heard 'Rock Lobster' by the B-52's for the first time... It sounds just like Yoko's music, so I said to meself, 'It's time to get out the old axe and wake the wife up!'"

Celebrity admirers of th B-52's also included Frank Zappa, William Burroughs, David Byrne, and, later, Dave Grohl. Out front were campy singers Fred Schneider, Cindy Wilson, and Kate Pierson, bouncing off music by Ricky (Cindy's brother) and drummer Keith Strickland. They were behind classics such as "Planet Claire" and "Private Idaho" on *The B-52's* (1979) and *Wild Planet* (1980), hinged on Ricky's rhythm guitar.

Though Schneider left few in doubt, Wilson and Strickland were not openly gay. "People just didn't go there," said the drummer. "But in our personal lives, we were out."

Strickland and Wilson's last songs together graced *Bouncing Off The Satellites* (1986). On October 12, 1985, Wilson succumbed to complications from AIDS at Memorial Sloane-Kettering Hospital in New York City. He was thirty-two years old. He is buried at Oconee Hill Cemetery in his hometown of Athens, Georgia.

The band's fortunes skyrocketed with 1989's "Love Shack," "Roam," and *Cosmic Thing*, likened by Strickland to "funerals in New Orleans where they have a jazz band and everybody parties and celebrates."

"Ricky's influence and spirit was so much a part of this..." said Pierson. "After this tragedy there was a sense of rebirth."

RIGHT Ricky Wilson live at the Greek Theater in Los Angeles, 1979.

RICKY NELSON
(ERIC HILLIARD NELSON)
PLANE CRASH

Born: May 8, 1940

Died: December 31, 1985

He'd been bitten by the showbiz bug early, starring with his real-life mother (singer Harriet Hilliard) and father (bandleader Ozzie Nelson) in popular radio/TV show *The Adventures Of Ozzie And Harriet*. A girlfriend's crush on Elvis prompted the teenage Ricky Nelson to try his hand at singing, too; afforded hefty publicity on the TV show, both sides of his debut single "A Teenager's Romance"/"I'm Walkin'" made the *Billboard* Top Ten. It heralded a string of hits—including two U.S. chart toppers in "Poor Little Fool" (1958) and "Travelin' Man"/"Hello Mary Lou" (1961), by which time Ricky had become Rick—and though Nelson's teen-heartthrob good looks might have suggested otherwise, his rockabilly-inflected records (featuring future Elvis guitarist James Burton) revealed a genuine talent.

In 1972, Nelson, fronting the country rock Stone Canyon Band, ratcheted up a surprise million seller with "Garden Party." The song was inspired by the heckling he'd received in fall 1971 at a Madison Square Garden gig for not playing his old hits—though in the 1980s Nelson made a good living from the nostalgia circuit.

In 1985, en route to Dallas from Guntersville, Alabama, Nelson's DC-3 airplane ran into trouble: a gas heater at the back started smoking, then fire broke out. The airplane plunged earthwards, missing a farmhouse, striking power cables and a tree, and losing a wing before crashing. Both pilots managed to escape, though severely burned; however, Nelson, his twenty-seven-year-old fiancée, and four of the Stone Canyon Band lost their lives.

It was later learned that pilots had had to make two emergency landings with the plane in the six months since Nelson had purchased it from its previous owner, Jerry Lee Lewis. In doing so, lifelong aviophobe Nelson had broken two rules he'd set for himself: always fly with a commercial airline, and never fly on a propeller-driven airplane.

RIGHT Nelson giving them his best in 1981.

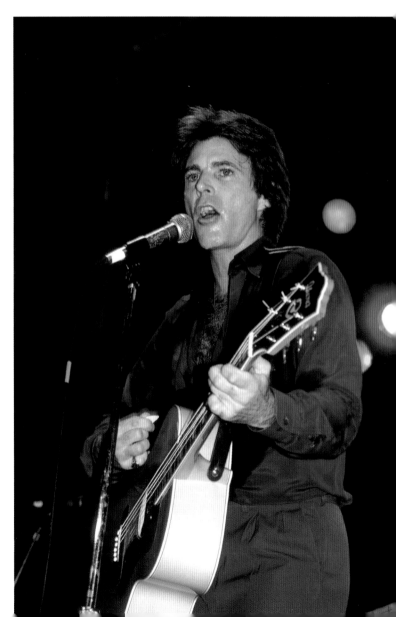

PHIL LYNOTT
(PHILIP PARRIS LYNOTT)
HEART FAILURE AND PNEUMONIA

Born: August 20, 1949

Died: January 4, 1986

"I am anti-drugs," Phil Lynott proclaimed in one of his final interviews, "… for other people."

Of hard rock's wild men, Lynott may be the best loved. From Jon Bon Jovi to Henry Rollins, his long-legged, twinkling-eyed, cowboy-cum-poet image entranced generations of fans.

Born in England's Birmingham, Lynott was raised in Moss Side in Manchester before moving to Dublin, Ireland. His dark skin—a legacy of his absentee Brazilian father, who he did not meet until the late 1970s—made him a target of racism, but he was quick to immerse himself in boozing, brawling, and bragging. In 1969, he formed Thin Lizzy, becoming their bassist, singer, and figurehead. "I tasted freedom," he said, "and I really liked it."

The band's breakthrough came in 1976. With Britain adrift in pre-punk blandness and the United States awash in disco, *Jailbreak* and its anthem "The Boys Are Back In Town" were breaths of fresh air.

"I tasted freedom, and I really liked it..."

Of 1977's *Bad Reputation*, producer Tony Visconti recalled: "I didn't expect a stretch limo to pull up outside my modest home and two inebriated rock stars to get out, waving large opened cans of Fosters lager. The rock stars were Phil Lynott and [guitarist] Scott Gorham… They were three sheets to the wind—maybe four! But they were laughing and friendly."

The darker side was revealed by tour manager Frank Murray: "He'd do all this coke to keep him awake until five in the morning, and then take a load of sleeping pills to get himself to sleep. Then there'd be someone knocking on his door a few hours later trying to get him on the bus… Consequently, he'd usually be in a really foul mood, and he'd be looking for a fight."

In 1978, Lynott played with Sex Pistols Paul Cook and Steve Jones in side project The Greedy Bastards. "Phil," observed Bono of then-support band U2, "was about to slide into the abyss." By 1979, heroin had entered the picture. "Phil was becoming harder and harder to work with," said guitarist Gary Moore. "You couldn't get him out of his hotel room, for a start… Scott used to call us the most unprofessional professional band in the business, and he was dead right." That year's *Black Rose* included the telling "Got To Give It Up."

In the midst of all this chaos, Lynott somehow managed to launch a solo career, despite the fact that Lizzy were still doing well, commercially. *Solo In Soho* was a success in 1980, but 1982's *The Philip Lynott Album* was a flop.

With Lynott and Gorham wracked by abuse, Lizzy bowed out with 1983's *Thunder And Lightning*—ironically, their strongest album for years—and a farewell tour. Lynott formed Grand Slam, only to encounter betrayed Lizzy fans and disinterested record companies. His wife left him, taking their two daughters.

His final hit was the Gary Moore collaboration "Out In The Fields" in 1985. On Christmas Day, he was admitted to Salisbury Hospital in Wiltshire with a kidney and liver infection, induced by drink and drugs. On January 4, 1986, he died of heart failure and pneumonia. He was thirty-six years old. He is buried at St. Fintan's Cemetery in Sutton, Dublin.

"Honesty was my only excuse," he had sung on Thin Lizzy's debut. "I took my life in my own hands and I abused it."

RIGHT Phil Lynott performing at Wembley Empire Pool in London, England, 1978.

RICHARD MANUEL
SUICIDE BY HANGING

```
Born: April 3, 1943
Died: March 4, 1986
```

In the early 1960s—along with Robbie Roberston, Levon Helm, Rick Danko, and Garth Hudson—keyboardist, singer, songwriter, and drummer Richard Manuel cut his rock 'n' roll teeth backing larger-than-life rocker Ronnie Hawkins up and down the length of North America. As The Hawks, the fivesome worked up a lean, thrilling powerhouse of a sound—and partied with a vengeance afterwards. "Ahhh, boy," Manuel later recalled, "lots of 'Bring out the wine and turn the music up,' lots of people in one room just sweating."

By 1965, their fearsome live reputation had attracted the attention of Bob Dylan, then looking to break out of acoustic-based folk and into loud, electric rock 'n' roll. The gargantuan sound they made together during their mid-1960s tour met with shrieks of protest from Dylan's folk fans, but *Time* dubbed it "the most decisive moment in rock history."

Dylan's motorcycle accident in July 1966 forced rock 'n' roll's premier poet to spend a spell recuperating at his home in Woodstock, New York. While he did, The Hawks (now renamed The Band) gathered around him, and together they brewed up a new rootsy Americana that flew in the face of psychedelia. Dylan's pared-down, countrified *John Wesley Harding* (1968) marked the first official change of direction, but The Band's debut *Music From Big Pink* (1968) was perhaps more remarkable. Touching soul, R&B, rock, and country, it proved hugely influential (presaging a "return to roots" for both The Beatles and The Rolling Stones) and, along with follow-up *The Band* (1969, featuring Manuel's fragile "Whispering Pines"), made the group's name.

Key to their success was Manuel's keyboard skills and high, soulful voice. His take on Ray Charles' "Georgia On My Mind" had originally inspired The Hawks to add him to their ranks, and his pleading falsetto could be unbearably poignant—note his vocal on "I Shall Be Released" and "Tears Of Rage" from *…Big Pink*. ("He was like Patsy Cline, just blessed with that voice," Helm reflected in 2000. "Rick and myself, in the beginning, were there just to rest Richard up.") Outside the studio, however, the depressive Manuel could be wilfully self-destructive. He'd started drinking at the age of seven; by the time of *…Big Pink*, he was regularly sinking quarts of Grand Marnier, his drinking toast a blithe "Spend it all!" according to Helm.

Of The Band's 1970s highlights, live offering *Rock Of Ages* (1972) was a standout, and their triumphant, star-studded final gig in San Francisco in 1976 (filmed as *The Last Waltz* by Martin Scorsese) was another. Drug and alcohol abuse dogged Manuel, though, and he entered detox in 1979.

When The Band re-formed in the early 1980s (minus Robertson), Manuel sang lead vocals. On March 4, 1986, having boozed and snorted some cocaine after a gig at the Cheek To Cheek Lounge, Winter Park, Florida, and having given no cause for concern that night, Richard Manuel hanged himself in the bathroom of the Quality Inn motel in Winter Park, Florida, while his wife slept next door. He left no note, but given his track record, such an outcome was perhaps sadly inevitable. Or, in the words of Libby Titus, one-time paramour of Levon Helm: "Self-deprecating, funny, soulful, sweet, extremely self-destructive, major alcoholic. He had zero information how to live."

RIGHT Manuel photographed at home in 1969.

CLIFF BURTON
(CLIFFORD LEE BURTON)
TOUR BUS CRASH

Born: February 10, 1962

Died: September 27, 1986

"I decided to devote my life to music," said Cliff Burton, "and not get sidetracked by all the other bullshit that life has to offer."

For Clifford Lee Burton, those distractions included fame and idolatry. "He hated all this being put on a pedestal bullshit," said drummer Lars Ulrich. Burton told his own sister never to call him a rock star.

Recruited from San Francisco band Trauma, Burton joined Metallica in 1982. "We heard this wild solo going on and thought, 'I don't see any guitar player up there,'" recalled singer James Hetfield. "It turned out it was the bass player, Cliff, with a wah-wah pedal and this mop of hair."

Unashamed hippy Burton—a school friend of Faith No More's equally idiosyncratic Jim Martin—was so vital to the early Metallica that Hetfield and Ulrich relocated from L.A. to his native San Francisco. His showcase solo became "(Anesthesia) Pulling Teeth" on 1983's *Kill 'Em All*. He also cowrote classics such as "For Whom The Bell Tolls" from *Ride The Lightning* (1984) and the title track of *Master Of Puppets* (1986).

Burton, Hetfield, Ulrich, and guitarist Kirk Hammett played their final show together in Stockholm on September 26, 1986. The next morning, at dawn, their tour buses were driving through Sweden en route to Copenhagen when one of the vehicles swerved, overturned, and crashed.

The driver blamed the accident on black ice, a claim Hetfield disputes: "All I knew was, he was driving and Cliff wasn't alive anymore." Burton, thrown from his bunk and crushed beneath the bus, was twenty-four. "It's not new that people in rock 'n' roll die," said Ulrich, "but usually it's self-inflicted... He had nothing to do with it. It's so useless. Completely useless."

The memorial service on October 7, 1986, featured "Orion"—a cut inspired by Burton, which Metallica would not play again for twenty years. The bassist was cremated and his ashes scattered in the San Francisco bay.

Burton's "To Live Is To Die" was included on 1988's *...And Justice For All*, and a 1987 video was titled *Cliff 'Em All*.

"You burn out from going too slow and getting bored."

In the band's 2004 movie *Some Kind Of Monster*, original guitarist Dave Mustaine says simply, "I wish Cliff was here" to a tearful Ulrich. Mustaine paid tribute to Burton with "In My Darkest Hour" on his band Megadeth's *So Far, So Good... So What!* (1988). "I went straight to the dope man," he said. "Got some shit and starting singing and crying and writing this song."

In 2007, Swiss metal band Krokus endured a bus crash, also en route to Copenhagen. "We were a lot luckier than Metallica," said singer Marc Storace. "They lost a great friend and a great bass player on a stretch of road which was very close to where we were."

Remembered as the bell-bottomed bassist with windmilling hair, Burton told one interviewer: "You don't burn out from going too fast. You burn out from going too slow and getting bored."

LEFT Metallica in 1985, from left to right: Kirk Hammett, James Hetfield, Lars Ulrich, and Cliff Burton.

PETER TOSH
(WINSTON HUBERT MCINTOSH)
SHOT BY ROBBERS

Born: October 19, 1944

Died: September 11, 1987

Having built his first guitar, the teenage Peter Tosh tried his hand at a solo career playing ska in the early 1960s under such pseudonyms as Peter Touch. His lot improved after he became one-third of The Wailers, alongside fellow Trenchtownites Bob Marley and Bunny Livingston. Though Marley is the more revered songwriter today, it was the talented Tosh who tutored him in

"I did not come on this Earth to be a background vocal..."

songcraft and guitar playing. Their 1964 debut single "Simmer Down," recorded for the Studio One label, sold 75,000 copies in Jamaica alone—but although they were successful enough to challenge The Maytals as Jamaica's top group, The Wailers saw little in the way of royalties. In fact, Tosh and Livingston quit in 1973, just as they began to make serious money—partly because they felt Marley was being groomed for solo stardom by their label, Island Records. ("I did not come on this Earth to be a background vocal," Tosh sniffed.)

A committed Rastafarian and devout marijuana consumer, Tosh named his debut solo album *Legalize It* (1976), its title track a strident plea for cannabis legalization (the cover showed the guitarist crouching in a field of the stuff, pipe in hand); it immediately attracted attention—and a blanket ban on Jamaican radio. Tosh's commercial success was to be dwarfed by Marley's, though the following year he charted with "Stepping Razor" (from *Equal Rights*, featuring Sly Dunbar and Robbie

Shakespeare). A strong set at the 1978 One Love Peace Concert (during which he smoked a spliff onstage and criticized Jamaica's leading politicians) resulted in Tosh's signing with Rolling Stone Records, and the same year he notched another hit, a duet with head Stone Mick on The Temptations' "(You Gotta Walk And) Don't Look Back." In March 1988, his album *No Nuclear War* received a Grammy for Best Reggae Performance—but by then, Peter Tosh was dead.

A fiery man with a short fuse, Peter Tosh regularly attracted controversy, and violence. He was frequently beaten by the Jamaican police (including a ninety-minute mauling after the One Love concert), but his end came at the hands of thieves, three of whom visited his house in Kingston's upper-middle-class parish of St. Andrew one evening in September 1987, talked their way inside, and demanded money. Tosh scoffed at them, and was first badly beaten for his trouble, then shot twice in the forehead, along with his herbalist Wilton "Doc" Brown and DJ Jess "Free-I" Dixon. Tosh's assassin, ex-con Dennis "Leppo" Lobban (whom Tosh had previously befriended), turned himself in and, after an eleven-minute jury deliberation, was sentenced to hang.

Tosh's violent demise surprised few—least of all Stones guitarist Keith Richards. "I let him use my house years and years ago and suddenly, apparently, he thought it was his," he recalled. "I got in touch with him and said, 'I'm coming down to the house, I need it for myself,' and he said, 'If you come anywhere near here I'll shoot you.' So I said, 'You'd better make sure you know how to use that gun and make sure you get the fucking magazine the right way round 'cause I'm gonna be there in half an hour.' And he left... "

RIGHT Peter Tosh onstage at the Roxy Theatre, Los Angeles, California, in May 1979.

HILLEL SLOVAK
DRUG OVERDOSE

Born: April 13, 1962

Died: June 25, 1988

Playing guitar for the Red Hot Chili Peppers may seriously damage your health. Dave Navarro fell off the wagon. John Frusciante nearly died. And Hillel Slovak—their original guitar hero—*did* die.

Born in Haifa, Israel, Slovak came to the United States when he was four, and hooked up with singer Anthony Kiedis, bassist Michael "Flea" Balzary, and drummer Jack Irons after high school in the Los Angeles band What Is This? They evolved into the Red Hot Chili Peppers, although Slovak and Irons stuck with What Is This? and did not grace the band's 1984 debut (ironically, produced by one of Slovak's heroes, Andy Gill of Gang Of Four).

Slovak returned for *Freaky Styley* (1985)—produced by funk overlord George Clinton—and was a major contributing factor in the Peppers' evolving funked-up sound.

Clinton and Kiedis had a colorful history with drugs; on the subsequent tour, Slovak, too, became an addict. He made a final album, *The Uplift Mofo Party Plan* (1987), and covered his idol Hendrix's "Fire" on *The Abbey Road E.P.* (1988). On June 25, 1988, he died of a heroin overdose in L.A., at the age of twenty-six. He is buried at Mount Sinai Memorial Park Cemetery.

The Peppers enlisted John Frusciante, who idolized Slovak. "Knock Me Down" (on 1989's *Mother's Milk*) and "My Lovely Man" (on 1991's *Blood Sugar Sex Magik*) are about his predecessor.

Slovak's brother published *Behind The Sun: The Diary And Artwork Of Hillel Slovak* in 1999. The guitarist's plans for an underwear range called Slippity Slop Scrotum Stoppers, however, never came to fruition.

LEFT The Red Hot Chili Peppers in New York, 1985. From left to right: Cliff Martinez, Anthony Kiedis, Hillel Slovak, and Flea.

NICO
(CHRISTA PÄFFGEN)
BRAIN HEMORRHAGE

Born: October 16, 1938

Died: July 16, 1988

Nico's ice-maiden beauty (which "made even the furniture moan," according to one-time Andy Warhol associate Mary Waronov) resulted in her modeling for Chanel in Paris, landing a minor role in Federico Fellini's *La Dolce Vita* (1960), and attracting French heartthrob Alain Delon as a lover. All before anyone had heard her sing. But coupled with her Teutonic blonde cool, Nico's striking low vocals made her a prize pop package, and after putting her on film in *Chelsea Girls* (1966), Warholian sidekick Paul Morrissey teamed her with noir art-rock quartet The Velvet Underground. Although no conventional nightingale, Nico's strongly accented voice was oddly captivating, whether dispassionate and knowing on "Femme Fatale" or strident on "All Tomorrow's Parties" (both on The Velvet Underground's eponymous debut album). However, tensions with one-time squeeze Lou Reed led to her rapid departure.

Velvet's bassist/viola player/ex-lover John Cale produced her debut solo effort *Chelsea Girl* (1967) and follow-up *The Marble Index* (1969), a stark, avant-garde cult classic on which she first played the Indian harmonium (in which she'd been tutored by Ornette Coleman) that became an enduring accompaniment. But deep-rooted unhappiness eradicated any hope of a viable solo career. The melancholy chanteuse took up heroin in the late 1960s and the drug dominated her life thereafter, precipitating a gradual decline; seeing her perform at the Whisky a Go Go in L.A. in the 1970s, Waronov was shocked to see that Nico's teeth were rotting away. At one point, she moved to Manchester, England—simply to improve her supply—where she befriended renowned Mancunian poet John Cooper Clark.

Strangely enough, the drugs didn't kill her. Indeed, she was reportedly clean when, cycling on the Balearic island of Ibiza in 1988, she fell off her bicycle, struck her head, and suffered a brain hemorrhage.

ABOVE Studio portrait of the pre-Velvets Nico in 1961.

ROY ORBISON
(ROY KERTON ORBISON)
HEART ATTACK

Born: April 23, 1936

Died: December 6, 1988

If angels sang rock 'n' roll, it would sound like Roy Orbison. Now regarded as one of rock's true originals, Orbison's career path had more than its fair share of false starts.

Orbison started out country, with The Wink Westerners in 1949, but was later urged to switch to rockabilly by a fellow North Texas State student, Pat Boone. Rechristening his group The Teen Kings, Orbison scored a minor local hit with the rockabilly-esque "Ooby Dooby," recorded at Noman Petty's studio in Clovis, New Mexico (also favored by Buddy Holly). Through Johnny Cash, Orbison secured a deal with Sam Phillips' Sun Records. Although a reworked "Ooby Dooby" gave him a minor national hit there in 1956, his heart wasn't in rockabilly.

Relocating to Nashville, Tennessee, Orbison worked for a time as a songwriter for Acuff-Rose (who had once employed country giant Hank Williams). He notched up a string of unsuccessful singles while trying to nail a new sound that he could make his own, though his "Claudette" (written for his first wife) proved a hit for The Everly Brothers in 1958. He finally hit paydirt with a run of melodramatic pop classics, kicking off with 1960's "Only The Lonely," a song that had previously been rejected by both Elvis Presley and the Everlys.

Unlike Elvis, Little Richard, or even Buddy Holly, Orbison never wailed. Gifted with a three-octave range, he conveyed emotion by letting his pure, unforced vocals soar to luminous heights. "Typically, he'd start out in some low, barely audible range, stay there a while and then astonishingly slip into histrionics," Bob Dylan recalled in 2004. "His voice could jar a corpse…There wasn't anything else on the radio like him."

Orbison's "Running Scared" (1961) set a troubled lyric to a dramatic bolero beat; "Crying" (also 1961) and "It's Over" (1964) made sadness sound inexpressibly beautiful. Among such company, his bestselling "Oh, Pretty Woman" (1964), set off by one of the most instantly recognizable guitar riffs in rock, sounded uncharacteristically upbeat.

By 1964, Orbison was an established star, his trademark Ray-Ban Wayfarer sunglasses (originally donned to disguise his astigmatism), impeccable black coiffeur, and sharp-suited appearance as much a trademark as The Beatles' moptops and collarless suits. Indeed, The Big O toured Britain in 1963 with a very nervous Fab Four, who never relished the prospect of following such an emotionally powerful singer on stage. (John Lennon's original, much slower version of "Please Please Me" was a conscious piece of Orbison mimickery.)

Thereafter, however, the new generation of rock 'n' roll ushered in by The Beatles gradually turned its back on Orbison and his kind, though as with many rock 'n' rollers (Bill Haley, Chuck Berry, Gene Vincent, and Eddie Cochran, to name but four), Britain maintained its affection for him long after his appeal had waned in the United States, and he continued to tour there throughout the decade.

At the height of his success, Roy Orbison's world came crashing down. In 1966, his wife Claudette died in a motorcycle accident and, two years later, a fire at his home in Hendersonville, Tennessee, killed two of his three young sons. He subsequently fell in love again, with Barbara Wellhonen, whom he married in 1969; when the hits finally dried up, he moved to his new wife's home country of Germany. The late 1960s and '70s represented a lean

RIGHT If angels sang rock 'n' roll… Roy Orbison in his prime.

ABOVE The Fab Five. From left to right: Roy Orbison, Jeff Lynne, Bob Dylan, Tom Petty, and George Harrison.

period for Orbison, and it wasn't until the following decade that his star rose once more, by which time he had relocated to the United States again. Don McLean took a faithful cover of "Crying" to No.1 in the UK in 1980, the same year that Orbison was picked as a support act for the Eagles and had a hit duet with Emmylou Harris, "That Loving You Feeling Again," which won a Grammy. Director David Lynch picked up on the dark underbelly of Orbison's oeuvre when he used "In Dreams" in a memorably sinister scene in *Blue Velvet* (1986). To crown it all, Orbison found considerable chart success as a member of 1980s supergroup The Traveling Wilburys, alongside Bob Dylan, George Harrison, Tom Petty, and Jeff Lynne.

Mystery Girl (1989), the title track of which was written by Bono and The Edge, provided Roy Orbison with a welcome UK No. 2, while "You Got It" (1989) went Top Ten; both were solo, and alas, posthumous hits. On a visit to his mother's home in Hendersonville, on December 6, 1988, Orbison suffered a massive heart attack (he had had a triple heart bypass ten years earlier).

Some of pop's finest moments have been those mini epics that seem to squeeze the exquisite pains of love into three time-stopping minutes—think "The Sun Ain't Gonna Shine Anymore," "You've Lost That Lovin' Feelin'," or "Stay With Me Baby." All owe a debt to Roy Orbison, who made heartbreak a thing of beauty.

PETE DE FREITAS
MOTORCYCLE ACCIDENT

Born: August 2, 1961

Died: June 14, 1989

Port Of Spain-born Pete de Freitas owed his place on the drum stool with Liverpudlian legends Echo And The Bunnymen to the fact that the band's previous source of percussion—a drum machine—had broken down. After joining, he completed a unit that became one of the UK's most revered post-punk bands.

Purveying an epic strain of psychedelia-tinged guitar pop, and blessed with Ian McCulloch's majestic vocals, the Bunnymen scored a string of hits at the start of the 1980s, including "The Back of Love" (1982), "The Cutter" (1983), and "The Killing Moon" (1984, from the acclaimed, semi-orchestral *Ocean Rain*), all driven by de Freitas' vigorous drumming.

The following year saw the release of one of their finest singles, the mesmeric "Bring on the Dancing Horses," but by then, the hedonistic, privately educated rocker was tiring of the music biz and quit, decamping for an indulgent break in New Orleans, where—for reasons best known to de Freitas—he renamed himself "Mad Louie" and blew all his Bunnymen earnings. By 1986, however, he was back in the fold.

In truth, the Bunnymen's best was now behind them and, after the so-so *Echo And The Bunnymen* (1987)—which provided a breakthrough in the United States—frontman McCulloch quit in 1988, a move in part inspired by his father's unexpected death. To the ire of diehard fans, the three remaining Bunnies continued.

Shortly after McCulloch's defection, de Freitas was en route for rehearsals on his motorcycle when he collided with a car, dying from his injuries shortly after. He was twenty-seven years old.

RIGHT Bunny boy de Freitas on the roof of the HMV store on London's Oxford Street in July 1987.

ANDREW WOOD
HEROIN OVERDOSE COUPLED WITH A CEREBRAL HEMORRHAGE

Born: January 6, 1966

Died: March 19, 1990

If the Melvins were godfathers of grunge, Andrew Wood was its godmother. Pearl Jam owe their existence to him (if he were still with us, Pearl Jam probably would never have been formed), but their earnestness was not for Wood. Engineer-turned-Nirvana-producer Jack Endino called him "the only stand-up comedian frontman in Seattle."

Born in Mississippi, Wood moved to Washington state as a youth. His first notable band, formed in 1980, was Malfunkshun, in which he dubbed himself "L'Andrew the Love Child." They were derailed by his 1985 spell in rehab for cocaine, then abandoned with the advent of Mother Love Bone in 1988. Fusing Guns N' Roses-esque viciousness with Led Zeppish grandeur, MLB's debut *Apple* was grinding on "Stardog Champion," glacial on "Crown of Thorns," and great throughout.

Introduced to drugs in high school, Wood graduated to heroin in Seattle, the scene of his demise. Before the release of the recording, Wood overdosed, and spent three days in a coma. His brother, also in Malfunkshun, recalled: "During the time they had him hooked up to life-support, he had a hemorrhage aneurysm and lost all brain function…and [the doctors said] you may as well pull the plug." He died at the age of twenty-four.

Members of Mother Love Bone united with Soundgarden for the tribute album *Temple Of The Dog*, then enlisted *Temple* singer Eddie Vedder to become Pearl Jam. Others paid tribute too, notably Alice In Chains with the hit "Would?" The singer was also immortalized in the acclaimed 2005 documentary *Malfunkshun: The Andrew Wood Story*.

RIGHT Mother Love Bone in Seattle, Washington, March 1990. From left to right: Andrew Wood, Jeff Ament, Stone Gossard, Greg Gilmore, and Bruce Fairweather.

STIV BATORS
(STEVEN JOHN BATOR)
INTERNAL INJURIES SUSTAINED AFTER BEING STRUCK BY A TRUCK

Born: October 22, 1949

Died: June 4, 1990

Inspired by Iggy Pop, Bators cofounded Frankenstein in 1975 in Ohio. After an eye-opening trip to New York at the invitation of Johnny Thunders, Frankenstein evolved into The Dead Boys, a much punkier proposition, in 1976. Their Pistols-esque legacy included "Sonic Reducer," covered by Pearl Jam, and "Ain't It Fun," a hit for Guns N' Roses. Bators was also involved in Rocket From The Tombs, which posthumously became an influential band.

Broke, and unnerved by the near-fatal stabbing of drummer Johnny Blitz, The Dead Boys finished in 1979. Bators relocated to L.A., made *Disconnected* (1980), and moved again, this time to the UK. He united with Sham 69 survivors in The Wanderers, then formed The Lords Of The New Church with Damned guitarist Brian James. They made three albums and a jaw-dropping mutilation of Madonna's "Like A Virgin," but are celebrated for their unhinged gigs. In 1983, a stunt in which Bators hung himself with a microphone cord, backfired when the wire tightened—rendering him clinically, albeit briefly, dead. The trick had already proved perilous in The Dead Boys when "the audience grabbed him and started pulling" according to guitarist Jimmy Zero. "He was about ten seconds from being killed."

The Lords imploded in 1988 and Bators relocated yet again, to Paris. There, in 1990, a truck struck him. Iggy Pop-ishly impervious to pain, Bators walked away—only to die of internal injuries in his sleep.

"Once you've actually died on stage…" he once mused, "how do you top that?"

RIGHT Stiv Bators performing with The Dead Boys at The Roundhouse, Camden, London, in December 1977 as part of their UK Invasion tour.

STEVIE RAY VAUGHAN
HELICOPTER CRASH

Born: October 3, 1954

Died: August 27, 1990

"The way I like to look at it," said Stevie Ray Vaughan of his blistering live act, "is if that's the last time I ever got to play, I'd better give it everything I've got."

With Eric Clapton dallying in album-oriented rock, Stevie Ray Vaughan kept the blues banner flying in the 1980s. Mick Jagger plucked him from the clubs of Austin, Texas, and a set at the 1982 Montreux Jazz Festival caught David Bowie's eye.

Bowie enlisted him for *Let's Dance* (1983) and tried to lure Vaughan into his band. Instead, the guitarist forged ahead with his group Double Trouble, making four albums from 1983 to 1989. Along the way, he kicked his debilitating taste for cocaine and whiskey. "It's a big world out there," he said, "With enough pain and misery in it, without me going around and helping it out by hurting myself and, consequently, those that care about me."

"I'd better give it everything I've got..."

On August 26, 1989, he played at the Alpine Valley Music Theater in East Troy, Wisconsin, encoring with fellow fret-burners Clapton, Robert Cray, Buddy Guy, and his brother Jimmie (with whom Vaughan recorded 1990's *Family Style*). In the early hours of the next morning, he boarded a helicopter bound for Chicago. Moments after take-off at 12:40 A.M., the chopper crashed in fog, killing all aboard. Clapton and Jimmie Vaughan helped the coroner identify the bodies. Vaughan was thirty-five.

"Stevie is the best friend I've ever had," said Buddy Guy, "the best guitarist I ever heard and the best person anyone will ever want to know."

RIGHT Stevie Ray Vaughan performing at the Warfield Theater in San Francisco in 1984.

STEVE CLARK
(STEPHEN MAYNARD CLARK)
RESPIRATORY FAILURE INDUCED BY DRINK AND DRUGS

Born: April 23, 1960

Died: January 8, 1991

"It was upsetting," said Def Leppard's Joe Elliott, "but it wasn't a shock. Steve's was a death waiting to happen."

"Steamin'" Steve Clark was integral to Leppard's early success. In 1979, the guitarist threatened to quit if the fledgling band did not play live. The quintet's perseverance paid off when they conquered America with 1983's *Pyromania*.

Though drummer Rick Allen's loss of an arm is the best documented of their misfortunes, there were other casualties. Guitarist Pete Willis was ousted—and Clark sank into abuse. Producer Mutt Lange chose the teetotal Phil Collen—Willis' replacement—to handle most of the guitar on *Hysteria*. Unemployed for much of the album's torturous gestation, Clark unsuccessfully checked into rehab in 1987.

On tour, he was—reported *Guitar World*—"on a round-the-clock regimen of vodka, schnapps, beer, cocaine, painkillers, and tranquilizers." "There was fuck all we could do to help him," said Elliott, "short of tying his hands behind his back. Steve had survived one of his sessions with double the alcohol John Bonham had in his bloodstream when he died."

On January 8, 1991, Clark was found dead of respiratory failure at his London home. He was 30 years old. "A very heavy drinker who seemingly had abused drugs and regrettably paid the price," said the coroner.

"White Lightning" on Leppard's *Adrenalize* was dedicated to Clark. "I knew he had a problem," said Ozzy Osbourne. "I never expected it to end like this though… It's just very sad."

ABOVE Def Leppard in 1983, from left to right: Steve Clark, Phil Collen, Joe Elliott, Rick Savage, and Rick Allen.

Behind the scenes

MARTIN HANNETT
HEART FAILURE

Born: May 31, 1948

Died: April 18, 1991

ABOVE He's got control...Martin Hannett, around 1979.

"I admire producers who go over the top when there is really no reason to go over the top," Martin Hannett once said. Though the likes of Joe Meek are more celebrated, the eccentric Hannett produced some of Britain's most important records.

Joy Division were his jewel. "They were a gift to a producer, cos they didn't have a clue," he told writer Jon Savage in 1989. Though Hannett's mission was "to make it appealing," his digital effects made *Unknown Pleasures* (1979) and *Closer* (1980) sound icy, eerie, and harsh. Twenty-five years on, their legacy remains, from Nine Inch Nails to Interpol.

Hannett—sometimes credited as Martin Zero—also helmed the fledgling Buzzcocks (1977's classic *Spiral Scratch* EP), U2 (1980's

"11 O'Clock Tick Tock"), New Order (1981's *Movement*), and The Stone Roses (1985's *Garage Flower*). His last widely acclaimed work was Happy Mondays' *Bummed* (1988).

Hannett's obsessiveness was fueled by a love both of technology and of drugs. Despite telling Savage "I didn't get into a 'lot of drugs' situation until about '83," he started using heroin in the late 1970s: "I suppose it got to be a lot cos your tolerance builds up...As Anthony Burgess says, they took away our opium and gave us beer and football."

Falling out with Joy Division/ New Order's boss Rob Gretton, and fellow Factory Records directors Tony Wilson and Alan Erasmus, exacerbated Hannett's woes. He supplemented heroin with alcohol—and died of heart failure on April 18, 1991.

STEVE MARRIOT
(STEPHEN PETER MARRIOTT)
SMOKE INHALATION SUSTAINED IN HOUSE FIRE

Born: January 30, 1947

Died: April 20, 1991

As a twelve-year-old, London East Ender Marriott had performed in the stage production of Lionel Bart's *Oliver!,* and taken minor roles in Peter Sellers' *Heaven's Above* (1963) and several teen B-movies. However, his musical break came in early 1965. Working at East Ham's J60 Music Shop, he sold a bass to Ronnie Lane; the two struck up a friendship, and soon Marriott was singing with Lane's band, The Outcasts, also featuring drummer Kenney Jones. His talent for showmanship was evident early on (Marriott destroyed a piano at an early gig), and with their formidable frontman the redubbed Small Faces (with Jimmy Winston, then Ian MacLagan on keyboards) were soon whipping up a storm in London clubs.

From 1965 on, they released some of the 1960s' most enduring singles, from early Mod faves "Whatcha Gonna Do About It?" (1965) and "All Or Nothing" (1966, their only UK No. 1) to the prime psychedelic pop of "Here Come The Nice" and "Itchycoo Park" (both 1967) and the quirky, very English *Ogden's Nut Gone Flake* (1968), a UK chart-topper. Eager to pursue a less pop-oriented direction, Marriott quit in 1969, starting up the bluesy Humble Pie with guitarist Peter Frampton, but their initial success didn't last; thereafter, Marriott involved himself in sundry musical projects without ever recapturing his 1960s heights. (The remaining trio recruited Rod Stewart and Ron Wood and went as ultimate early 1970s lads' band The Faces.)

Having returned from working with Frampton in Los Angeles in April 1991, a jet-lagged and tipsy Marriott fell asleep in his sixteenth-century Essex home, lit cigarette in hand. The neglected cig set off a fire from which the woozy Marriott could not escape (prescription pills had also dulled his instincts) and he perished from inhaling smoke.

RIGHT Marriott serves up Humble Pie at Madison Square Garden, New York city, 1972.

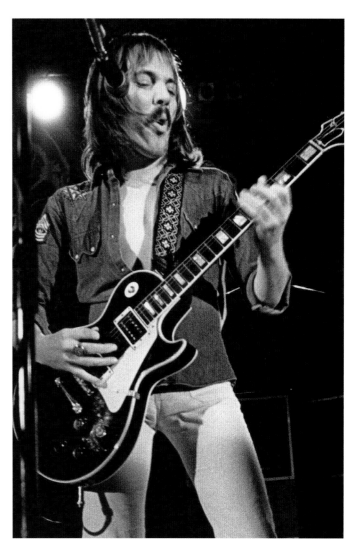

GENE CLARK
(HAROLD EUGENE CLARK)
HEART ATTACK

Born: November 17, 1944

Died: May 24, 1991

Clark was the Byrd who wouldn't fly—and the one with the best tunes. The Byrds' jangly folk-rock cover of Dylan's "Mr Tambourine Man" was a worldwide number one in 1965, but in that first flush of fame the only Byrd with serious songwriting chops was Gene Clark, who formed the band with Roger McGuinn and David Crosby, with Chris Hillman and Michael Clark joining shortly after. Their debut album boasted Clark's storming "Feel A Whole Lot Better," though the bittersweet "I Knew I'd Want You" was more characteristic. "Set You Free This Time," from follow-up *Turn! Turn! Turn!* demonstrated Clark's gift for deft wordplay, and he made a major contribution to the group's finest moment, "Eight Miles High."

By March 1966, however, Clark's songwriting royalties were causing friction ("We were all so busy that we really didn't notice how many songs Gene had written until the first album came out and he bought a sports car," McGuinn recalled). This, coupled with his phobia of flying, led to his quitting.

Clark's solo career had its share of high points. Debut *Gene Clark And The Godsin Brothers* (1967) was a strong set, and his two albums with Doug Dillard—especially *The Fantastic Expedition Of Dillard And Clark* (1968)—were excellent country-rock excursions. *White Light* (1971) is an understated minor classic of singer-songwriting, while the stunning *No Other* (1974)—an ambitious, richly produced set of songs—remains his finest release. None, however, was a hit.

Clark had been a serious boozer and flirted with drugs for many years. The hard living caught up with him in April 1988, when he underwent an operation to have most of his stomach removed. Genuine attempts to straighten himself out were followed by destructive binges, sometimes on heroin or crack cocaine. Little surprise, then, that in May 1991 he was found on the floor of his home in Sherman Oaks, California; an aneurysm had brought on a fatal heart attack.

Perhaps he was simply too sensitive to be a star. Byrd bandmate Chris Hillman thought so: "Gene Clark was a really sweet soul who got waylaid by everything negative and the fight just got taken out of him… Sometimes I think it would've been better if he'd have stayed in Missouri, led a local band and had kids, and never come to Hollywood."

ABOVE The Byrds onstage in 1979 (from left): Gene Clark, Roger McGuinn, Chris Hillman.

Behind the scenes

Tragic beginning, tragic end; helluva life in between. Shortly after young Wolfgang (a Russian Jew) was born, his father perished in an accident, and the child lived in orphanages in Germany and Paris before emigrating to New York (a sister died en route from their Parisian orphanage; his mother died in a concentration camp). There, Wolfgang Grajonca became Bill Graham ("I wish I'd never changed it," he mused in 1968. "Bill Graham is a nothing name"), and went on to become the most influential concert promoter in the history of popular music.

Graham's business sense first showed itself when he put on a gig featuring the Grateful Dead and Allen Ginsberg. This was to raise funds for the San Francisco Mime Troupe (an award-winning theater of rambunctious political satire that often attracted attention for its socialist bent), who had

fallen foul of U.S. obscenity laws. From benefit organizer, Graham swiftly expanded to become out-and-out promoter, pioneering light shows, merchandizing, and other mainstays of today's rock industry. His mixture of acts was no less innovative, an avowed aim "to broaden the musical taste of the public. A kid comes to hear The Doors, but he also hears The Staple Singers."

To name the acts he put on at his Fillmore West (San Francisco) and Fillmore East (New York) venues is to list the most important U.S. bands of the era—the aforementioned Dead, Janis Joplin, The Doors, Jimi Hendrix, Santana, and Frank Zappa And The Mothers Of Invention—as well as incoming Brits such as Cream, The Who, and Led Zeppelin.

Graham went on to promote some of these acts in the 1970s (and mount The Band's final concert, immortalized in Martin

BILL GRAHAM
(WOLFGANG GRAJONCA)
HELICOPTER CRASH

Born: January 8, 1931

Died: October 25, 1991

Scorsese's *The Last Waltz*), as well as organizing Rolling Stones tours and the U.S. leg of Live Aid in the early 1980s, and managing Van Morrison and Santana. His aggressive no-bullshit business approach made him many enemies, but also $100 million a year by 1990.

Graham's eventful life came to an end one night after a Huey Lewis And The News gig in Concord. He was flying home by helicopter when the aircraft hit a transmission tower around 25 miles north of San Francisco during a heavy storm. He died in the crash, along with his partner Melissa Gold, and pilot Steve Kahn.

ABOVE Bill Graham at the finale of the U.S. Live Aid in Philadelphia, 1985.

FREDDIE MERCURY
(FARROKH BULSARA)
BRONCHIAL PNEUMONIA
BROUGHT ON BY AIDS

Born: September 5, 1946

Died: November 24, 1991

"When I go on stage," Freddie Mercury told *Melody Maker* in 1981, "whether I'm rich or starving, I want to give my all. I want to go on there and die for the show!"

Some stars are celebrated because of their early death. Freddie Mercury is no such star. Queen made him famous, Live Aid made him a legend, and death made him immortal.

Farrokh Bulsara first made music in his native Zanzibar, in school band The Hectics. Relocating to Britain, he joined guitarist Brian May and drummer Roger Taylor in Smile in 1970. His stage name paid tribute to the messenger of the gods, but Mercury was also, in astrological terms, his rising planet. With bassist John Deacon, Smile became Queen—whose triumphs like "Bohemian Rhapsody" obscure a discography packed with gems.

"I want to go on there and die for the show!"

Mercury's solo career is less celebrated. In 1973, he adopted the Gary Glitter-spoofing pseudonym Larry Lurex and, with May and Taylor, recorded a flop cover of The Ronettes' "I Can Hear Music." A decade later, with the argumentative Queen at daggers drawn, he resumed a solo career with 1984's "Love Kills" and 1985's "I Was Born To Love You." On the solo album *Mr. Bad Guy* (1985), Mercury thanks his band-mates "for not interfering." Its "Made In Heaven"—a flop single at the time —was later resurrected as the title track of a Queen album.

A much more memorable 1985 event was a little show called Live Aid. Initially wary, Queen were talked into it by Bob Geldof: "I said tell the old faggot it's going to be the biggest thing that ever fokkin' happened!" Though America remained unswayed, Europe remembered that it loved Queen. "It was the perfect stage for Freddie," said Geldof. "He could ponce about in front of the whole world."

The band's subsequent *Magic* shows of 1986 proved them masters of stadium rock. The tour ended—as did Mercury's touring history—with a spectacular performance at Knebworth in England's Hertfordshire, in front of 120,000 fans.

Mercury's solo career ticked over with a cover of The Platters' "The Great Pretender" in 1987 and a titanic team-up with opera singer Montserrat Caballe on the splendidly silly "Barcelona." Mercury's final solo single in his lifetime was 1989's forgotten "How Can I Go On?"

Meanwhile, Queen resolved some of their squabbles by crediting songs to the group rather than individual writers. "It's got to the point where we're all actually too old to break up," said Mercury. "Can you imagine forming a new band at 40? Be a bit silly, wouldn't it?" Among the results of this rediscovered sense of purpose was 1991's *Innuendo*—Mercury's last album in his lifetime.

The singer had long led a self-confessedly "extremely promiscuous" life, fueled by fine wine and cocaine. "It's like you never grow up," Brian May told *Mojo*. "We've all suffered... Freddie, obviously, went completely AWOL, which is why he got that terrible disease. He wasn't a bad person, but he was utterly out of control for a while." In 1983, Mercury met Jim Hutton, his only long-term lover except for early girlfriend and lifelong confidante Mary Austin. Of his excesses, he said: "I stopped all that and started growing tulips." However, in 1990, the man who once said he "lived for sex" told his family he was HIV positive and had AIDS.

RIGHT Freddie Mercury in full flow onstage in the 1980s.

"We were sitting in his bedroom having coffee," recalled his brother-in-law, "when he said suddenly, 'What you have to understand… is that what I have is terminal. I'm going to die.' We saw these marks on his ankles and knew he was ill. After that, we talked no more about it."

Among his final recordings were Roger Taylor's "These Are The Days Of Our Lives" and "The Show Must Go On" by May. Recalled the guitarist, "I said, 'Do you think that's okay? Can you sing that?' And he went, 'Darling, I can sing that and I will give it my all.' Because he knew what it was all about and it didn't need to be said." In a heartbreaking video for Taylor's song, an almost ghostlike Mercury mouths "I still love you" to the camera.

"He chose the time to die," Mary Austin told the *Daily Mail*. "He knew it was coming, that it was closer than it had ever been before. Then he suddenly said, 'I've decided that I've got to go!' The quality of his life had changed so dramatically and he was in more and more pain every day... One day he decided enough was enough and stopped all the medical supplements that were keeping him going... He looked death in the face and said, 'Fine, I'll accept it now—I'll go.'"

Mercury died of bronchial pneumonia in London's Kensington, on November 24, 1991. He was 45. He was cremated at a modest service in west London, attended by Elton John; a single red rose adorned his coffin. Wreaths came from Ringo Starr, Boy George, U2, and David Bowie.

Mercury won even greater adoration after his passing. "Bohemian Rhapsody" topped the British chart again. A star-studded Wembley Stadium tribute concert in 1992 saw the crowd join in his videotaped audience participation routine as lustily as if he had been physically present.

Posthumous albums included 1995's *Made In Heaven*, whose poignant "Mother Love" was the last song Mercury recorded. The musical *We Will Rock You* plays to packed houses, and May and Taylor even revived the Queen name for tours with singer Paul Rodgers. A statue of Mercury stands in Montreux, Switzerland, where Queen recorded their last albums.

Doubtless Mercury would relish the fuss. But, as he said in 1981, "I've never been one to analyze myself too much. Sometimes it's best to leave well alone, dear."

ABOVE Tributes from Queen fans on the doors of Mountain Studios, Montreux, Switzerland, where Queen recorded their final albums.

RIGHT Onstage at the Milton Keynes Bowl, England, in 1982.

ERIC CARR
(PAUL CHARLES CARAVELLO)
COMPLICATIONS BROUGHT ON BY CANCER

Born: July 12, 1950

Died: November 24, 1991

Even in the makeup-slathered, fire-breathing, blood-spitting Kiss, "Rusty Blades" was too ridiculous a name. Instead, Paul Caravello became "Eric Carr" on joining the New York noise merchants (he subsequently checked into hotels under the "Blades" alias). Carr's original makeup—a hawk—was also abandoned, owing to its resemblance to *Sesame Street*'s Big Bird, and he became "The Fox."

Succeeding in the auditions to replace drummer Peter Criss in 1980, Carr remained friendly with his predecessor. "He respected him very much," said Carr's sister, "and Peter was a perfect gentleman to Eric." Carr's thunderous, Bonhamesque drumming— the best Kiss ever had—is showcased on 1982's cranium-crunching *Creatures Of The Night*.

Carr contributed barnstormers such as "All Hell's Breakin' Loose" to the Kiss catalog, and sometimes stepped in for Gene Simmons on bass. He also sang a version of Criss' hit "Beth."

Diagnosed with cancer in 1990, Carr endured months of surgery to treat various tumors on his heart and lungs. "It all sounds pretty nasty," he said at one point, "but here I am. I've got an 11-inch scar on my chest. I'm ready to get laid." But as his condition worsened, he grew isolated from Gene Simmons and Kiss's co-founder Paul Stanley, who regarded Carr as a junior. Nonetheless, he contributed harmony vocals to their hit reworking of "God Gave Rock 'N' Roll To You," before dying on November 24, 1991. The death of Freddie Mercury on the same day meant that Carr's death was shamefully ignored.

"It's like a dream come true… " Carr said of Kiss. "I wish that everybody, sometime in their life, could have an experience like this."

RIGHT The 5' 7" Fox stands tall after a solo with Kiss.

GG ALLIN
(JESUS CHRIST ALLIN, LATER RENAMED KEVIN MICHAEL)
DRUG OVERDOSE

Born: August 29, 1956

Died: June 28, 1993

Jesus Christ Allin was born to a disturbed father in New Hampshire in 1956. Though his mother renamed him Kevin Michael ("GG" was his brother's mispronunciation of "Jesus"), Allin grew up a misfit, and turned to rock 'n' roll to "destroy and fuck up everything that ever got in my way."

Leading the Jabbers, he made *Always Was, Is And Always Shall Be* (1980), the best introduction to his discography (which ranged from Stooges-style punk to Hank Williams, Jr.-inspired country). The Jabbers, however, disbanded when Allin proved uncontrollable. He spent the ensuing decade in heroin-fueled chaos.

Allin became famous for his notorious stage shows, during which he would perform transgressive acts, such as defecating and eating the results, performing naked, masturbating, and taunting and assaulting the audience and other band members. Consquently, he enjoyed a media profile entirely disproportionate to his success. On chat show *Geraldo*, he declared: "My flesh, blood, and body fluids are a communion to the people." His stage shows were regularly stopped by the police after just a few songs.

Having long threatened to commit suicide onstage, Allin instead died of a heroin overdose at a party on June 28, 1993, in New York. Fellow partygoers had photographs taken with his body. At his funeral, he was laid out—unwashed—in his leather jacket and jockstrap. Attendees put drugs in his mouth and whiskey in his casket.

"My body can't control what's inside of it," he told Doug Levy, who interviewed him in jail in 1992. "Why it can't be killed is beyond me... But I guarantee you when I get outta here this time, I'm gonna put it to the test."

RIGHT GG Allin performing with the MurderJunkies at The Wreck Room, Atlanta, Georgia, in February 1992.

FRANK ZAPPA
(FRANK VINCENT ZAPPA)
PROSTATE CANCER

Born: December 21, 1940

Died: December 4, 1993

"Americans are really suspicious of anything cerebral," said *Simpsons* creator Matt Groening, "and Zappa didn't disguise his intelligence well enough. Frank Zappa was my Elvis."

Some mavericks, like Sun Ra and Jandek, amass an extraordinary body of work without ever impinging on the mainstream. Frank Zappa's catalog of nearly 100 albums is unexplored territory for most rock fans, yet they have him to thank for Alice Cooper, Steve Vai, Bart Simpson, and tireless campaigning against music censorship.

Born to a Greek-Sicilian household in Baltimore, Maryland, Zappa moved to California when he was nine. There he played in school and bar bands, and scored the 1962 movie *The World's Greatest Sinner*. With proceeds from the latter, he opened his own studio in Cucamonga—which promptly folded when he was framed and busted for producing pornography. This triggered his battle against societal hypocrisy and legislated morality, and made him concentrate on his band, the Muthers (renamed, at corporate insistence, The Mothers Of Invention).

The Mothers reflected the eclecticism of a man who counted blues legend Howlin' Wolf and electronic composer Edgar Varèse among his influences. Their first album was the influential *Freak Out!* (1966), followed by 1967's *Absolutely Free* and 1968's *Lumpy Gravy*, which was Zappa's first solo album with an orchestra. That year also also brought both the R&B tribute *Cruising With Ruben And The Jets* and the *Sgt. Pepper*-skewering *We're Only In It For The Money* (John Lennon, hardly a fan of *Pepper* himself, jammed with Zappa in 1971, and may have had a celestial chuckle when Zappa covered "I Am The Walrus" on his final tour in 1988).

Seeking to eclipse San Francisco as the hotbed of the musical counterculture, Zappa established the L.A.-based Bizarre and Straight labels, his protégés including Tim Buckley, Tom Waits, Alice Cooper, and high school friend Captain Beefheart.

The excellent solo album *Hot Rats* (1969) showcased his extraordinary guitar skills, and signaled the end of The Mothers in their original lineup. His output—twenty-one albums in the 1970s alone, of which 1973's *Over-Nite Sensation*, 1974's *Apostrophe (')* and 1975's *One Size Fits All* are recommended to newcomers— was fueled by nothing stronger than nicotine and caffeine. "To me, a cigarette is food," said the staunchly anti-drug Zappa. "I live my life smoking these things, and drinking the 'black water' in this cup here." He gave as much credence to anti-smoking

"Cancer can bother you to death. I'm fighting for my life. So far, I'm winning..."

campaigns as he did to other attempts to restrict freedom: "The whole pitch about smoking has gone from being a health issue to a moral issue, and when they reduce something to a moral issue, it has no place in any kind of legislation, as far as I'm concerned."

Sheik Yerbouti (1979) gave Zappa exposure outside his fanatical fan base, thanks to the disco parody "Dancin' Fool" and controversial "Jewish Princess," for which he was obliged to defend himself against the Anti-Defamation League. Zappa and his daughter Moon Unit hit with the hard-rock spoof "Valley Girl"

RIGHT With The Mothers Of Invention on the "Mothers Day Tour," May 1970.

in 1982, while 1981's *Tinseltown Rebellion* introduced prodigious axman Steve Vai. Zappa's own interest in the guitar—and the costs and trials of running a band—declined as he relied more on synthesizers and samplers.

In 1985, he testified in front of a Senate committee, arguing against efforts—led by Al Gore's wife Tipper—to attach warning stickers to albums. His own *Jazz From Hell* (1986) was itself stickered, owing to the saucily titled—but entirely instrumental— "G-Spot Tornado."

Fans who stuck with him through experiments with classical and Synclavier-generated music were rewarded in 1988 with *Guitar*—a smorgasbord of solos—and the start of his six-volume live retrospective, *You Can't Do That On Stage Anymore*. "I have a low tolerance for wasting time," he said.

In 1990, Zappa made the news again, invited to the then-Czechoslovakia by its leader Václav Havel, an ardent rock fan and pioneer of the anti-communist movement. "In Prague," he reported, "I was told that the biggest enemies of the Communist Czech state were Jimmy Carter and me. A student I met said that

he was arrested by the secret police and beaten. They said they were going to beat the Zappa music out of him."

Zappa even planned to run for president of the United States but, in 1990, was diagnosed with prostate cancer. "It had been there for anywhere from eight to ten years," he told *Playboy*. "By the time they found it, it was inoperable."

Years of painful treatment—amid which he was gratified to receive "a sweet letter" from Tipper Gore—ensued, although he managed to attend the premiere of his orchestral work, *The Yellow Shark*, in September 1992. "I'm not dead," he announced, "and I have no intention of checking out this week or within the foreseeable future." "Have you thought of stopping work?" asked *The Guardian*. "What would I do?" replied Zappa, "Play golf?"

"Cancer can bother you," he admitted to *Pulse* in one of his final interviews. "It can just bother you to death. I'm fighting for my life. So far I'm winning. I've already beaten the odds. When the cancer was first diagnosed, the doctors didn't give me too long to go. But I've surprised everybody by sticking around this long."

However, on December 4, 1993, the man who famously paraphrased Varèse's quote "The present-day composers refuse to die" on two early albums succumbed. After a private funeral service, he was laid to rest at the Westwood Village Memorial Park Cemetery. His grave—unmarked, to avoid vandalism—is near that of Roy Orbison. Asked about the afterlife by fan magazine *Society Pages*, he said: "If you start defining these things in nuts-and-bolts scientific terms, people reject it because it's not fun, y'know. It takes some of the romance out of being dead... But basically, I think when you're dead, you're dead. It comes with the territory."

His work continues to be issued by his family. "A composer's job essentially involves the decoration of fragments of time," he once said. "Without music to decorate it, time is just a bunch of boring production deadlines, or a collection of dates by which bills must be paid."

LEFT The Grand Wazoo rocks the Deutschlandhalle in Berlin, September 15, 1972.

ABOVE Zappa photographed by Lynn Goldsmith, aka Will Powers of "Kissing With Confidence" fame.

HARRY NILSSON
(HARRY EDWARD NELSON III)
HEART ATTACK

Born: June 15, 1941

Died: January 15, 1994

Rock stardom via banking? Such was the unlikely career path of singer-songwriter/pianist/guitarist Harry Nelson III. While employed at First National Bank in California, Nelson took to writing advertising jingles in his spare time (his mother had been a songwriter, too). Under the moniker Nilsson—the Swedish version of his surname—he recorded *Spotlight On Nilsson* (1966) debut LP that rather slipped under the radar, though it was enough to pique RCA's interest.

Major label debut *Pandemonium Shadow Show* (1968) heralded the arrival of a considerable talent, albeit one prone to whimsy. Highlights included Nilsson's complex medley of Beatles tunes, "You Can't Do That," while The Monkees had a hit with the nostalgic charm of "Cuddly Toy" (Monkeeman Mickey Dolenz was to remain a lifelong friend). Beatles aide Derek Taylor spread the word to his masters, and when John Lennon was asked at a 1968 press conference who his favorite American singer was, he answered "Nilsson." (Asked who his favorite American group was, Paul McCartney gave the same reply.)

Resurrected for the *Midnight Cowboy* soundtrack, Nilsson's light-and-breezy cover of Fred Neil's "Everybody's Talkin'"—which had earlier appeared on his second album, *Aerial Ballet*—gave him a *Billboard* No. 6 hit in 1969, and in 1970 he paid tribute to another leftfield songwriting talent with *Nilsson Sings Newman*.

The commercial high point of his career came in 1972, however, with *Nilsson Schmilsson*, featuring his best known song. "Without You" was another cover, penned by Badfinger's Pete Ham and Tom Evans, but Nilsson took their rather anemic original and fleshed it out into an emotional epic—heartbreak Hollywood style. Result: a transatlantic No. 1 and a Grammy for the writers. *Son Of Schmilsson* (1972) also sold well, though Nilsson's maverick talent was perhaps better illustrated by *A Little Touch Of Schmilsson In The Night* (1973)—a beautifully realized set of orchestrated pre-rock 'n' roll pop standards, produced by Derek Taylor.

An astute businessman, Nilsson invested wisely in property and movie distribution—his financial well-being offsetting the poor showing subsequent albums made on the charts. But he liked a drink too…

Enter John Lennon. Nilsson struck up a friendship with the ex-Beatle during Lennon's notorious year-long "Lost Weekend" away from Yoko Ono when he took to booze-fueled bachelordom. On one infamous occasion in March 1974, Lennon and Nilsson drunkenly heckled The Smothers Brothers' act at L.A.'s Troubadour club. The two singers remained lifelong friends; after Lennon was shot in 1980, Nilsson became a vigorous campaigner for gun control.

In 1991, Nilsson's financial adviser embezzled his earnings, leaving Harry and family with a paltry U.S. $300. In February 1993, Nilsson suffered a massive heart attack brought on by his long-term weakness for drink. He never fully recovered, but his shaky financial state forced him back into the studio for one final (as yet unreleased) album. Shortly after finishing his vocals, the great Schmilsson's heart finally gave out.

RIGHT Smokin'! Nilsson with ukelele in Hawaii, 1973.

136

KURT COBAIN
(KURT DONALD COBAIN)
SELF-INFLICTED GUNSHOT WOUND

Born: February 20, 1967

Died: April 5, 1994

"I figured he was in the wrong business," said Keith Richards. "What's so tough about being lead singer in one of the biggest rock 'n' roll bands in the world? You just deal with it."

Kurt Cobain's unhappy fairytale began in rain-soaked Aberdeen, 100 miles from Seattle, Washington. Cobain learned the guitar to keep him out of trouble after his parents divorced when he was seven. Reluctant to join the local logging and lumber industries, he dropped out of high school and set off to Seattle, where the streets were paved with heroin.

No one regarded his band Nirvana as the Next Big Thing. Nonetheless, the band convinced the Sub Pop label to issue 1990's *Bleach*, a fusion of Beatlesque melodies and Black Sabbath riffing.

At the behest of Sonic Youth, Nirvana abandoned Sub Pop for the MCA empire. If Cobain wanted to avoid the big time, he chose the wrong way to do it. He also selected producer Andy Wallace (who had worked with Jeff Buckley, Bruce Springsteen, and Prince) to sweeten *Nevermind* (1991), then complained that the album was too slick.

Nevermind dethroned Michael Jackson from the top spot on the *Billboard* album charts, thanks to "Smells Like Teen Spirit," an aping of the Pixies' loud-quiet-loud formula and Boston's "More Than A Feeling." True to form, Cobain despised the video that, courtesy of MTV, made him a star.

Along the way, he became entwined with Courtney Love. "I met him at a show about a year or something ago," she told *Sassy* in 1992. Love was promptly branded a gold digger, despite her band Hole enjoying greater success than Nirvana when they met.

Cobain, who first injected heroin in November 1990, lured Love back to the drug—not, as is suggested, the other way around. The press dutifully reported that his nodding off in interviews was due to narcolepsy, and that he took heroin to soothe stomach pains. Oddly, when Love admitted to taking the drug in *Vanity Fair*, she was vilified.

While their figurehead languished in narcotic oblivion, Nirvana became one of rock's most famous bands, despite being outsold by Pearl Jam and Guns N' Roses. Reduced to pranks like wearing a T-shirt emblazoned "Corporate magazines still suck" on a *Rolling Stone* cover, Cobain admitted, "I think we look ridiculous already."

"I wish I could have taken a class on becoming a rock star."

His daughter Frances Bean—the only thing that made Cobain happy—was born into chaos in August 1992. For the birth, Love had checked into an L.A. medical center where Cobain was detoxing. Reported Courtney's confidant Everett True: "Her husband followed her to the delivery room, weakened from his treatment and hooked up to an IV stand himself—and passed out just moments before Frances was born." The next day, Cobain allegedly tried to talk his wife into a double suicide, then left to buy heroin.

Nirvana's next album—the working title of which was *I Hate Myself And I Want To Die*—became *In Utero* (1993). Titles like "Radio Friendly Unit Shifter" signaled a turgid treatise on superstar woes. "I wish I could have taken a class on becoming a rock star," he whined. Prudently, however, Cobain ensured "Heart-Shaped Box" and "All Apologies"—*In Utero*'s most melodic moments— were remixed by R.E.M. producer Scott Litt.

LEFT Cobain during one of his notoriously enthusiastic performances.

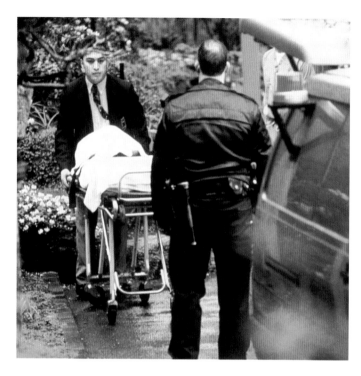

On tour, adding cellos and declining to play "Smells Like Teen Spirit" won Nirvana no friends. Adding cellos and declining to play "Smells Like Teen Spirit" did, however, make an *MTV Unplugged* performance their finest moment. Cobain revived songs by David Bowie and the Meat Puppets, and critics applauded his unearthing Leadbelly's "Where Did You Sleep Last Night?"—a song Love had regularly sung on tour with Hole.

Spotlighted by the media, by now unhappily married, strung out, and estranged from his band after reneging on an agreement to split royalties equally, Cobain attempted suicide in March 1994. Though the coma-inducing combination of Rohypnol and alcohol that he took in Rome was reported an accident, Love told *Spin* that Cobain had written a suicide note, mentioning how his psychotherapist "said that like Hamlet, he had to choose life or death, and that he's choosing death."

In April, Cobain fled another rehab facility and returned to Seattle. On the flight, he sat next to Duff McKagan of Guns N' Roses—whose Axl Rose he had taunted, schoolyard-style, for three years.

With Love out of town, Cobain bought drugs and obtained a shotgun. On April 8, an electrician at his Lake Washington home reported finding a body in a room above the garage. Cobain had pumped himself with heroin and died, the autopsy concluded, from a "self-inflicted shotgun wound to the head" on April 5.

Conspiracy theorists suggested Love had her husband killed, and questioned Cobain's elusiveness in his final week. "After the cat tried to off himself in Rome," said Keith Richards, "I was surprised that the people who were supposed to be taking care of him let him buy a shotgun and mope around for days." The claims about Love got the movie they deserved in Nick Broomfield's *Kurt And Courtney* (1998).

"I haven't felt the excitement of listening to as well as creating music... for too many years now... " Cobain wrote in his suicide note. "I feel guilty beyond words." Love read the note to mourners in Seattle, responding: "Then don't be a rock star, you asshole."

Cobain's mother—referring to Jimi Hendrix, Janis Joplin, and Jim Morrison having also died at twenty-seven—agreed: "Now he's gone and joined that stupid club."

Neil Young—whose "My My, Hey Hey (Out Of The Blue)" was quoted in Cobain's suicide note—recorded "Sleeps With Angels" in tribute. The Nirvana juggernaut rolled on with the live *MTV Unplugged In New York* (1994) and *From The Muddy Banks Of The Wishkah* (1996)—and, later, barrel-scraping compilations. Love issued fantastic albums while battling a press who vilified her for the self-absorption and abuse for which they deified Cobain.

In 2007, Frances Bean, now a teenager, wrote: "I'm not as mad at him anymore. I still wish he hadn't left me and my mom, but... I got some Nirvana shirts, and I've been wearing them."

ABOVE Police removing Cobain's corpse, April 1994.

RIGHT Kurt Cobain in concert with Nirvana at the Reading Festival in 1992.

LEE BRILLEAUX
(LEE COLLINSON)
THROAT CANCER

Born: May 10, 1952
Died: April 7, 1994

Formed in the UK on Essex's Canvey Island in 1971 around the formidable talents of South African-born Brilleaux (vocals, harmonica) and much-lauded guitarist Wilko Johnson, Dr Feelgood swiftly established themselves as a thrilling R&B act. (The name was probably a nod to a 1962 song by American blues artist Willie Perryman, who recorded under the pseudonym "Piano Red"). At a time when too many bands were consumed by high-art concept albums and brain-numbing solos, the Feelgoods' tight, hard-hitting sound—centered around Brilleaux's snarled vocals and Johnson's choppy guitar—came as a breath of fresh air (as heard on their taut debut single "Roxette"). They soon became leading lights on the pub rock circuit, their cropped hair, besuited appearance, and punchy sound anticipating punk stars The Jam and the new-wave bands that followed them. The United States remained resistant to their charms, but Dr Feelgood scored a UK No. 1 with the live album *Stupidity* (1976); three years later—and sans Johnson, who quit in 1977—they secured a UK No. 9 hit with the memorable "Milk And Alcohol."

Considered old hat by the early 1980s, the Feelgoods' day was over, though Brilleaux periodically took new variations of the group on the road, usually playing around 200 gigs annually. (Trivia fact: until 1982, when only Brilleaux remained of the original group, all Feelgoods save him had been named John.) Brilleaux's eponymously named solo effort was a no-hit in 1986. Brilleaux became ill in 1993 with throat cancer. He was playing with yet another Feelgood variation when he died—on Canvey Island, where it had all started.

RIGHT Like any self-respecting pub rocker, Brilleaux kept his drink close to hand.

VIV STANSHALL
(VICTOR ANTHONY STANSHALL)
HOUSE FIRE

Born: March 21, 1943

Died: March 5, 1995

English eccentric *par excellence*, Viv Stanshall (also known as Vivian) first made his name fronting The Bonzo Dog Doo-Dah Band, a 1960s rock institution that combined a love of music hall, dada, trad jazz, *The Goon Show*, sound effects, explosions, homemade props, crazy songwriting genius (care of Stanshall and Neil Innes), and a brilliantly off-kilter humor. Stanshall's wit and love of words, combined with his rich, plummy voice, was central to the Bonzos' charm. ("Viv used to phone Captain Beefheart on a fairly regular basis," recalled revered DJ John Peel. "You simply cannot imagine what their conversations could have been about…")

Stanshall's 1970s post-Bonzos career was a haphazard affair, his rich talent undercut by an entrenched insecurity and self-destructive drink binges—on which he was sometimes accompanied by Who loon, Keith Moon. Of his solo work, the extraordinary *Sir Henry At Rawlinson's End*—a tale of an aberrant aristocrat, later filmed with

Trevor Howard—was his best known, though his dulcet tones also adorned Mike Oldfield's mega-selling *Tubular Bells* (1973), heralding each instrument's appearance. (Oldfield was elated: "I mean, he was supposed to be rock 'n' roll's answer to Peter Cook, wasn't he?") Later, long-term admirers Pete Townshend of The Who and writer and personality Stephen Fry sponsored Stanshall's play *Stinkfoot* at London's Bloomsbury Theatre in 1988, though by then his alcoholism and addiction to Valium had made him both notoriously unreliable and exceptionally fragile (many of his belongings were stolen by beggars he'd encountered and invited back to his apartment).

On the morning of Sunday, March 5, 1995, Stanshall died in a fire at his London apartment, possibly from an overturned bedside lamp—exactly 100 years after the demise of the nineteenth-century Assyriologist Sir Henry Creswicke Rawlinson, who was the inspiration for Stanshall's cult classic.

RIGHT The Bonzos rock out—artily—at the ninth Jazz and Blues Festival at Plumpton, Sussex, England, in 1969.

EAZY-E
(ERIC LYNN WRIGHT)
COMPLICATIONS FROM AIDS

Born: September 7, 1963

Died: March 26, 1995

"I'm the type of nigga that's built to last," insisted Eric "Eazy-E" Wright on "Gangsta Gangsta," the cut that christened a genre. No one did more to put gangsta rap on the map—and, ultimately, make it the world's most popular music.

While his bandmates in Niggaz With Attitude—Ice Cube, Dr. Dre, MC Ren, and DJ Yella—were mostly middle class, Eazy was closer to the streets they rapped about; Ruthless Records was reportedly founded on the profits of his drug dealing. NWA exploded with *Straight Outta Compton* (1988), thanks to "Express Yourself" (based on a song by Charles Wright, sometimes misidentified as Eazy's father), and the controversial "Fuck Tha Police."

Assisted by NWA, his *Eazy-Duz-It* (1988) was another multi-million seller. The exit of Ice Cube, who complained of being cheated, could not stop NWA: 1989's *100 Miles And Runnin'* EP went gold, and *Efil4Zaggin'* (1991) topped the chart. But Dre's departure—with grievances similar to Cube—finished the group.

The Doctor decamped to Death Row, a label he cofounded with entrepreneur Suge Knight. Knight reportedly freed Dre from his contract with Eazy by visiting the Ruthless offices with associates armed with pipes and bats.

Eazy promptly pulled Dre's cuts from 1992's *5150: Home 4 Tha Sick* (featuring Black Eyed Peas' will.i.am, then part of the Ruthless roster) and the pair waged war on wax; Dre with *The Chronic* (1992), Eazy with *It's On (Dr Dre) 187um Killa* (1993). Though Dre won on sales, Eazy could crow about the subsequent success of

Ruthless act Bone Thugs-n-Harmony. He also courted controversy by supporting one of the L.A. cops accused of assaulting Rodney King, and attending a Republican Party fundraiser. "I paid $1,500 for $1,000,000 worth of press," he gloated.

But on February 24, 1995, he was hospitalized with what Cedars-Sinai Medical Center announced was asthma. Later diagnosed with AIDS (a condition that was stigmatized in the macho rap world), Eazy used his illness to stage a remarkable redemption. "I've got thousands and thousands of young fans that have to learn about what's real when it comes to AIDS... " he said in a passionate statement. "I'm not looking to blame anyone except myself. I've learned in the last week that this thing is real and it doesn't discriminate."

Dre and Cube visited Eazy in intensive care, while fans, reported British newspaper *The Independent*, "flooded the hospital with more calls than were received for the dying Lucille Ball in 1989." Eazy died on March 26.

For his funeral, Eazy was laid out in a gold coffin. Mayor Omar Bradley, who once denounced the rapper for discrediting his district, called him "Compton's favorite son." Of NWA, only Yella attended. Eazy is buried at Rose Hills Memorial Park in L.A.

Ruthless continued under Eazy's widow. Her husband is cited as an influence by The Game ("Los Angeles loved Eazy like that nigga was Caesar in Rome") and Kanye West. "Maybe," said Eazy in his final statement, "success was too good to me."

RIGHT Eazy-E sitting on the hood of his car in Compton, California, in 1994, a year before his untimely death.

SELENA
(SELENA QUINTANILLA-PÉREZ)
GUNSHOT

Born: April 16, 1971

Died: March 31, 1995

"It's a wound to the heart," said Abraham, father of Selena Quintanilla-Pérez, "that will be there till you die."

Born in Corpus Christi, Texas, Selena was singing with her father's band Los Dinos by the age of five. "I got ahead of everyone as far as career and being more mature about business," she recalled, "Even though I didn't know what the heck was going on."

Her sound was Tejano. "It's country music," she said, "It's jazz, it has roots of German polka, it also has Mexican music." Like Beyoncé (with whom she shared a bill in the early years of Destiny's Child), she was sexy onstage, strictly moral off.

"I got ahead of everyone... even though I didn't know what the heck was going on."

With a clothing boutique, and an eye on the fortunes of Gloria Estefan, Selena dreamed of mainstream success. Her popularity in the Latin market led her to perform for nearly 67,000 fans at the Houston Astrodome in 1995, and work with David Byrne on the soundtrack to *Don Juan DeMarco* (1995).

Meanwhile, friend Yolanda Saldivar graduated from running Selena's fan club to managing her boutique. The family were unaware Saldivar had been accused of theft by a former employer, failed to repay her college loan, and left a job as a nurse's aide under a cloud. In March 1995, Abraham found evidence of embezzlement. Selena told Saldivar to provide proof of her innocence when she got back from a business trip to Mexico.

Returning across the border, Saldivar called Selena, claiming she had been abducted and raped. On March 30, the singer visited Saldivar at her Corpus Christi motel. With Selena's husband present, Saldivar refused medical attention for the supposed rape and offered none of the evidence the singer had requested.

The next morning, Selena took Saldivar to the hospital, where she retracted the rape claim. The pair returned to the motel, where a maid heard shouting, then a gunshot. Selena fled to the lobby, bleeding from a wound in her back. She was dead on arrival at the hospital.

Saldivar insisted it was an accident. However, as the prosecution at her trial observed, she neither called 911 nor used her nursing training. Convicted of murder, she was sentenced to life imprisonment.

Thousands visited the Corpus Christi Convention Center, where Selena lay in a coffin surrounded by white roses. The family opened the casket to silence rumors that it was empty. She is buried at the town's Seaside Memorial Park.

The posthumous *Dreaming Of You* (1995) won the crossover success she had sought, entering the *Billboard* Top 200 at No.1. George W. Bush, then governor of Texas, passed a law against concealed handguns, and proclaimed April 16, the singer's birthday, "Selena Day."

Jennifer Lopez won widespread acclaim with the lead in the 1997 movie *Selena*. The singer's death, Lopez reflected, "was a reminder of how you never know what's going to happen, and how you'd better really live for today."

RIGHT Selena performing in 1994.

JERRY GARCIA
(JEROME JOHN GARCIA)
HEART ATTACK

Born: August 1, 1942

Died: August 9, 1995

His nickname was "Captain Trips," a reference to his early enthusiasm for psychedelics, and drugs played a large part in the life—and death—of The Grateful Dead's Jerry Garcia. All the more remarkable, then, that over a period of thirty years, his exceptional musicianship produced such a memorable body of work.

Garcia's earliest musical influences stemmed from his grandparents' interest in country music (he lived with them after his father drowned in 1948, an event that Garcia witnessed first hand), though it was his older brother's love of T-Bone Walker and Chuck Berry that inspired him to take up guitar. By 1965, he was playing at Ken Kesey's Acid Tests with The Warlocks—the future Grateful Dead. Their debut, 1967's *The Grateful Dead*, was a tight, speed-fueled affair, but they soon pushed into less charted territory—such as the jazz-tinged psychedelia of *Live Dead* (1969).

After years in the financial wilderness, the Dead's prodigious live schedule paid off. They made U.S. $11.5 million from concerts in 1985 and, by the 1990s, *Forbes* magazine cited them as some of the highest earners in the entertainment business.

However, the 1980s marked the start of a terminal slide for Garcia. A lifestyle of relentless touring, junk food, and hard drugs resulted in his slipping into a diabetic coma in 1986. On awakening, he had to painstakingly relearn how to play music.

In July 1995, he checked into the Betty Ford Clinic in Palm Springs to kick his heroin habit; after just two weeks, he felt well enough to leave the clinic. But the inevitable end came the following month at another rehab center in Serenity Knolls, California. An attendant found him dead in his bed. Garcia had had a heart attack in his sleep.

When word got out, the mayor of San Francisco ordered that flags be flown at half-mast. Appropriately enough for a man whose music was often described as "cosmic," a newly discovered star in the solar system was later named for him.

LEFT The Grateful Dead, live in 1982, from left to right, Jerry Garcia, Bill Kreuzman (on drums), Bob Weir, and Phil Lesh.

RIGHT Memorial services for Garcia were held in Golden Gate Park on August 13, 1995, with all the band members, Garcia's family and friends, and thousands of fans present.

SHANNON HOON
(RICHARD SHANNON HOON)
DRUG OVERDOSE

Born: September 26, 1967

Died: October 21, 1995

"By the time I was seventeen" declared Richard Shannon Hoon, "I realized I'd wasted years trying to be what my parents wanted me to be." So, in true rock 'n' roll style, he hopped on a Greyhound bus from Lafayette, Indiana, to L.A., and cofounded Blind Melon.

While the band struggled to write an album, Hoon visited Axl Rose, another Lafayette-to-L.A. pilgrim. He wound up gracing *Use Your Illusion*'s "Don't Cry."

Blind Melon's 1992 eponymous debut—psychedelia meets the Allman Brothers—fared poorly until a charming video for "No Rain," featuring a girl in a bee costume, took MTV by storm. But with success came abuse, which periodically forced Hoon off tour and into rehab or jail. "I just gave up hope," said his mother. "There were times I didn't think he'd live that long."

"There's a lot of things I need to take into consideration. Staying alive is one of them."

The problems continued after 1995's disastrous follow-up *Soup*, and Hoon once again checked into rehab. "Obviously now, being a father, there's a lot of things I need to take into consideration," he acknowledged. "Staying alive is one of them."

Blind Melon were in New Orleans—"a city where one's willpower is tested daily," said Hoon—when the singer died of a cocaine overdose on his tour bus. He was twenty-eight. Sales of *Blind Melon* promptly soared to four million copies. Hoon is buried at Dayton Cemetery in Indiana.

"He didn't want to die," mourned guitarist Rogers Stevens. "He was always sticking one toe into the gutter, and it just caught up with him this time."

LEFT Shannon Hoon performing at Woodstock in 1994.

Behind the scenes

Peter Grant left his life as a sheet metal worker to indulge his passion for showbiz. He worked as a stagehand, bouncer, stuntman, actor (including *The Guns of Navarone*), and wrestler, but found his niche as a manager for the likes of The Animals, Chuck Berry, Bo Diddley, and Jeff Beck.

In charge of the ailing Yardbirds, Grant persevered when, in 1968, Jimmy Page assembled a new lineup to honor tour commitments. The "New Yardbirds" became Led Zeppelin and, thanks to Grant's tactics (kind to the band, extremely unkind to promoters and record labels), ruled 1970s rock.

Grant urged the band to focus on albums and touring instead of singles and TV, making them impossibly rich and shrouded in mystery. "He was the first to make

sure the artist came first and that we got paid properly," recalled Phil Everly of The Everly Brothers. Feared in the business, Grant was beloved by musicians—namechecked onstage by both Robert Plant and Elvis.

Obesity and cocaine were already taking their toll on Grant's health when the death of John Bonham in 1980 brought Zeppelin to a halt. Grant retired, eventually cleaning up and slimming down. He succumbed to a heart attack while driving to his home in England's Sussex, and was buried in Somerset after a funeral attended by the surviving members of Led Zeppelin.

"I don't need a fancy office," he once said. "I don't need to put on a show. It's all bullshit. The only thing that impresses people is Led Zeppelin's music."

PETER GRANT
HEART ATTACK

Born: April 5, 1935

Died: November 21, 1995

ABOVE From left to right: Peter Grant with Led Zeppelin lead singer Robert Plant and bass guitarist John Paul Jones.

TUPAC SHAKUR
(TUPAC AMARU SHAKUR)
DRIVE-BY SHOOTING

Born: June 16, 1971

Died: September 13, 1996

"It's the game of life," Tupac Shakur said in 1996. "Do I win or do I lose? I know one day they're gonna shut the game down but I gotta have as much fun and go around the board as many times as I can before it's my turn to leave."

Pac's game did not get off to a promising start. His mother Alice Williams (later Afeni Shakur) was an active member of the Black Panthers and had been jailed, accused of plotting a race war. She was acquitted just before her son's birth—but then her new husband, Mutulu Shakur, was incarcerated.

The Harlem-born Pac was quiet and withdrawn as a child. "I read a lot," he said, "I wrote poetry." In 1984, he moved to Maryland and rapped as MC New York. In 1988, he moved again, this time to California. From then on, the West Coast was home.

Employed as a dancer and roadie for rappers Digital Underground, Pac graduated to a solo deal. But his debut album *2Pacalypse Now* (1991) was unremarkable, and the story might have stopped there had his darker side not prevailed.

Juice set it off. Pac's unnerving portrayal of a psychopath in the 1992 movie created a *Scarface*-esque icon and public image. That year, his headline-snaring woes began when a stray bullet from Pac's gun—reportedly fired by his half brother at a California festival—killed a six-year-old (the case was settled in 1995 without criminal charges being filed).

Meanwhile, *2Pacalypse Now*—found in the possession of a youth who shot a Texas cop—was denounced by Vice President Dan Quayle.

Strictly 4 My N.I.G.G.A.Z. (1993) capitalized on Pac's notoriety with bass-driven bloodlust. Contrarily, he starred in the romance *Poetic Justice* alongside Janet Jackson—only to complain that she insisted he take an HIV test before kissing him during filming, and ignored him afterward.

Menace II Society fanned the flames. Fired from the movie for trouble on set, Pac punched director Allen Hughes. Rounding off 1993, he was arrested for shooting at off-duty police in Atlanta, then charged with the sexual abuse of a fan in a New York hotel.

The chaos flowed into 1994. In the spring, Pac was arrested for drug possession and carrying a concealed weapon, and did fifteen days in jail for his attack on Hughes. More damagingly, New York rapper The Notorious B.I.G.—whom he had befriended in LA—enjoyed success that eclipsed his own. "Biggie is a Brooklyn nigga's dream of being West Coast... " Pac complained. "Doesn't Biggie sound like me? Isn't that my style coming out of his mouth?"

Despite the tension, *Thug Life Volume 1* (1994) and *Me Against The World* (1995) ditched bloodthirsty funk for soulful reflection. *Thug Life* included, in demo form, a duet with B.I.G. that failed to make the final cut. Meanwhile, Pac played a scene-stealing part in basketball movie *Above The Rim* (1994). "A gleaming portrait of seductive evil," said *Rolling Stone*.

In November 1994, awaiting the outcome of the 1993 sexual abuse case, Pac was robbed and shot at a New York studio. Though his codefendants in the case were the likeliest suspects, Pac implicated B.I.G. and producer Puff Daddy, who were in the building at the same time. Paranoia was eating him alive.

Pac left hospital against medical advice, and attended court in a wheelchair the next day. Convicted of sexual abuse, he was sentenced to prison for up to four-and-a-half years; *Me Against The World* (1995) became the first album to top *Billboard*'s chart while its maker was in jail. Largely abandoned by the rap

LEFT Tupac performing shortly before he died.

community, Pac instead enjoyed the support of Madonna (who he briefly dated), actor Mickey Rourke, and long-time friend Jada Pinkett.

With bail set at U.S. $1.4 million, however, a bigger benefactor was needed. Enter Suge Knight, hulking CEO of Dr. Dre's Death Row label. Early in 1996, Pac signed with the company, was freed from prison in New York, and began work in California.

In jail, he had claimed, "The vengeful Tupac is dead." But Suge Knight's loathing of Puff Daddy's empire fueled Pac's paranoia. As *All Eyez On Me* (1996) sent him into the multi-platinum bracket, he tipped over the edge.

In the single "Hit 'Em Up," Pac claimed to have slept with B.I.G.'s wife Faith Evans, and took fire at Biggie, his cohorts, and New York rappers Mobb Deep. Lavished in riches, drugs, and women, Pac envisaged himself as a general—"Makaveli"—in an East Coast-West Coast war.

On September 7, 1996, he attended a boxing match in Las Vegas. Afterwards, driving down the casino strip with Knight, he was hit by four bullets fired from a passing car. He spent six days on life support. "They revived him seven times," said Afeni, "and

then I asked the doctors to allow him to be." He was twenty-five years old. Conspiracy theories variously blamed Knight (at whose suggestion Pac had removed a bulletproof vest) and B.I.G. (killed, in possible retaliation, the following year). It was even suggested the rapper fabricated his death. The most plausible "evidence" for this included a video made a month earlier for "I Ain't Mad At Cha," depicting him being fatally shot. Pac's self-chosen artwork for *The Don Killuminati: The 7 Day Theory* (1996), the final album of his lifetime, imagines his crucifixion. And on Richie Rich's "Niggas Done Changed," also released in late 1996, Pac raps, "I've been shot and murdered, can't tell you how it happened... "

The case remains unsolved; the most frequently cited suspect was himself killed in 1998. Afeni buried her son's ashes on her North Carolina farm, planning later to take them to Soweto. Posthumous albums have made him one of rap's biggest sellers.

"Sometimes," said Reverend Jesse Jackson, who visited Pac in hospital, "the lure of violent culture is so magnetic that even when one overcomes it with material success, it continues to call. He couldn't break the cycle."

RIGHT Graffiti tributes to Tupac sprang up all over urban America.

LEFT Suge Knight's BMW, in which Shakur was shot, at the crime scene.

RANDY CALIFORNIA
(RANDOLPH CRAIG WOLFE)
DROWNED

Born: February 20, 1951

Died: January 2, 1997

Randy California's mother, Bernice Pearl, had grand plans for her boy to be an entertainer. Pearl's brother Ed had founded the Ash Grove, L.A.'s leading folk/blues venue, and Randy learned his prodigious guitar skills first hand from the likes of Mississippi John Hurt and John Lee Hooker. Schoolmate (and future bandmate) Jay Ferguson recalls him as a "fourteen-year-old kid with braces, who was just a genius at playing great Delta blues." Indeed, Jimi Hendrix (who dubbed him "California") wanted to take Randy to London with him in 1966 after they played together in Jimmy James And The Blue Flames; California—still a minor—couldn't go.

Instead, he cofounded another five-piece outfit, Spirit, with his fortysomething stepfather Ed Cassidy on drums. Drawing on rock 'n' roll, blues, and jazz, they were a powerful live proposition, and by mid-1967 were packing out Monday nights at the Ash Grove. A contract with Lou Adler's Ode Records swiftly followed, but relationships between band and label were troubled (Adler slapped orchestration on their eponymous debut album without warning them). Spirit's finest offering—1970's innovative *Twelve Dreams of Dr. Sardonicus*—bombed and the band split that year.

California had been an aficionado of LSD, then cocaine—not great for a troubled soul under pressure since childhood to succeed—and his mental health suffered accordingly. During one performance in England, he stopped playing, and cut up his arms with a razor in the dressing room afterwards. In April 1973, he jumped from London's Chelsea Bridge into the Thames below. Though he swam to safety on that occasion, water was eventually to prove his downfall. In early 1997, on a visit to his mother, he was swept out to sea at Molokai, Hawaii, reportedly while trying to save his twelve-year-old son, Quinn, from drowning. His body was never recovered.

LEFT He played with Spirit. California onstage at the Reading Festival, 1979.

BILLY MACKENZIE
(WILLIAM MACARTHUR MACKENZIE)
SUICIDE BY DRUG OVERDOSE

Born: March 27, 1957

Died: January 22, 1997

Although never major-league contenders, The Associates provided a welcome injection of inspired avant-gardism to early 1980s UK pop. Central to their impact was singer Billy MacKenzie whose multi-octave range and arresting delivery marked him out as a genuine original (reportedly he was the subject of The Smiths' "William, It Was Really Nothing"). For a good example, listen to "Party Fears Two," their biggest hit (UK No. 9), which hitched a brilliant keyboard riff to bizarre lyrics sometimes sung, sometimes shrieked, sometimes shouted.

MacKenzie and sidekick Alan Rankine blew a £60,000 (U.S. $120,000) advance in two months creating its parent album, *Sulk* (1982). They purchased state-of-the-art synthesizers, submerged a drum kit in water and urinated in a guitar (to see what they would sound like), and—perhaps unsurprisingly—snorted a lot of cocaine. The resultant album— a dense, imaginative, sumptuous beast—remains a critics' favorite. "Is it an object lesson in how not to make a record?" mused bassist Michael Dempsey in April 2007. "Well, yes. Except that it worked."

Not for long. The hits soon dried up. MacKenzie quit a UK tour one day before its start, and spurned a U.S. $600,000 advance from an American label; the band broke up, his solo projects came to naught, and in the mid-1990s he was declared bankrupt. By 1996, a troubled MacKenzie was living back with his parents in Auchterhouse, Dundee, but his mother's death in the summer sent his spirits plummeting further.

Billy MacKenzie ended his life with an overdose of prescription pills in the family garden shed. His father, Jim—who had found his son wrapped in a duvet, clasping a photo album—later burned down the shed.

RIGHT Billy MacKenzie backstage, with dog, in 1982.

BRIAN CONNOLLY
(BRIAN FRANCIS CONNOLLY)
KIDNEY FAILURE

Born: October 5, 1945
Died: February 9, 1997

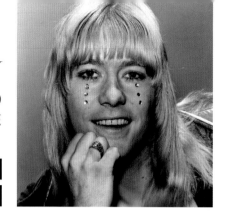

"It was all wine, whiskey, and song with me," said Brian Connolly of his success with Sweet. "The rest I spent foolishly." Born near Glasgow, Connolly was adopted at birth—making actor Mark McManus, famed in Britain as TV's *Taggart*, his brother. (He reclaimed "Connolly" on learning his birth mother's surname.)

After replacing future Deep Purple star Ian Gillan in cover band Wainwright's Gentlemen, Connolly formed Sweetshop with drummer Mick Tucker and bassist Steve Priest. By 1970, with guitarist Andy Scott, they had become Sweet.

"Funny Funny" broke Britain, while the United States was won over by "Little Willy." But, sick of such bubblegummy confections, Sweet toughened up for 1973's "Hell Raiser" and UK No.1 "Blockbuster"; 1974's "Teenage Rampage"; and 1975's "Ballroom Blitz" (which Quentin Tarantino considered for the *Reservoir Dogs* torture scene before settling on "Stuck In The Middle With You" by Stealer's Wheel).

More than Bowie (whose "The Jean Genie" is eerily similar to "Blockbuster"), Sweet epitomized "glam rock," the swishy subgenre that spawned a million bands from Kiss to Guns N' Roses. Connolly's platinum-blond hair was among their visual trademarks.

After the harder "Fox On The Run" and "Action" (covered by Def Leppard), disco and punk decimated Sweet's success, though they remained popular in Germany. Despite a freak return to transatlantic Top Tens with 1978's "Love is Like Oxygen," their days were numbered. The singer accused the band of recording backing tracks in a key he could not reach, and left in 1979.

In the early 1980s, a young Nikki Sixx tried to interest him in his band London. Connolly advised him to keep his day job. Sixx proceeded to find fame with Mötley Crüe, while the Sweet man languished in obscurity.

Claiming he had "never been into drugs," Connolly instead became an alcoholic. In 1981, he suffered the first of multiple heart attacks—though not the thirteen in a twenty-four-hour period that his ex-wife claimed. "I know I did the impossible," he said of his survival, "but that *is* impossible."

By the end of the decade, he and Scott were both fronting revival bands called Sweet. "Little by little he stabbed me in the back," Connolly told British newspaper *The Independent*. Fleeting reunions proved abortive. "It's like an egg," opined Scott. "It's been fried."

In the 1990s, Connolly's health continued to suffer. In January 1997 he suffered another heart attack but promptly discharged himself from hospital, only to be readmitted a week later for a final visit. He died of kidney failure on February 9, in England's Slough, at the age of fifty-one.

Andy Scott and Steve Priest attended his funeral at Denham in Buckinghamshire. Mick Tucker—who died of leukemia in 2002—sent his condolences. Messages were also received from stars such as Brian May and Ritchie Blackmore. The coffin left the church to "The Sixteens"—one of Connolly's Sweet favorites—and Connolly was cremated in Ruislip. "Brian's work inspired me very much," wrote Def Leppard's Joe Elliott, "and he will be sorely missed."

RIGHT: Brian Connolly, downing a yard of ale in 1975.

THE NOTORIOUS BIG
(CHRISTOPHER GEORGE LATORE WALLACE)
DRIVE-BY SHOOTING

Born: May 21, 1972

Died: March 9, 1997

"I was a full-time, 100 per cent hustler," boasted Brooklyn-born Christopher Wallace in an early biography. But when a 1991 drug run to North Carolina led to nine months' incarceration—his second jail term—he made part-time rapping a full-time concern.

Borrowing the nickname "Biggie Smalls" from the 1975 movie *Let's Do It Again*, the six-foot-three-inch, 280-pound Wallace became formally known as The Notorious BIG. A 1992 demo tape found its way to Sean "Puff Daddy" Combs, then building his Bad Boy label. "I thanked God," said Puffy later, "not because He sent me a dope rapper, but because He sent me somebody who cared for me."

"People know that Biggie ain't on the corner selling drugs. Why would anyone want to hear about that? I got other problems now."

Biggie's debut *Ready To Die* (1994) was an instant classic and is regarded as the best of his work. Hits like the autobiographical "Juicy" and self-mythologizing "Big Poppa" even led to a cameo with Michael Jackson. But as his reputation rocketed, his friendship with another rapper soured.

Fellow New Yorker Tupac Shakur met Biggie while filming *Poetic Justice* in 1993. "We just clicked off the top," Biggie recalled, "and were cool ever since."

But that turned out to be wishful thinking. Pac's reputation was built on notoriety, rather than critical acclaim or upwardly mobile sales. As *Ready To Die* sold millions, and Biggie was acclaimed as

the finest MC since Ice Cube, the egotistical Pac grew first jealous and then enraged. To make matters worse for him, in November 1994 he was shot and injured during a robbery at a Times Square studio—where Biggie and Puffy happened to be working at the same time.

Convinced he had been set up, the hotheaded rapper boiled over in fury: "[Biggie] knows how much he borrowed from me," he ranted. "He owed me more than to turn his head and act like he didn't know a nigga was about to blow my fucking head off."

Pac's paranoid theories earned a wry response from Puffy: "If I'ma set a nigga up, which I would never do, I ain't gonna be in the country. I'ma be in Bolivia somewhere." Of the whole affair, Biggie said simply, "I can't believe that he would think that I would shit on him like that."

With Pac and his boss Suge Knight out for blood, battle lines were drawn. In New York, Biggie, Puffy, and their protégés Junior M.A.F.I.A., alongside Nas and Mobb Deep, faced vitriol from artists on Knight's California-based Death Row label. "Pretty soon," prophesied Death Row cofounder Dr. Dre, "niggas from the East Coast ain't gonna be able to come out here and be safe."

Pac channeled his loathing into "Hit 'Em Up"—in which he claimed to have slept with Biggie's wife Faith Evans—and "2 Of Amerikaz Most Wanted," the video for which viciously caricatured Puffy and Biggie.

Meanwhile the latter—despite breaking his leg in a car accident, and being arrested for harassing autograph hunters, and possessing drugs and weapons—focused on his second album. "I call the album *Life After Death*," he told the *Los Angeles Times*. "Because on *Ready to Die*, I was dead, yo. There was

RIGHT Biggie performing in 1997.

nothing but anger coming out, about everything. But now, I can't do that no more. People know that Biggie ain't on the corner selling drugs. Why would anyone want to hear about that? I got other problems now."

Tupac's death in 1996 apparently shocked the rap world to its senses. "Him being gone," Biggie opined, "I think's it's time for us to be forgiving." But in the early hours of March 9, 1997, Biggie was partying in downtown L.A., having been in the city preparing for the album's release. At around 12:45 A.M. he left the party—only to be shot by a drive-by assailant. He was dead on arrival at Cedars-Sinai Medical Center.

A popular theory suggests the shooting was retaliation for Tupac's similarly unsolved death—a lawsuit brought by Biggie's estate even implicated the Los Angeles Police Department. "We may never find out who killed Biggie," said Faith Evans, "but we know a proper investigation wasn't carried out."

Fittingly, Biggie's funeral was larger than life. A motorcade carrying his body—dressed in a white suit and hat—rode through packed streets of the Brooklyn neighborhood where he grew up. At a ceremony in Manhattan—attended by Dr. Dre—Evans sang a gospel tune and Puffy delivered the eulogy; the pair later collaborated on the tribute "I'll Be Missing You." Biggie's ashes were divided between his mother and Evans.

"I wanna see my kids graduate… " he said shortly before his death. "I want to watch them get old. You're not going to get to see that if you're out there wilding."

LEFT The funeral procession passes fans and police on St. James Place in Bedford-Stuyvesant in Brooklyn, New York, where Biggie once lived.

LAURA NYRO
(LAURA NIGRO)
OVARIAN CANCER

Born: October 18, 1947

Died: April 8, 1997

Laura Nyro's career might have ended with her debut at The Monterey International Pop Festival in June 1967, when the nineteen-year-old singer-songwriter was roundly heckled. Perhaps understandably: her style was more intimate nightclub than hippie-fest, her band was under-rehearsed, and Nyro had chosen to wear a long black gown from which projected an angel's wing. (*Mojo* magazine later dubbed her "the Bronx Ophelia.")

But Nyro's dense melodies and multi-octave vocal dexterity were soon winning her new friends. Post-Monterey comfort came care of music biz wunderkind David Geffen, who promptly offered his services as manager. ("She wore purple lipstick, Christmas balls for earrings, strange clothes," he recalled. "But [she was] very talented.") Her second album, *Eli And The Thirteenth Confession* (1968) fared well, and the quality of Nyro's output saw a string of her songs chart, albeit in other hands: Barbra Streisand went Top Ten with Nyro's "Stoney End" (from her 1966 debut *More Than A New Discovery*), while The Fifth Dimension sold two million copies of her "Stoned Soul Picnic" in 1968 (one of around sixty versions, including those by Aretha Franklin and Sinatra) and took "Wedding Bell Blues" to No. 1. Three Dog Night's "Eli's Coming" (No. 10 on the *Billboard* singles chart) remained her favorite cover.

Nyro retired from live performance at the ripe old age of twenty-four (making an acclaimed return in the 1980s), though she continued to record. Meantime, she concentrated on bringing up her son Gil, applying herself to feminism, animal and civil rights, and promoting ecological awareness.

Her mother had died from ovarian cancer at the age of forty-nine; the same disease claimed Laura Nyro at the same age in Danbury, Connecticut, on April 8, 1997.

RIGHT The Bronx Ophelia in New York in 1975.

JEFF BUCKLEY
(JEFFREY SCOTT BUCKLEY)
DROWNED

Born: November 17, 1966

Died: May 29, 1997

His father Tim cast a long shadow over the life and work of his son; that both came to an untimely demise seems only to underline the connection. All the more impressive, then, that before his death Jeff Buckley had firmly established himself as one of his own generation's most outstanding artists.

In truth, father and son had no relationship to speak of; they met once after one of Tim's concerts in 1972, but two months later Tim Buckley was dead of a drug overdose. Jeff had inherited the musical genius gene, though. ("First there was my mother's breasts, then music," he declared in an interview.) A stint at the Musicians' Institute in Los Angeles set him on the road, but he first came to public notice

"A pure drop in an ocean of noise."

at a 1991 tribute performance for his father at St. Anne's Church in Brooklyn, where he sang three of Tim's songs.

After a brief stint in arty left field band Gods And Monsters with ex-Beefheart guitarist Gary Lucas, Buckley struck out solo on the New York cafe/folk club scene, swiftly gaining a reputation as a stunning singer-songwriter and interpreter. His adroit guitar playing drew on blues, jazz, Eastern traditions, folk, and rock; his mesmerizing vocals could spin from a whisper to a wail in a single line, never sounding forced, drawing on influences as diverse as Robert Plant, Nusrat Fateh Ali Khan, and all points in between. Witness his deconstruction of Van Morrison's "The Way Young Lovers Do," from the *Live At Sin-É* (1993) EP.

Buckley's 1994 debut album *Grace* hardly set the charts alight—but who measures genius in units? Originals such as the supple, restless "Mojo Pin" and poignant "Lover, You Should've Come Over" indicated an articulate, imaginative talent. Of the covers, "Lilac Wine" and "Corpus Christi Carol" possessed an arresting delicacy, while Buckley's masterful take on Leonard Cohen's "Hallelujah" is now seen as definitive.

Touring and record company expectations for a more successful follow-up dragged Buckley down, however—as did the fact that he was now inevitably being compared to his famous father. Sessions in New York and Memphis—including some produced by ex-Television guitarist Tom Verlaine—were aborted or scrapped, partly due to Buckley's perfectionism.

The outlook seemed more optimistic by mid-1997. On Thursday, May 29, Buckley and friend Keith Foti set off for their Memphis rehearsal rooms. They got lost and wound up by the Wolf River. Here, they got out a ghetto blaster and Buckley sang along to Led Zep's "Whole Lotta Love" as Foti accompanied him on acoustic guitar. Endearingly willfull to the last, the singer then jumped into the river, fully clothed, and floated on his back—still singing. A tugboat and a barge passed by, and Foti shouted out a warning; Buckley swam out of the way. Foti turned to move the ghetto blaster, and when he turned back Buckley had vanished, caught up in the vessel's undertow.

Six days later, his body surfaced at the foot of Memphis' famed Beale Street, home of the blues. A sad, premature end for a man whose voice Bono once described as "a pure drop in an ocean of noise."

RIGHT Jeff Buckley playing live at the Reading Festival in England.

JOHN DENVER
(HENRY JOHN DEUTSCHENDORF, JR.)
PLANE CRASH

Born: December 31, 1943

Died: October 12, 1997

"I like John Denver," Jefferson Starship's Grace Slick reportedly said. "The kid's got a good voice. I don't give a shit that he looks like a fucking turkey."

Born in Roswell, New Mexico, Henry John Deutschendorf, Jr.—son of a strict Air Force pilot—took up the guitar as a child. By 1964, he was playing in the folk clubs of L.A., and had changed his name to Denver in tribute to the mountains of Colorado.

His first success was as the writer of folk trio Peter, Paul, and Mary's 1967 U.S. chart-topping "Leaving On A Jet Plane" (the guitar part of New Order's 1989 "Run" resembles the one in this track—as that band found to their legal cost). Signed to RCA, his own career flourished in the 1970s with smashes like "Take Me Home, Country Roads" and "Annie's Song"—the latter reportedly written, in ten minutes, for his second wife after the near breakup of their marriage. Denver's *Greatest Hits* (1973) has sold over nine million copies in the United States alone.

His gentle music and image—blond hair and granny glasses—inflamed the ire of rock critics. "He's the balladeer for the masses," sniped *Rolling Stone* in 1972, "sweet-voiced, ingenuous, and completely devoid of human characteristics." Two years later, the same writer admitted, "These characteristics undercut his efforts to be a Tom Paxton-style protest singer, but in the last few years he's transformed into a competent and, in retrospect, rather original pop record maker."

The innocuous image disguised a complex man. His marriages were jeopardized by his inability to communicate, yet he engaged huge audiences, and was a passionate campaigner against nuclear energy, famine, and threats to the environment. He forged a memorable association with the Muppets and, in 1985, formed an unlikely triumvirate with Frank Zappa and Twisted Sister's Dee Snider against congressional attempts to censor music.

He also made what were, in pop terms, pioneering visits to Africa, the Soviet Union, and China. Appropriately for a man born in the UFO hotspot Roswell, he was intrigued by space, and fruitlessly tried to participate in the ill-fated *Challenger* shuttle mission of 1986. When Denver's success waned, he survived bouts with drink and drugs, and even a plane crash, to emerge sober and still popular in the 1990s.

On October 12, 1997, he was piloting a newly purchased experimental aircraft, reportedly with the intention of "buzzing" his friend Clint Eastwood's home, when he crashed into California's Monterey Bay. The accident was variously blamed on Denver's failure to refuel the plane, his unfamiliarity with its controls, and the plane's design. His ashes were scattered over his beloved Rocky Mountains in Colorado after 2,000 people attended a funeral service at the Faith Presbyterian Church in the Denver suburb of Aurora. "Many in the audience," reported CNN, "wept when the first song, 'On The Wings Of A Dream,' was played, a tune whose first line is, 'Yesterday, I had a dream about dying.'"

RIGHT John Denver's body is carried from the beach on a surfboard stretcher.

MICHAEL HUTCHENCE
(MICHAEL KELLAND JOHN HUTCHENCE)
SUICIDE BY HANGING

Born: January 22, 1960
Died: November 22, 1997

"I'm very happy," Michael Hutchence told *The Face* magazine in 1991. "I've got to this stage in my life and I'm not dead. I haven't got married and divorced and done all that palimony business, you know, all that mess. There's no drugs or drinking problems. So I think, 'Phew, I've survived.' I really have. I've come through intact."

The globetrotting life of a rock 'n' roller was in the singer's blood. Born in North Sydney, Australia, in 1960, he spent his youth in Hong Kong, where his father worked. At eight, he made his recording debut, providing the voice for a Japanese toy. In 1972, the family returned to Sydney and Hutchence met the Farriss brothers—keyboard player Andrew, guitarist Tim, and drummer Jon; with bassist Garry Gary Beers and guitarist and saxophonist Kirk Pengilly, they became INXS in 1979.

Extensive touring helped escalate sales in their homeland. By 1983's *Shabooh Shoobah*, they were Australian stars. America fell with "What You Need" from *Listen Like Thieves* (1985), and the world was theirs with 1987's *Kick*. "Need You Tonight," "New Sensation," "Devil Inside," and "Never Tear Us Apart" were international hits, helped by Hutchence's charm and sex appeal.

In 1989, the group took a break. Hutchence cut his hair, played Shelley in the movie *Frankenstein Unbound* (having also starred in 1987's *Dogs In Space*) and recorded the *Max Q* album with Ollie Olsen. "There's a self loathing that makes you take excessive unnatural drugs," he told *NME*, "and just lately I've come to realize that I can do without them. At the moment, with no girlfriend, no drink, and no drugs, I'm probably the straightest man in rock and roll!"

Working on *Max Q*, he successfully pursued Kylie Minogue, then in the process of shedding her soap opera origins for a sexier persona. "He just was incredibly charismatic," said Kylie. "Very intelligent, generous, funny. Fabulous storyteller. He just was larger than life. But humble with it. I met him at a point where I was just ready to look at the world. It was like he took my blinkers off."

"Suicide Blonde"—allegedly inspired by Kylie—trailed 1990's *X*. The single and album were INXS's final international smashes; 1992's excellent *Welcome To Wherever You Are* and 1993's *Full Moon, Dirty Hearts* bombed in the United States. Elsewhere, sales continued to rise, but Hutchence became better known for his girlfriends than his music.

Kylie gave way to supermodel Helena Christensen, by whom he was introduced to U2. "He was great fun to hang out with," remembers Bono. "You could be silly or serious with him. We'd be sitting at the table from one o'clock in the afternoon to one o'clock in the morning, talking and laughing. Occasionally Michael and myself might run amok. We slept on a few beaches coming home from the clubs in Cannes."

In 1995, Hutchence began an affair with Paula Yates, the pair having conducted a lascivious interview on British breakfast television. With Yates still married, the couple became easy targets for the tabloids. "We tried to keep in touch as much as possible," recalled U2's The Edge, "but it was difficult. He wasn't around as much and he was involved with Paula Yates, who was married to Bob Geldof, another good friend of ours. There were other complications because it transpired that he and Paula were involved with substances that maybe made them less social."

Amid their doomed, druggy romance came the birth of the couple's daughter, Heavenly Hiraani Tiger Lily, in 1996. But Hutchence was in a downward spiral—titling his final INXS album

RIGHT In the UK on INXS's "Get Out Of The House Tour" in July 1993.

Elegantly Wasted (1997) seemed less wry than ghastly. Preparing to tour Australia, he was found dead, alone in a hotel room, on November 22, 1997. He was thirty-seven years old.

"The deceased was found at 11:50 A.M. naked behind the door to his room," reported the coroner. "He had apparently hanged himself with his own belt and the buckle broke away and his body was found kneeling on the floor and facing the door. It has been suggested that the death resulted from an act of autoeroticism. However, there is no forensic or other evidence to substantiate this suggestion."

Amid a messy custody battle for Yates' children with Geldof, Hutchence called the Live Aid star on the morning of his death. Geldof described the singer as "hectoring and abusive and threatening." He had also mixed alcohol, cocaine, Prozac, and other prescription drugs. The coroner concluded: "The deceased was in a severe depressed state… combined with the effects of the substances that he had ingested. I am satisfied that the deceased intended to and did take his own life."

"You pay the price if you want to experiment and lose control," Hutchence once said.

The funeral, on November 27, 1997, at St. Andrew's Cathedral in Sydney, began with INXS's "By My Side," and featured Nick Cave singing his own "Into My Arms." Hutchence was cremated; his father, mother, and Yates each receiving a third of his ashes. His father scattered his share in Rose Bay, Sydney. Yates died in 2000 of an accidental heroin overdose.

Hutchence's cenotaph reads: "A sensitive and loving soul who touched hearts around the world—So dearly loved—So sadly missed—'Stay Young.'" The latter refers to an anthemic single on 1981's *Underneath The Colours* (a self-titled solo album was released posthumously).

On the first anniversary of his death, a memorial was unveiled at the Northern Suburbs Crematorium. Etched in bronze upon it are his handwritten lyrics to "Shine Like It Does" from *Listen Like Thieves*. Hutchence subsequently inspired "Afterglow" by INXS—who eventually replaced him in 2005 with J.D. Fortune, hired following a U.S. television talent contest to find a new frontman—and "Stuck In A Moment You Can't Get Out Of" by U2. "He would have been very good at getting old," said Bono, "very debonair, and his rascal side would have kept the place on its toes."

LEFT Hutchence gets down and dirty onstage.

RIGHT Michael Hutchence's coffin is carried by pallbearers, including his bandmates from INXS, at his funeral in Sydney, Australia.

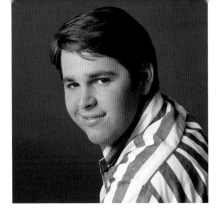

CARL WILSON
(CARL DEAN WILSON)
LUNG AND BRAIN CANCER

Born: December 21, 1946

Died: February 6, 1998

Spinal Tap bassist Derek Smalls famously characterized his role of intermediary between the "fire" and "ice" of fellow bandmates as akin to that of "lukewarm water." Carl Wilson would surely have concurred.

A founder member of The Beach Boys, Carl Wilson provided Chuck Berry-style guitar breaks on the band's sparkling feelgood early singles (1963's "Surfin' USA"; and 1964's "Fun, Fun, Fun," and "I Get Around"). His high, clear voice was an essential element in The Beach Boys' smooth harmonies too, though overshadowed by the lead vocals of cousin Mike Love and brother Brian.

When Brian abruptly abandoned touring (partly out of fear of flying, although repeated LSD trips, marijuana, and an inherently fragile mental state didn't help), Carl assumed a greater role in the band's live performances. His higher profile was reflected in the number of lead vocals he now took, including his sublime reading of "God Only Knows," once cited by Paul McCartney as his favorite pop song.

When parent album *Pet Sounds* (1966)—which Brian regarded as his best work yet—flopped Stateside, he had a breakdown, one exacerbated by the fraught and incomplete recordings for 1967's *Smile* album. (Taken from those sessions, "Good Vibrations," featuring another arresting Carl vocal, provided a transatlantic No. 1 in 1966.) Hedonistic third brother Dennis was providing problems of his own in the late 1960s, regularly squabbling with Mike Love and hanging out with sinister hippie Charles Manson. Carl was the calm at the storm's center, keeping the band a working unit and finding the time to deliver more stunning

contributions—on 1969 single "I Can Hear Music," his clear-blue sky of a vocal seems to soar above those background tensions.

The Beach Boys' credibility plummeted during the high-water mark of hippiedom, but revived somewhat at the start of the 1970s with the release of *Surf's Up* (1971). The mesmerizing title track—a leftover from the *Smile* sessions—attracted much attention, but Carl's innovative "Free Flows" was remarkable in its own right, featuring synths and a free-'n'-easy sax solo alongside those trademark harmonies. Follow-up *Carl And The Passions/So Tough* (1972), a nod to one of the band's early monikers, referenced his increasing profile.

Stimulated by the unexpectedly successful compilation *Endless Summer* (1974), The Beach Boys evolved into an oldies act. ("We just surrendered to it," Carl admitted later. "We'd gone through so many changes over the idea of oldies over the years, and now it was obvious what the people wanted us to play. Really obvious.") They cleaned up on the nostalgia circuit, though if anything their newfound lease on life only increased the internecine bickering. Carl quit in 1981, but after two solo albums (*Carl Wilson*, 1981; *Youngblood*, 1983) he rejoined the fold, providing lead vocals for The Beach Boys' last (and, inexplicably, biggest) hit, "Kokomo," featured in Tom Cruise's movie *Cocktail* (1988).

Although aware that he had contracted lung cancer, Carl continued to tour with The Beach Boys into the 1990s, undergoing chemotherapy and taking doctors on the road with him during the band's thirty-seventh annual tour in 1997. All to no avail: the cancer spread to his brain and he died the following year.

LEFT Barefoot Beach Boys in California, 1962. From left to right: Dennis Wilson, David Marks, Carl Wilson, Mike Love, and Brian Wilson.

173

ROB PILATUS
(ROBERT PILATUS)
HEART FAILURE

Born: June 8, 1965

Died: April 2, 1998

Pop forgives its stars anything except miming—and the most famous whipping boys are Milli Vanilli.

The duo—Fabrice Morvan and New York-born model Robert Pilatus—were masterminded by Frank Farian, svengali behind 1970s record-breakers Boney M.

Milli Vanilli scored an international smash with 1988's "Girl You Know It's True," title track of an album that sold six million copies in the United States alone. "Musically we are more talented than any Bob Dylan," Pilatus told *Time* magazine. "Musically we are more talented than Paul McCartney. I'm the new Elvis."

But in 1989, a technical mishap at an MTV performance made it clear Morvan and Pilatus were miming to pre-recorded vocals. When they insisted they be allowed to sing on the next album, Farian announced they had not sung on the first, and a Grammy award was duly withdrawn.

"Musically we are more talented than Paul McCartney. I'm the new Elvis."

Regarded as a joke by the public, and an embarrassment by the music industry, the duo was ostracized. Pilatus slashed his wrist in an L.A. hotel and threatened to jump off a balcony, then upped his drinking and cocaine intake to numb the pain. He was subsequently arrested for assault and imprisoned for attempted car theft.

After a spell in rehab, Pilatus returned to Germany—only to be found, by Farian, dead in a Frankfurt hotel room. The cause of death, often listed as a suicide, was heart failure owing to a cocktail of alcohol and prescription pills. He is buried in Munich, where he grew up.

LEFT Fabrice Morvan and Robert Pilatus on stage.

WENDY O. WILLIAMS
(WENDY ORLEAN WILLIAMS)
SUICIDE BY GUNSHOT

Born: May 28, 1949

Died: April 6, 1998

"She was definitely one of a kind," said Joey Ramone. "You just didn't see many girls swinging chainsaws."

Ex-porn star and macrobiotic cook Wendy Orlean Williams was enlisted to front The Plasmatics in 1978. Though the band made fine, punkily metallic music, they were best known for their shows. Wendy chainsawed guitars and blew up cars, while lighting rigs collapsed and guitarists swung above the stage. "Makes Kiss look like greasy kid stuff," marveled *Billboard*. The group were duly banned in London, while the mohawked singer—in a leather bikini, with whipped cream or electrical tape over her nipples—was arrested in Milwaukee for simulating masturbation with a sledgehammer handle.

Beneath the trappings was a fierce intelligence and anti-consumerist message, albeit delivered with sandpaper vocals. Her finest album was 1984's solo *W.O.W.*—which, with credits for Gene Simmons, Ace Frehley, Eric Carr, and Paul Stanley, is essential for Kiss fans.

When her fame faded, Wendy worked with animals, but despaired of her waning fortunes and society's hypocrisies. On April 6, 1998, she entered woods near her Connecticut home, fed the squirrels, and shot herself. Tammy Wynette—whose "Stand By Your Man" Wendy demolished with Motörhead in 1980—died the same day.

"For me, much of the world makes no sense," read her suicide note, "but my feelings about what I am doing ring loud and clear to an inner ear and a place where there is no self, only calm. Love always, Wendy."

RIGHT With Plasmatics guitarist Richie Scott, in the early 1980s. "The Plasmatics," said Wendy, "give me a chance to get this violence out of me."

175

DUSTY SPRINGFIELD
(MARY ISOBEL CATHERINE BERNADETTE O'BRIEN)
BREAST CANCER

Born: April 16, 1939

Died: March 2, 1999

Part of pop's magic is that it enables people to reinvent themselves. Thus it was with convent girl Mary O'Brien, whose love of American soul and R&B music—coupled with a truckload of talent—transformed her into possibly the greatest female white soul singer pop has known.

As a teenager in England, she had performed in a folk duo and cabaret trio, but it wasn't until 1960 that her career truly took off. She formed The Springfields with brother Dion and Tim Field; seeking a more authentically folk-sounding name, Mary became Dusty. On a Springfields tour of the United States, she became smitten with the sound of black R&B and soul and had soon relaunched herself as a solo star in that vein. ("When I first started, I copied every black singer. One week I was Baby Washington, next week I was the lead singer of The Shirelles.") Her folksy look got a makeover too, replaced by voluminous beehive hair and heavy "panda-eye" makeup.

Debut hit "I Only Want To Be With You" (1963) became one of the first "British Invasion" hits in the United States, alongside The Beatles. Thereafter, Dusty produced a string of pop gems, some courtesy of songwriters Burt Bacharach and Hal David; her smouldering take on their "The Look Of Love" has never been bettered. Few white female singers of the day could match Dusty's power, emotion, and exquisite vocal control—witness "You Don't Have To Say You Love Me," her first UK No. 1. Like many songs in her oeuvre, it's a tour de force of frustration, heartbreak, and longing.

"There is a sadness there in my voice," she reflected in later life. "Comes with being Irish-Scottish. Automatically melancholy and mad at the same time." Such sentiments pepper the work of her glory years ("I Just Don't Know What To Do With Myself," "If You Go Away," "Some Of Your Lovin'") and—unsurprisingly—she swiftly earned a sizeable gay following.

Her 1969 album *Dusty In Memphis* should have seen Dusty's star take off Stateside. Aside from single "Son Of A Preacher Man" (a masterpiece of understated sexuality), though, it flopped— a crime, as the producers (including Atlantic's Jerry Wexler) and superlative musicians at Muscle Shoals studio had created a superbly sympathetic background for her voice. Her exquisite vocals, and the carefully crafted, upmarket pop she excelled at, seemed simply out of touch in the hippie era.

When the hits dried up, the demons stepped in. The 1970s saw the former icon move to New York then Los Angeles, lose direction to booze and drugs, and—ignominiously—work as a session singer.

Her renaissance came late. In 1987, she guested on "What Have I Done To Deserve This" (UK No. 2) by long-term fans The Pet Shop Boys, and the appearance of "Son Of A Preacher Man" in Quentin Tarantino's *Pulp Fiction* (1994) once more reinvigorated interest in this queen of melodrama. That same year, however, she was diagnosed with breast cancer. She was awarded an OBE in 1999, but by then was too ill to attend the ceremony at Buckingham Palace, and died six weeks later.

RIGHT Dusty Springfield, 1970.

RICK DANKO
(RICHARD CLARE DANKO)
NATURAL CAUSES

Born: December 29, 1942

Died: December 10, 1999

Ontario-born Rick Danko's life as a jobbing musician started at the age of fourteen. Three years later, he was in Ronnie Hawkins' rambunctious backing group The Hawks, initially playing rhythm guitar, then bass. After leaving Hawkins in 1963, the formidable live outfit went on to become Bob Dylan's band.

Having made musical history on Dylan's controversial "electric" world tour of 1965/'66, they did it again by evolving an exhilarating country-soul-blues-folk-rock hybrid at Dylan's retreat in Woodstock, New York. ("We hadn't really thought up a name until *Big Pink* in 1968," Danko later revealed. "But [we] used to see these posters up on marquees and it always said just 'Bob Dylan and band,' so we thought it was quite funny just to call ourselves 'The Band.'")

The group swapped roles, alternated harmonies, and "With these multiple voices and jumbled instruments we discovered our sound," drummer Levon Helm recalled. This radical, highly influential change of direction informed The Band's *Music From Big Pink* (1968, featuring Danko/Dylan cowrite "This Wheel's On Fire") and *The Band* (1969), Danko's soulful country-inflected falsetto a major element.

They reunited with Dylan for a 1974 tour and the acclaimed *Before The Flood* collaboration, but split two years later. Danko's 1977 eponymous solo album was the first (and best) by a Band member. Along with his ex-comrades, he endured an ongoing battle with drug addiction but remained musically active, rejoining a Robbie Robertson-less Band in the 1980s and playing alongside Helm in Ringo Starr's celebrity touring outfit.

Rick Danko passed away in his sleep (overweight, but clean of drugs) on December 10, 1999.

BELOW Danko (right) on stage with Paul Butterfield in 1980.

MARK SANDMAN
HEART ATTACK

Born: September 24, 1952

Died: July 3, 1999

"One of the sexiest bands around," said PJ Harvey of Morphine. The Boston band was led by Mark Sandman, who served time as a cab driver and on an Alaskan fishing boat before turning to music.

Though eclipsed by fellow Bostonians the Pixies, Sandman's mid-1980s rock trio Treat Her Right enjoyed a local hit with "I Think She Likes Me." When that group ended, he busied himself with projects like the improvisational band Supergroup, before forming Morphine.

Like Treat Her Right, Morphine eschewed guitars in favor of Sandman's bass and baritone drawl, saxophone, and drums. Sandman drily labeled their sound "low rock" and "implied grunge." After three albums for Rykodisc, notably 1993's *Cure For Pain*, they were one of the first signings to the DreamWorks label. Sandman also played in several spin-off bands, including the Hypnosonics.

On July 3, 1999, Sandman was onstage with Morphine at the Giardini del Principe in Palestrina, near Rome, jokily reciting lyrics to an old song in Italian, when he collapsed of a heart attack. He was pronounced dead on arrival at hospital. He was forty-six.

Of his funeral, Chris Ballew of Presidents Of The United States Of America (another Supergroup alumni) wrote, "Dana Colley, the baritone sax player from Morphine, and Russ Gershon, from the Either/Orchestra, both got their instruments and stood under the tree next to Mark's grave. They played disembodied horn sections from songs by Morphine and the Hypnosonics. The lack and void was huge."

RIGHT Mark Sandman of Morphine, around 1995.

CURTIS MAYFIELD
(CURTIS LEE MAYFIELD, JR.)
DIABETES-INDUCED COMA

Born: June 3, 1942
Died: December 26, 1999

Mayfield cofounded the vocal trio that became The Impressions in 1956 and their first hits—"For Your Precious Love" (1958) and "It's All Right" (1963)—were pop, pure and simple. His passionate and active support of the civil rights movement soon began to filter into Mayfield's recorded work, though—witness 1964's "Keep On Pushing," the majestic "People Get Ready" (1965), and black-pride clarion call "We're A Winner" (1967). The Impressions' influence was widespread—a Jamaican tour left an indelible mark on the fledgling Wailers: "We used to practice off Curtis Mayfield and The Impressions, even tried to look like 'em," revealed Peter Tosh later. (Bob Marley later subtly acknowledged Mayfield in the song "One Love/People Get Ready.") Anticipating black-music icons from Stevie Wonder to Prince, Mayfield wrote, sang, and produced his music.

Racial tension and civil strife in his country—specifically the desperate state of black ghettos—informed Mayfield's final Impressions LP and his solo debut *Curtis*, both released in September 1970. But he offset the gloom with a triumphantly upbeat single, "Move On Up" (1971), a classic slice of soul punctuated by bright brass orchestration and topped with Mayfield's characteristically sweet, understated vocal.

The height of his mainstream success came when the ex-Impression was asked to compose a soundtrack for an upcoming low-budget film, *Superfly* (1972). He turned in a riveting set of songs, exquisitely (and gently) sung reflections on street drug culture from the memorable title track to the softly sinister "Pusherman" and stark "Freddie's Dead," and the album racked up two million sales. Ironically, and in common with other "blaxploitation" flicks of the time, the film perversely

seemed to celebrate the gangster lifestyle. "Visually, I thought, 'This is a cocaine informercial,'" the singer fulminated. "I tried to go straight in the lyrics. I tried to tell the stories of the people in depth."

Despite the commercial windfall, Mayfield kept his eyes on the real deal. *Back To The World* (1973) highlighted the plight of black servicemen back from Vietnam to face the misery of inner-city desolation, a theme he continued on *There's No Place Like America Today* (1975). The rise of feelgood disco was just around the corner, however; suddenly, Mayfield's sharp-eyed urban critiques were as welcome as a protest singer on the dance floor. The Reaganomics of the following decade depressed him, though by 1990 he was music-making again, this time with Eazy-E and Ice-T on *The Return Of Superfly*.

The start of Curtis Mayfield's end was due to appalling bad luck. While he was performing to a 10,000-strong crowd in Brooklyn on August 13, 1990, a gust of wind sent a lighting rig crashing down onto Mayfield, destroying three of his vertebrae, and paralyzing him below the neck. Then, during his hospitalization, his house burned down.

It's a mark of the phenomenal positivity of the man that he endured, recuperating to the extent that he could produce a warmly received final album, 1996's Grammy-nominated *New World Order*, recorded with superhuman patience, line by line. By then, diabetes had set in, necessitating the amputation of his right leg and leading to a coma from which Mayfield never emerged. He died in North Fulton Regional Hospital, Roswell, Georgia, on December 26, 1999.

Ain't *that* a man.

RIGHT Platform soul—Mayfield in the early 1970s.

BIG PUN
(CHRISTOPHER LEE RIOS)
HEART ATTACK

Born: November 9, 1971

Died: February 7, 2000

A broken home and heroin-addicted mother formed the grim origins of Christopher Lee Rios. Born to Puerto Rican parents in New York, he tried boxing and drug dealing to escape the confines of the Bronx; a talent for basketball was stymied by his weight gain.

Turning to rap, he called himself Big Moon Dawg and hooked up with rapper Joseph Cartagena, aka Fat Joe. "First I look at him," recalled Joe. "I'm like, damn, this nigga's a big nigga!" But like The Notorious BIG and Joe himself, Christopher made a virtue of his bulk: equal parts thick-set thug and larger-than-life ladies' man. Renamed Big Punisher, he snared attention in 1995 with verses on Joe's *Jealous One's Envy* (1995) and a Funkmaster Flex mixtape.

Signed to Wu-Tang Clan's label Loud, his debut single, "I'm Not A Player"—remixed for mainstream success as "Still Not A Player"—proved him as adept at commercial rap as he was with gun talk. "They were comparing me to Biggie and Pac," said Pun of his newfound admirers, "because that's what those two would do. They would rhyme hardcore, then also rhyme party songs."

Loud bolstered his reputation with "BIG PUN" banners across New York, leading authorities to crack down on promotional posters, and album artwork featuring a scantily clad model dressed as the Statue of Liberty. The consequent controversy pushed *Capital Punishment* (1998) to double platinum, making Pun the first Latino solo rapper to move a million. "He definitely put a bar that you gotta raise to," said Xzibit, "if you gonna be a Latin MC... Pun is the bar."

Behind the scenes, success took its toll. "Everybody thought we were living the life and I was Miss Princess," said his abused wife Liza Rios. "In real life we went blow for blow... he was not happy with himself." Depression contributed to his overeating and Pun's weight ballooned in line with his Grammy-nominated ego.

Hitting 600 pounds, he became breathless—audible on *Yeeeah Baby* (2000)—and narcoleptic, and found it hard to walk. On February 7, 2000, he developed breathing difficulties and died before reaching hospital. He was twenty-eight. "We've got to take care of our health," said Fat Joe, "because Pun was too young to go like that." *Endangered Species* (2001) wrapped up his discography and the 2002 documentary *Still Not A Player* portrayed his rise and fall in grisly detail.

Lil' Kim, Puff Daddy, LL Cool J, and hundreds of fans attended a public viewing at the Ortiz Funeral Home in the Bronx before Pun was laid to rest at the district's Woodlawn Cemetery.

"He was a source of pride for the Latin community, a great artist, and a great person," said Jennifer Lopez, on whose "Feelin' So Good" Pun appeared at the time of his death. "We will miss him terribly."

LEFT Big Pun, blinged up and ready to go, January 1999.

IAN DURY
(IAN ROBIN DURY)
COLON CANCER

Born: May 12, 1942
Died: March 27, 2000

"Sex And Drugs And Rock And Roll" is Ian Dury's most famous contribution to music, although he modestly declared, "Life coined the phrase, and I nicked it off life." But the canon of the man Suggs of Madness called "the people's Poet Laureate" boasts plenty of other gems.

Dury contracted polio at seven. The crippling disease, he told *Village Voice*, "made me mentally aggressive." A witty wordsmith, he loved jazz and Gene Vincent, and studied art under *Sgt. Pepper*… sleeve designer Peter Blake.

Contempt for art school bands prompted Dury to form Kilburn And The High Roads (one of the most respected bands on the pub-rock circuit) in 1971. Despite a support slot with The Who, sales never matched acclaim, and they disbanded in 1975. However, a union with guitarist Chaz Jankel led to 1977's classic "Sex And Drugs And Rock And Roll" and *New Boots And Panties!!*

Fronting funky new band The Blockheads, Dury hit the UK Top Ten in 1978 with "What A Waste" and No. 1 with "Hit Me With Your Rhythm Stick." "Reasons To Be Cheerful, Part 3" gave him another smash in 1979.

Finally successful, Dury, said a former manager, "turned from being really nice to being a real pain in the arse." The Blockheads split while infidelity finished his marriage; he subsequently spent two years with actress Jane Horrocks. Scorning the UN's "Year of the Disabled" in 1981, he released "Spasticus Autisticus"—whose then-shocking lyrics proved, he said, "a career wrecker."

In the 1980s, music took second place to stage and screen. His celluloid CV includes *The Crow: City Of Angels* with Iggy Pop and *Hearts Of Fire* with Bob Dylan. Dury's voice also graced a long-running British TV commercial: "Hello Tosh, gotta Toshiba?"

The Blockheads reunited in 1990, leading to 1997's glorious *Mr. Love Pants*. But in 1996, Dury was diagnosed with cancer of the colon. When secondary tumors struck his liver, he was told the condition was terminal. His reaction: "Oh blimey."

Undaunted, he busied himself with charity campaigning and The Blockheads, raising an eyebrow when Bob Geldof—then a DJ—announced his death in 1998. Dury played his last show—*New Boots And Panto*, supported by Kirsty MacColl—at the London Palladium on February 6, 2000, dying just weeks later (MacColl died the same year, hit by a speedboat while swimming with her sons, see page 187).

Robbie Williams, whom Dury inspired and befriended, was among mourners at his funeral. Horses drew his coffin through North London, via Kilburn High Road. Members of Madness were his pallbearers at Golders Green crematorium. Irreverent wreaths included a pint of Guinness and condoms. *Ten More Turnips From The Tip*, unfinished when he died, was released in 2002. Robbie Williams sang its love song, "You're The Why," featuring Dury's last lyrics.

"I haven't shaken my fists at the moon," Dury told British newspaper *The Independent* in 1998. "I'm fifty-six and mustn't grumble. I've had a good crack, as they say. Do I ever feel sorry for myself? No. Sorry for yourself is for wankers, innit?"

RIGHT Ian Dury with The Blockheads at the Hope and Anchor pub in Islington, North London.

Behind the scenes

JACK NITZSCHE
(BERNARD ALFRED NITZSCHE)
HEART ATTACK

Born: April 22, 1937

Died: August 25, 2000

ABOVE Jack Nitzsche (left) in a recording studio with Darlene Love and Phil Spector.

From working with Phil Spector to winning an Oscar, via The Rolling Stones, Chicago-born composer and arranger Bernard Alfred "Jack" Nitzsche had an extraordinary career.

Having migrated to Hollywood, Nitzsche got his first break via Sonny Bono, with whom he wrote "Needles And Pins" for Jackie DeShannon (later to be covered by the Ramones). He helped build Phil Spector's "Wall of Sound" on classics such as Ike and Tina Turner's "River Deep Mountain High," and had an instrumental hit of his own, 1963's "The Lonely Surfer."

Nitzsche is all over The Rolling Stones' early output, from tambourine on "Satisfaction" to the choral arrangement on "You Can't Always Get What You Want" and the soundtrack of the Mick Jagger-starring 1970 movie *Performance*.

Nitszche's work with Neil Young included *Buffalo Springfield*, 1972's *Harvest*, and a role in Young's band Crazy Horse. But, after a grim tour for *Harvest*, the relationship cooled. Nitzsche later dated Young's ex-partner, actress Carrie Snodgress, whom he was arrested for assaulting in 1979. Although he scored movies from The Monkees' *Head* to *One Flew Over The Cuckoo's Nest*, drink and drugs made his output erratic.

Despite an Oscar for 1982's "Up Where We Belong" from *An Officer And A Gentleman* and a reunion with Young on 1992's *Harvest Moon*, Nitszche's work rate had slowed by the time of his death in L.A. from cardiac arrest, blamed on a recurring bronchial infection. He was buried at Hollywood Forever Cemetery. Phil Spector delivered the closing eulogy.

KIRSTY MacCOLL
(KIRSTY ANNA MacCOLL)
HIT BY SPEEDBOAT

Born: October 10, 1959

Died: December 18, 2000

"She has great songs and a crackin' bust," said Morrissey. "The Noel Coward of her generation," concurred Bono.

The talent of Londoner Kirsty MacColl, daughter of folk star Ewan MacColl, showed itself early on, and Kirsty was signed at just 16. Her debut single, "They Don't Know," was released in 1979, but it was a flop until Tracey Ullman's cover in 1983. However, MacColl scored big with 1981's "There's A Guy Works Down The Chip Shop Swears He's Elvis."

Throughout her career, MacColl's fame and talent were stymied by stagefright, and she retreated to backing vocals with stellar acts such as Talking Heads and The Smiths. Via her husband, producer Steve Lillywhite, she sang with The Rolling Stones and picked the running order for U2's *The Joshua Tree*.

After a starring role on 1987's seminal Christmas favorite "Fairytale Of New York" with the Pogues, MacColl resumed her solo career with 1989's *Kite* (featuring a hit reworking of The Kinks' "Days"). *Electric Landlady* (1991), which, like *Kite*, featured Johnny Marr of The Smiths, *Titanic Days* (1993), the hit's compilation *Galore* (1993) and the critically acclaimed *Tropical Brainstorm* (2000) followed.

After making this album, MacColl was holidaying with her partner and children in Cozumel, Mexico, when, in an area reserved for swimmers, she was hit and killed by a speedboat. She had pushed her son out of its way, sacrificing herself in the process. The speedboat belonged to one of Mexico's wealthiest businessmen. Although the driver was convicted of culpable homicide, many questions arising from the investigation remain unanswered and her family continues to campaign for justice.

At a private funeral, Fauré's *Requiem*, The Beach Boys' "Good Vibrations," her own "Good For Me," and Blue Boy's "Remember Me" reflected MacColl's diverse tastes. A public memorial service at London's St Martin in the Fields was attended by stars including Bono and The Edge, and climaxed with an airing of her own "Don't Come The Cowboy With Me, Sonny Jim."

LEFT Kirsty MacColl with Shane MacGowan of The Pogues.

JOHN PHILLIPS
HEART FAILURE

Born: August 30, 1935

Died: March 18, 2001

During their mid-1960s heyday, The Mamas And The Papas produced some of the best sun-kissed West Coast pop this side of Brian Wilson's Beach Boys. Central to the foursome's success was John Phillips, coauthor (with wife Michelle) of their debut hit "California Dreamin'" (1966, No. 4 on the *Billboard* charts), on which sublime harmonies were combined with heart-tugging melancholy—a combination to which Wilson himself was no stranger. "They had just come down off about eighty acid trips, they were funky and dirty, and yet they sang like absolute angels," recalled producer Lou Adler, of an early encounter with the fine-blend foursome.

"Monday, Monday" (also 1966, *Billboard* No. 1) provided a sublime follow-up (though of the four, only Phillips liked it); "Words Of Love," "Dedicated To The One I Love" (previously a Shirelles hit), and "Creeque Alley" (an account of their rise to fame) maintained the group's hit quota throughout 1967. They rapidly established themselves as prime practitioners of flower power pop, though their contemporary harmonic blend and psychedelic outfits showed their debts to earlier golden ages of popular song.

Phillips' best year was 1967. Riding high in the charts with his band, he also helped to organize 1967's memorable Monterey Pop Festival and wrote another anthemic paean to California—"San Francisco (Be Sure To Wear Some Flowers In Your Hair)," a worldwide smash for Scott Mackenzie.

But it wasn't all sunny-side up. Phillips had married Californian beauty Holly Michelle Gilliam in 1962—she joined his group The Journeymen, which evolved via folk rock into The Mamas And The Papas—but their marriage was fracturing by the late 1960s.

Indeed, Michelle had actually been fired in 1966, though she and her husband were swiftly reconciled. They finally divorced in 1969. (Michelle had even less success with her next husband—Dennis Hopper; they split after eight days of marriage in 1970.)

As with The Monkees, The Mamas And The Papas' hits dried up almost as soon as they'd arrived. Riven by drugs and multifarious infidelities, the group disbanded in July 1968, though they reunited for 1971's contractual-obligation album, *People Like Us*. Phillips had made a promising start to solo life with 1970's acclaimed country-rock set *John The Wolfking Of L.A.*, but thereafter his career stalled, hampered by his burgeoning drug addiction, which saw him spend much of the following decade in a zonked-out daze (he later confessed to shooting heroin and cocaine "almost every fifteen minutes for two years"). Heroin and Dilaudid disrupted his mid-1970s sessions with Keith Richards and Mick Jagger, released posthumously as *Pay Pack And Follow* (2001). Following a 1980 cocaine bust, Phillips spent time on an anti-drugs lecture tour along with his daughter Mackenzie who had similar problems. (Another daughter, Chynna, was one third of successful 1980s outfit Wilson Phillips.) With ex-bandmate Denny Doherty, he toured a version of The Mamas And The Papas in the 1980s (that included Mackenzie) and cowrote unexpected (albeit uninspired) Beach Boys' chart-topper "Kokomo" in 1988.

Unsurprisingly, Phillips was not in the best of health at the turn of the century. He'd undergone a liver transplant in 1992, and a hip replacement in 1997, though in the end it was a viral kidney infection that led to the heart failure that claimed him in March 2001.

RIGHT Phillips onstage at the Mill Run Theater, Chicago, during a 1982 Mamas And Papas reunion tour.

CURSED BAND
RAMONES

THE DEPARTED

JOEY RAMONE
(Jeffry Ross Hyman)
Lymphatic cancer
Born: May 19, 1951
Died: April 15, 2001

DEE DEE RAMONE
(Douglas Glenn Colvin)
Drug overdose
Born: September 18, 1952
Died: June 5, 2002

JOHNNY RAMONE
(John Cummings)
Prostate cancer
Born: October 8, 1948
Died: September 15, 2004

- -

One-two-three-four! Fatalities in the Ramones have yet to match their legendary onstage intro—but with three members down, and another five to go, one may well have died in the time it has taken you to read this.

In their twenty-two years together, the Ramones proved rock's most influential post-1960s band. A stellar lineup on 2003's tribute album *We're A Happy Family* includes Red Hot Chili Peppers, Metallica, U2, Green Day, Kiss, and Tom Waits.

Long before The Sex Pistols were a twinkle in Malcolm McLaren's eye, the Ramones cut a punky swathe through pomp and disco. They borrowed their black leather and bowl haircuts from the early Beatles, melodies from 1960s girl groups, and riffing from every band that made feedback more important than fretwork—then hammered the result into two-minute blocks of rock. "Loud, fast, and stripped down to the core," said *We're A Happy Family*'s compiler Rob Zombie. "The Ramones will forever be cemented in my brain as four teenage punks in black leather and blue jeans ready to crack your skull with a baseball bat."

Singer Joey, guitarist Johnny, bassist Dee Dee, and drummer Tommy convened in 1974, adopted the group surname, and unleashed *Ramones* in 1976. Classics like "Beat On The Brat" stamped a template for the thirteen studio albums to follow. Of the myriad live albums and compilations, 1979's *It's Alive* and 1999's *Hey! Ho! Let's Go* are the most highly rated.

For two decades, they toured relentlessly, burning through four drummers (Tommy quit to be their producer and was

RIGHT The Ramones, photographed around 1980.

FAR RIGHT The Ramones performing onstage in the 1970s.

"Yeah, I'm still in the best band in the world."

replaced by Marky, Richie, and Elvis—the latter Blondie's Clem Burke) and two bassists (Dee Dee was replaced by one of his own fans, CJ).

Joey died in New York on April 15, 2001—Easter Sunday— from cancer that had rendered him visibly ailing for the previous five years. He is buried in New Jersey's Hillside Cemetery. At a New York tribute concert, Steven Van Zandt declared, "Jeffry Hyman died so that Joey Ramone could live."

Dee Dee—a long-time drug user, bearing a tattoo reading "Too tough to die"—was found dead in Hollywood on June 5, 2002, of a heroin overdose. Johnny—who is often credited with running the band—died in L.A. on September 15, 2004, of prostate cancer. He and Dee Dee are buried at L.A.'s Hollywood Forever Cemetery.

All three founder members' headstones bear both their given and Ramones names—a gracious end to the tensions within the band in its final years. "Me and Joey basically didn't speak for a long time," Johnny explained to *Rolling Stone*, "[but] I would still get up there every day, look at Joey, start to play and know, 'Yeah, I'm still in the best band in the world.'"

JOHN LEE HOOKER
DIED IN SLEEP

Born: August 22, 1917
Died: June 21, 2001

Delta Blues giant John Lee Hooker was born in Coahoma County, near Clarksdale, Mississippi—stopping-off place for countless blues legends including Bessie Smith, Muddy Waters, Howlin' Wolf, and Robert Johnson. Hooker's stepfather, Will Moore, was a blues guitarist who had worked with Charlie Patton, and Hooker's own distinctive droning guitar style, often based around one chord, stemmed from Moore: "What I'm playing now, he taught me," Hooker revealed in 1990. "Nobody else plays this style; I got it all to myself."

The young Hooker was a devout churchgoer, singing with various local choirs, but left home at the age of fourteen, traveling north and joining the Army. After moving to Detroit, he drifted south again, to Memphis (where he began playing blues), Cincinnati (where he sang with gospel groups and worked as a theater usher), and back to Detroit to work in an automobile factory and—aided by a local record-store owner—produce a demo record. That record—the rudimentary but riveting "Boogie Chillen" (1948, a million-seller and winner of the W.C. Handy Hall of Fame Award)—married country blues to its electrified R&B urban cousin, and proved a landmark of the genre.

In the 1940s, now fronting his own band, Hooker delivered a grab-bag of blues classics, including "Hobo Blues" and "Crawling King Snake Blues" (both 1949, the latter revisited by The Doors on 1971's *L.A. Woman*). The following year, he even scored a pop hit with "I'm In The Mood." By now, he'd established his trademark style—a laconic, almost somnambulant drawl complemented by dextrous, unpredictable guitar picking. "I can play straight changes on twelve or eight bars; I can do that if I really want to, but I don't because I'm *known* not to," he explained years later. "The people eats it up the way *I* do it." "Boom Boom" (1962) provided another crossover hit, while an appearance at the Newport Blues Festival the same year cemented his status.

The British Invasion of pop groups during 1964 introduced many white Americans to blues material, and artists, that had been under their noses for decades, and Hooker's career was afforded a new lease on life. ("Oohhh, I felt good when your bands started doin' my tunes," he told journalist Charles Shaar Murray in 1990; "seemed like ever' band over there was doin' them.") Later that

"The people eats it up the way I do it."

decade, he relocated to San Francisco, pairing up with blues-rockers Canned Heat for *Hooker 'N' Heat* (1971) his first *Billboard* hit. For the remainder of his life, he toured relentlessly, clad in trademark hat and sunglasses—an uninviting appearance that disguised a dry but warm sense of humor. His albums were patchy, though 1989's *The Healer* was a strong set that united the blues veteran with admirers such as Bonnie Raitt and Carlos Santana, and secured him a Grammy for "I'm In The Mood."

Countless blues artists died penniless, unrecognized, and before their time. Refreshing, then, to note that John Lee Hooker enjoyed adulation and plaudits aplenty, was financially secure, and died of natural causes in his sleep, two months short of his eighty-fourth birthday.

RIGHT John Lee Hooker in Los Angeles, California, 1981.

AALIYAH
(AALIYAH DANA HAUGHTON)
PLANE CRASH

Born: January 16, 1979

Died: August 25, 2001

"It's hard to say what I want my legacy to be…" said Aaliyah (Arabic for "highest, most exalted, the best") shortly before her death. "I want people to look at me as a full-on entertainer, and a good person."

Aaliyah Dana Haughton was born in Brooklyn but raised in Detroit. R. Kelly—to whom Aaliyah was introduced via her aunt, Gladys Knight—helmed her debut *Age Ain't Nothing But A Number* (1994) and its hit "Back And Forth." The album went platinum within months.

To familial horror and tabloid delight, the pair married in August 1994. Aaliyah, just fifteen—twelve years Kelly's junior—claimed to be eighteen. Her parents reportedly annulled the marriage; neither she nor Kelly discussed their relationship.

Without him, she was teamed with up-and-coming hitmakers Timbaland and Missy Elliot. They floated Aaliyah's haunting vocals over soon-to-be trademark stuttering sounds for 1996's multi-platinum *One In A Million*, an evolution continued by subsequent hits "Are You That Somebody" and "Try Again." The latter came from the movie *Romeo Must Die* (2000), in which Aaliyah appeared opposite Jet Li.

Aaliyah went from strength to strength. She won the title role in *Queen Of The Damned* (after screen-testing with scenes from *Macbeth* and *Salome*), was contracted to star in the *Matrix* sequels, released another hit album—*Aaliyah* (2001)—and planned a collaboration with Trent Reznor of Nine Inch Nails.

On August 25, 2001, Aaliyah was due to leave the Bahamas, having shot a video for "Rock The Boat." She detested small planes, but—anxious to return to boyfriend Damon Dash—declined the offer of a private jet and boarded a light aircraft. On takeoff from Abaco Island, it flew 200 feet, crashed, and caught fire. All nine aboard died.

An autopsy revealed cocaine and alcohol in the system of the pilot, who had been sentenced to probation for crack possession twelve days before the crash. Investigators said the plane was at least 700 pounds overweight. Aaliyah died of burns and a blow to the head. "Even if she had survived the crash," said the pathologist, "recovery would have been near impossible."

"Thousands lined the streets of New York City to watch the twenty-two-year-old singer's funeral entourage," reported the *Milwaukee Journal Sentinel*, "an occasion that might have qualified for the city's largest show of collective grief that year had not the events of Sept. 11 overshadowed it days later." Her silver-plated coffin was carried in a horse-drawn, glass-paneled hearse. Puff Daddy, Usher, Jay-Z, Lil' Kim, Gladys Knight, and Mike Tyson were among the mourners. After the service, Aaliyah's mother released white doves while fans sang "One In A Million."

Aaliyah promptly topped the *Billboard* chart, while "More Than A Woman" became a UK No. 1. *Queen Of The Damned* opened to praise for its star amid trashing of the movie itself, and "Aaliyah" made it into an annual list of America's most popular baby names.

"I can see why God wanted you closer to Him," said rapper and *Romeo Must Die* co-star DMX, "because you truly were an angel on Earth."

LEFT Aaliyah performing at Shoreline Amphitheater in Mountain View, California, in 1998.

GEORGE HARRISON
THROAT CANCER

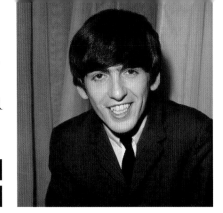

Born: February 25, 1943

Died: November 29, 2001

Overshadowed during his Fabs years by the twin pop powerhouses of John Lennon and Paul McCartney, George Harrison's contribution to the evolution of The Beatles was nevertheless immense. Initially, that contribution was limited to his clean, economic guitar riffs—often with a country and western twang—that decorate early Beatles singles. In 1964, Harrison employed his electric twelve-string Rickenbacker 360 guitar on the *A Hard Day's Night* soundtrack. Inspired by the bright, jangly tones, Roger McGuinn bought the same model and used it to create The Byrds' trademark sound.

As the first Beatle to balk at the claustrophobic pressures (and tedium) of pop superstardom, Harrison's enquiring mind did much to move the group into new directions. Bored on the set of *Help!* in 1965, he picked up a sitar and became fascinated by its haunting sound. His subsequent tutelage under sitar maestro Ravi Shankar, and increasing fascination with all things Eastern, filtered back to The Beatles via Harrison's "Love You To" and "Within You Without You." It led to his interest in transcendental meditation, prompting the whole group to visit India to study under the Maharishi Mahesh Yogi in 1968.

Harrison's songwriting was improving apace too: "If I Needed Someone" (an homage to The Byrds' "The Bells Of Rhymney"), "Long, Long, Long," "While My Guitar Gently Weeps," and "Here Comes The Sun" rivaled Lennon and McCartney's best. Frank Sinatra called "Something" "the greatest love song of the last fifty years," although at first he'd thought it was a Lennon-McCartney tune.

Following the break-up of The Beatles in 1970, Harrison launched his solo career in style, with the critically acclaimed *All Things Must Pass* (1970) and worldwide No. 1 "My Sweet Lord" (1971), a reflection of Harrison's devout spirituality. He practiced what he preached too, attracting a stellar lineup of stars (including Bob Dylan and Beatle buddy Ringo) to raise money for starving refugees with 1971's Concert for Bangladesh. He also branched into movie production, forming Handmade Films, which stepped in at the eleventh hour to back Monty Python's controversial movie *Life Of Brian*.

The death of John Lennon in 1980 hit Harrison hard, and prompted the affectionate tribute "All Those Years Ago" (1981) on which all three remaining ex-Beatles played. They reconvened again in 1994 (as "The Threetles," in Harrison's phrase) for two singles built around Lennon demos—"Free As A Bird" and "Real Love." (Another old-school reunion, in 1987, had seen Harrison join The Traveling Wilburys alongside luminaries such as Bob Dylan and Roy Orbison, to considerable commercial success.)

Harrison almost went the same way as Lennon on December 30, 1999, when Michael Abram broke into his home in Henley-on-Thames and stabbed him several times, puncturing his lung. (Abram, who had declared he was on a "mission from God," was later declared insane and cleared of attempted murder.)

The end wasn't far away, though. Back in 1997, Harrison had undergone radiation treatment and surgery for throat cancer, which he attributed to his years of smoking. In May 2001, he had surgery for lung cancer; two months later he underwent radiotherapy for a brain tumor. By then, the writing was clearly on the wall. Harrison finally succumbed to cancer on November 29, 2001, at his friend Gavin de Becker's house in Los Angeles.

RIGHT The Traveling Wilburys (minus "The Big O"). From left to right: Tom Petty, Bob Dylan, George Harrison, drummer Jim Keltner, and Jeff Lynne.

STUART ADAMSON
(WILLIAM STUART ADAMSON)
SUICIDE BY HANGING

Born: April 11, 1958

Died: December 16, 2001

ABOVE Stuart Adamson onstage with Big Country in Liverpool, England, in 1986.

Stuart Adamson first found fame with Scottish New Wavers The Skids, whose third, breakthrough single—"Into The Valley" (1979)—remains a punk-pop gem. Hits "Masquerade" and "Working For The Yankee Dollar" followed, but three albums in, tensions between guitarist Adamson and lead singer Richard Jobson led to Adamson's somewhat premature departure.

It proved a shrewd move. As The Skids faded into obscurity, Adamson's new outfit—Big Country—found success as purveyors of distinctively Scottish stadium rock. Their epic sound—big guitars (a twin-ax attack dubbed "bagpipe-like," to Adamson's chagrin), big choruses—scored them a string of UK hits, including "Fields Of Fire (400 Miles)" (UK No. 10), "In A Big Country" (UK No. 17), "Chance" (UK No. 8), and "Wonderland" (UK No. 9) within a year. Debut LP *The Crossing* (1983) made the UK Top Three and broke them Stateside; sophomore release *Steeltown* (1984) entered the *Billboard* charts at No. 1.

When the tides of pop changed, however, Big Country found themselves swiftly stranded. In the wake of acid house and indie-dance bands, their trademark brush-cuts and plaid seemed hackneyed; they split in 1999.

Adamson began a long spiral downwards, with alcoholism and severe depression as unwelcome companions. In November 1999 (now living in Nashville, Tennessee) he vanished temporarily, although reports that his family knew of his whereabouts led some to speculate that he was attempting to battle his addiction in rehab. On November 7, 2001 (a drunk-driving charge now hanging over him), he disappeared again—to Hawaii—leaving a note for his son, Callum, which read "Back by noon, Sunday." His second wife, Melanie Shelley, reported him missing on November 26, then filed for divorce. The following month, Adamson hanged himself in a room at Honolulu's Best Western Plaza Hotel. "I still hold him in tremendous respect," admitted erstwhile bandmate Jobson in 2007. "His talent was what that band was about."

ZAC FOLEY
(ZACHARY SEBASTIAN REX JAMES FOLEY)
DRUG OVERDOSE

Born: December 9, 1970

Died: January 2, 2002

While "Stairway To Heaven" has its admirers, the era-defining classic most likely to fill a dance floor is "Unbelievable" by EMF.

Born in England's Gloucestershire, bassist Zac Foley claimed he had been expelled from school just for having long hair. Along with keyboard player Derry Brownson, drummer Mark Decloedt, singer James Atkin, and guitarist Ian Dench, he formed Epsom Mad Funkers, more commonly known as EMF.

Dismissed as imitators of Jesus Jones, EMF eclipsed their progenitors with 1990's "Unbelievable," which topped the *Billboard* singles chart and paved the way for 1991's million-selling *Schubert Dip* (the release of which was delayed when Yoko Ono objected to a sample of Mark Chapman reciting lyrics by John Lennon).

Though EMF scored another nine UK hits, the worldwide success of "Unbelievable" became something of an albatross. Foley—fans' favorite after pin-up Atkin—amused himself by stuffing fruit under his foreskin (as illustrated in *Select* magazine) but, by the time of 1992's *Stigma*, "was pumping myself full of anything." One album later, EMF imploded.

Foley formed Carrie (as in Carrie "Princess Leia" Fisher), which—like the musical endeavors of his former bandmates—met no acclaim whatsoever. EMF duly reformed in 1991, but Foley's substance abuse continued.

He died in London's Camden from an overdose of heroin, cocaine, ecstasy, barbiturates, and alcohol—"a combination," *Q* reported the coroner as saying, "usually found in dead people." He was thirty-one.

"It's such a waste," said Foley's brother. "What is that they say about the light that burns twice as bright? That was Zac."

LEFT EMF: crazy kids. Clockwise from top right: James Atkin, Zac Foley, Mark Decloedt, Derry Brownson, and Ian Dench.

LAYNE STALEY
(LAYNE THOMAS STALEY)
DRUG OVERDOSE

Born: August 22, 1967

Died April 5, 2002

"This girl walked up to me and said, 'You're not dead,'" Layne Staley of Alice In Chains reported in 1996. "And I said, 'No, you're right. Wow.'"

Staley spent a decade constructing his own obituary. On *Dirt* (1992), he sang, "What's my drug of choice? Well, what have you got?" As comfortable with gentle harmonies as with metallic roaring, he sounded, said Rage Against The Machine's Tom Morello, "like an angry angel."

Alice In Chains—from a daydream of Staley's about a metal band in drag—convened in Seattle in 1987. Relentless touring made *Facelift* (1990) a slow-burning success. Their fortunes were bolstered by 1992's movie *Singles*, from whose soundtrack "Would?"—a reference to Andrew Wood, Mother Love Bone's singer who died of a heroin overdose (see page 118)—was a hit.

"There's more to life than being fucking rock stars."

Though *Dirt* sold millions, a 1993 tour proved their last. "The girls, the free drugs, the free beer... I got all that shit during the first record," said Staley. "It didn't satisfy me. There's more to life than being fucking rock stars." For the singer—happiest "rearranging my apartment and taking photographs"—that meant art and heroin.

"We would have done anything he wanted to have helped him," drummer Sean Kinney told *Rolling Stone*. "Sadly... what he wanted was for us to leave him alone." After 1994's *Jar Of Flies*—a *Billboard* chart-topping sequel to 1992's acoustic *Sap*—Alice

vanished. Rumors obliged their management to deny that Staley had lost fingers to gangrene, or died. Instead, he joined members of Pearl Jam and Screaming Trees for *Above* (1995), credited to Mad Season. On its eerie "River Of Deceit," Staley sang simply, "My pain is self-chosen."

Alice managed a final album in 1995. Though it warned "You'd be well advised not to plan my funeral till the body dies," Staley proved neither able nor inclined to tour. Their last live outings, in 1996, were an *MTV Unplugged* and four shows supporting Kiss. "I see a lot of you are dressed up like Kiss," the scarily sick-looking singer cracked to one audience, "but none of you are dressed up like me. What's up with that?"

His final releases were a soundtrack cover of Pink Floyd's "Another Brick In The Wall" and two songs—"Get Born Again" and "Died"—for a box set. "Staley never recovered," reported *Blender*, "from the 1996 drug-related death of his girlfriend, [*Dirt* cover star] Demri Murphy."

On April 19, 2002, police broke into Staley's Seattle apartment after his mother reported not having seen him for two weeks. They found him on his couch "in an advanced state of decomposition." An autopsy concluded he had overdosed on a mixture of heroin and cocaine, known as a speedball, two weeks earlier—eight years to the day after Kurt Cobain's suicide. At his funeral, Soundgarden's Chris Cornell, with Ann and Nancy Wilson of Heart, sang The Rolling Stones' "Wild Horses."

"I'm gonna be here for a long fuckin' time," Staley told *Rolling Stone*. "I'm scared of death... of where I would go."

RIGHT Alice In Chains performing on *MTV Unplugged* in 1996.

LISA "LEFT EYE" LOPES
(LISA NICOLE LOPES)
CAR ACCIDENT

Born: May 27, 1971

Died: April 25, 2002

"I like it when you kiss both sets of lips," quips Lisa "Left Eye" Lopes on TLC's first hit. The mischievous rapper distinguished TLC from legions of R&B girl groups, and helped make them one of music's best-selling female acts.

Born in Philadelphia, Lopes moved wherever her army father was stationed. "I lived in Panama where it was predominantly Spanish people or army kids," she remembered—a multi-cultural influence on her 2001 single "The Block Party." She was converted to rap at fourteen: "I'm not the best singer in the world. Rapping is more fun for me."

In 1990, she hooked up with Tionne "T-Boz" Watkins and Rozonda "Chili" Thomas in TLC, assembled by R&B singer Pebbles. Brainstorming stage names, Lopes remembered, "A man once told me... my left eye was more beautiful than my right."

Ooooooohhh... On The TLC Tip (1992) went triple platinum, but the band's gimmicky sound and image—Lopes wore condoms over her eye—augured poorly for their longevity. However, CrazySexyCool (1994) and Fanmail (1999)—bolstered by hits like "Waterfalls" and "Unpretty"—sold many millions more.

Meanwhile, Lopes—the "Crazy" in CrazySexyCool—became charismatically pugnacious. In 1993, she was arrested for fighting with police. In 1994, she had a fateful argument with football-player boyfriend Andre Rison: "I decided to barbecue his tennis shoes. I threw them in the bathtub because I thought the fire would contain itself that way, but it immediately blazed out of control and then the whole house burnt down." Lopes was put on ten years' probation and ordered into rehab.

TLC filed for bankruptcy in 1995 to escape their ties with Pebbles, and cracks began to appear when Lopes objected to producer Dallas Austin (Chili's future husband). Later, resentful of her diminished role, Lopes challenged her bandmates to issue solo albums and to then let the public decide who's best. "Sisters argue and they kiss and make up," said T-Boz.

She launched a solo career with Supernova (2001) and, as NINA (New Identity Non-Applicable), signed to Death Row boss Suge Knight's new label. "She wasn't afraid to go against the grain," said Knight. Lopes also worked with renegade rappers Method Man and Tupac Shakur.

In 2002, Lopes was in the Central American country Honduras, where she planned a home. "She would always try to get me to go..." said Lil' Kim. "There's a purifying lake [and] a man out there who was a witch doctor or something who she would go to." But on April 25, Lopes was driving a rented vehicle when she lost contol, hit two trees and tumbled off the road. She died at the scene of a fractured skull.

Thousands attended her funeral in Lithonia, Georgia, including T-Boz and Chili, Usher, Janet Jackson, Whitney Houston, and Alicia Keys. Mary Mary performed one of Lopes's favorites, "Shackles (Praise You)." Engraved on the casket was her "Waterfalls" rap: "Dreams are hopeless aspirations in hopes of coming true; believe in yourself, the rest is up to me and you."

LEFT Performing "Too Much Booty" for the MTV Music Video Awards at New York's Metropolitan Opera House in September 1999.

JOHN ENTWISTLE
(JOHN ALEC ENTWISTLE)
HEART ATTACK

Born: October 9, 1944

Died: June 27, 2002

"The sudden ending with the line of coke and the hooker in Las Vegas…" Roger Daltrey reflected in the UK newspaper *The Observer*. "Is it that bad at fifty-seven? What's the alternative? The alternative may be very slow and smelly, as George Orwell said."

Keith Moon is The Who's most famous casualty, but John Entwistle played a key role in the band for nearly four decades. He wrote fan favorites like "Boris The Spider" and "Heaven And Hell," and was crucial to powerhouses like "My Generation," "Won't Get Fooled Again," and "The Real Me."

Having attended the same school as Pete Townshend, Entwistle reunited with the guitarist in singer Roger Daltrey's band the Detours—who, with Moon on drums, evolved into The Who. Entwistle's flamboyantly fiery technique earned him the nickname "Thunderfingers." "We were a three-piece band with a singer, so we had a lot of ground to cover," he explained to *Goldmine*. "I eventually became a lead bass player."

Immoveable onstage—memorably in a skeleton suit—he became known as "The Ox." Offstage, he shared Moon's appetite for destruction but let the drummer take the blame for trashed hotels. His black humor leavened Townshend's pretension: witness "My Wife" on *Who's Next* (1971) and "Fiddle About" on *Tommy* (1969).

Entwistle distanced himself from internal power struggles: "I let Pete and Roger argue about who was the most important person in the band." Nonetheless, his dissatisfaction led him to consider offers from Hendrix ("I had to say no because that was a good week with The Who") and The Moody Blues. He also, around 1966, considered a supergroup with Keith Moon, Jeff Beck, and Jimmy Page, yet conceded it would go down "like a lead Zeppelin." Page took note.

Entwistle was the first to undertake a solo career with 1971's *Smash Your Head Against The Wall*. "I had been smashing my head against the wall trying to get songs on the Who albums," he explained.

Townshend split the band in 1982. "John Entwistle was very resentful…" he said. "He'd got used to living high, and his money supply was cut off… He didn't want to live less high. He preferred to be dead."

Even after The Who reunited, Entwistle continued making his own music, and toured with Ringo Starr and Roger Daltrey. But on the eve of The Who's 2002 U.S. tour, he was found dead in a Las Vegas hotel room. The coroner, noting both a "significant amount of cocaine" and evidence of heart disease, said, "That's a bad combination."

"If he could have written an ending for himself it would have been very similar to the one he had," noted Daltrey wryly. "I just hope that God has got his earplugs ready." Entwistle was buried in Stow-on-the-Wold, in Gloucestershire, England.

At the seventh concert of the rescheduled tour, Townshend announced they would stop dedicating shows to Entwistle: "It's not working. He hasn't shown up."

RIGHT Promotional appearance at the Duke of York's Barracks, King's Road in London's Chelsea, November 12, 1966.

JAM MASTER JAY
(JASON WILLIAM MIZELL)
GUNSHOT

Born: January 21, 1965

Died: October 30, 2002

"Run-DMC first said a DJ could be a band," rapped Public Enemy in 1988. Their inspiration: Jason "Jam Master Jay" Mizell.

Mizell grew up in Queens, New York, with small-time criminals. "I had to be their friend," he told biographer Bill Adler, "in order not to be scared of them." Tagging along on a burglary, Jay was narrowly missed being shot by a security guard's gun. Shaken, he turned to the theoretically safer world of deejaying. "First parties I deejayed when I was thirteen…" he remembered. "Hip hop has always been about playing live and working a crowd."

With rappers Joseph "Run" Simmons and Daryl "DMC" McDaniels, he steamrollered onto the scene with 1983's "It's Like That" and "Sucker MCs." Where predecessors like Grandmaster Flash were funky, Run-DMC were heavy—long before rap-rock reared its head, they did it first. "We didn't want to be like the soft R&B," Jay said, "We wanted to go hardcore."

Run-DMC (1984) and *King Of Rock* (1985) went gold, then *Raising Hell* (1986)—thanks to its resurrection of Aerosmith's "Walk This Way"—became the first hip hop album to go platinum. The band also inspired the Beastie Boys. "Back when we started," said Jay, "you couldn't even hear rap on the radio. We've helped bring rap where it is now, which is everywhere."

His skills were celebrated in "Jam Master Jay" ("We got the master of a disco scratch") and "Peter Piper" ("Goddamn that DJ made my day"). Run-DMC scored further smashes with *Tougher Than Leather* (1988), *Down With The King* (1993), and Jason Nevins's reworking of "It's Like That." In 1996, Jay met Queens rapper Curtis Jackson, taught him about structuring songs, and convinced him he could make it. Jackson became 50 Cent.

On October 30, 2002, Jay was at his studio in Jamaica, Queens, when two men entered. Accounts vary: in one, the men greeted Jay with a hug; in another they burst into the studio. But one of the men shot Jay in the head at point-blank range and fled.

A *Playboy* article—"The Last Days Of Jam Master Jay," available online—suggests Jay, reportedly deeply in debt, may have been the middleman in a drug deal that went wrong. Another theory held that Jay was targeted for his links with trouble magnet 50 Cent.

LL Cool J and Chuck D, who compared Jay's death to that of John Lennon, were among fans for the funeral at Allen A.M.E. Cathedral in Queens. DMC rapped "Jam Master Jay," with the audience shouting the title. Wreaths included one shaped like turntables, while pallbearers wore Jay's trademark Shell Toes (Adidas debuted a Jam Master Jay sneaker in 2003). Kid Rock led an all-star tribute—featuring Grandmaster Flash—at a VH1 awards show.

"This is not a person who went out looking for trouble," said Dr. Dre. "He's known as a person that builds, that creates, and is trying to make the right things happen."

RIGHT Run-DMC rockin' their ever-present Adidas. From left to right: Run, Jam Master Jay, and DMC.

JOE STRUMMER
(JOHN GRAHAM MELLOR)
HEART ATTACK

Born: August 21, 1952

Died: December 22, 2002

"Joe was as huge an inspiration to me now as he was in 1977," said Iggy Pop in 2002. "He combined cool with an uncompromising stance, infused reggae into punk and taught a whole generation of us more about politics than any number of teachers or politicians."

Born the son of a diplomat in Turkey, John Graham Mellor brought intelligence and eclecticism to The Clash, the band he formed with Mick Jones and Paul Simonon after an inspirational early show by The Sex Pistols. "Strummer" came from his rhythm guitar playing in pre-Clash hopefuls The 101'ers.

After the Stones and before U2, The Clash was rock's most important band. They are celebrated by stars as diverse as Rage Against The Machine and Billy Bragg for their lyrics, which championed left-wing politics in a time when the right was on the rise. But they also wrote glorious songs for albums rightly regarded as classics, from 1977's punky *The Clash* to 1982's head-spinning *Combat Rock*. Even albums whose merits are debated yielded gems such as "The Call Up" on 1980's *Sandinista!* and "This Is England" on 1985's *Cut The Crap*.

When the band imploded, Strummer kept busy. He scored Alex Cox's movies *Sid And Nancy*, *Straight To Hell*, and *Walker*, made 1989's well-received *Earthquake Weather*, substituted for Shane MacGowan in The Pogues, collaborated with a range of artists from Black Grape to Johnny Cash, and formed a fine new band, The Mescaleros.

Throughout the decades, he resisted offers to re-form his old band, partly to prevent their legacy "from being besmirched or cheapened" and partly out of loyalty to drummer Topper Headon, whose health was too poor for him to participate.

Strummer avoided most rock 'n' roll clichés, except an enduring fondness for marijuana. But on December 22, 2002, shortly after walking his dogs, he succumbed to an undiagnosed heart defect at his farmhouse in England's Somerset. "That heart of his always worked too hard," said Pete Townshend.

An amazing array of stars paid tribute, from Pearl Jam to David Bowie, Neil Tennant to Bruce Springsteen, and the Beastie Boys to Brian May.

Clash men Mick Jones and Paul Simonon were among mourners at his funeral, held in the band's spiritual home, West London. Also in attendance were twenty-four firemen, paying respects to the man who played one of his final gigs in support of their strike. That show saw Strummer and Jones reunited onstage for the first time in nearly two decades.

Strummer's final album was celebrated in a 2004 *Interview* article, featuring—in a reflection of his influence—Elton John and Bono. "The most maddening of clichés has come to be true," said Bono, "which is that *Streetcore*... is probably his best." "It is a truly great album, " agreed Elton, "even though Joe sounds contented on *Streetcore*, I don't think he ever stopped searching for new sounds, new ideas."

LEFT The Clash—Paul Simonon, Joe Strummer, and Mick Jones— rocking the United States.

MICKEY FINN
(MICHAEL NORMAN FINN)
LIVER AND KIDNEY DISEASE

Born: June 3, 1947

Died: January 11, 2003

Playing percussion for Marc Bolan can, it would appear, shorten your life.

When Bolan was making his name as a tousle-haired hippie-poet songster in Tyrannosaurus Rex, his bongo-playing accomplice was Steve "Peregrine" Took. Born Stephen Ross Porter, Took renamed himself after a character in J. R. R. Tolkein's *The Hobbit*, in a move redolent of those whimsical days. Took stayed with The Corkscrew-Haired One for 1968 debut album *My People Were Fair And Had Sky In Their Hair But Now They're Content To Wear Stars On Their Brows* (whimsical days…) and a trio of minor hit singles, but—with abysmal timing—quit at the end of a U.S. tour and ran off with a fan. (Took's frustration that his own songwriting potential was being sidelined may also have played a part in his decision.)

Obscurity beckoned, though Bolan's manager Tony Secunda did help Took eventually to secure royalties he was owed from his days as Bolan's bongocerro. Sad to say, those belated royalties probably hastened Took's end. Celebrating his newfound wealth on October 27, 1980, the thirty-one-year-old spent the night boozing, taking morphine, and greedily eating cherries, which proved to be his undoing; in one of rock 'n' roll's more unlikely deaths, he choked on a cherry pit.

Took's loss was Mickey Finn's gain. Along with 300 others, long-haired looker Finn answered an ad Bolan had placed in *Melody Maker* for "a gentle young guy who can play percussion, i.e. bongos and drum-kit, some bass guitar, and vocal harmony." It's more than possible that Finn's good looks—along with his Triumph 650cc motorcycle—won Bolan over. By 1970, Tyrannosaurus Rex had become T-Rex and Bolan had swapped his acoustic guitar for a Gibson Les Paul.

From 1970 on, T-Rex were a hit machine, racking up a string of solid-gold classic singles that included "Ride A White Swan" (1970, UK No. 2), "Hot Love," "Get It On" (both 1971, both UK No. 1s), "Jeepster" (1971, UK No. 2), "Telegram Sam" (1972, UK No. 1), and "Metal Guru" (1972—another No. 1). By 1975, however, Bolan's majestic run as glam-rock's beglittered king was at an end and there were divisions in the T-Rex camp (following the introduction of drummer Bill Legend, Finn's percussive role began to shrink). After recording *Bolan's Zip Gun* (1975), Finn took his bongos elsewhere…

As it happened, those bongos headed straight into the heartland of pop wilderness. The 1980s saw Finn work on sessions for fly-by-nights The Blow Monkeys and The Soup Dragons. In 1997, he teamed up with some of Bolan's other backing musicians for a reunion concert (minus Bolan, who had been killed in a car accident in 1977, see page 60). The response from loyal T-Rex fans was encouraging, and an inspired Finn formed tribute band Mickey Finn's T-Rex, which included T-Rex session drummer Paul Fenton and occasionally Marc's son Rolan.

Alas, the new lease of life led to naught. Hampered with kidney and liver complaints—brought on by his years as a booze hound—Mickey Finn passed away at Mayday Hospital in Croydon on January 11, 2003; the precise cause of his death is not known.

RIGHT Mickey Finn performing with T-Rex in 1973.

NINA SIMONE
(EUNICE KATHLEEN WAYMON)
CANCER

Born: February 21, 1933

Died: April 21, 2003

"I want to be remembered," Nina Simone declared in 1997, "as a diva from beginning to end who never compromised in what she felt about racism and how the world should be, and who to the end of her days consistently stayed the same."

Born Eunice Kathleen Waymon in Tryon, North Carolina, she played piano and accompanied singers in the Methodist church where her mother preached. On beginning her professional career, she needed a stage name to hide her path from the same parent: "Nina" came from a boyfriend's nickname for her, "Simone" from the French actress Simone Signoret.

"I want to be remembered as a diva from beginning to end."

Though classically trained, Simone regarded her music as folk and blues, and resented being ghettoized as "jazz." "Jazz means black and jazz means dirt," she told *Details*, "and that's not what I play." Like Billie Holiday, she recorded the anti-racist "Strange Fruit," yet scorned comparisons with her predecessor: "What an insult! Because she was a drug addict! They only compared me to her because we were both black—they never compared me to Maria Callas, and I'm more of a diva like her than anybody else."

Simone made her recording debut in 1957, released as *Little Girl Blue*, aka *Jazz As Played In An Exclusive Side Street Club* (1958). The album featured her hit interpretation of the George and Ira Gershwin classic "I Loves You Porgy," and the song that became a milestone in her career, "My Baby Just Cares For Me." When

a rerelease of the latter revived her career in the late 1980s, she railed against audiences who had come to hear it.

Although her mainstream chart impact was minimal—1960's live *At Newport* reached No. 23 in *Billboard*—Simone put her stamp on songs in the 1960s. The Animals are the best-known devotees—her versions of "The House Of The Rising Sun" and "Don't Let Me Be Misunderstood" inspiring theirs.

However, online resource The Nina Simone Web also cites "Lilac Wine" (Jeff Buckley: "Nina does it best… she's the king"), "Wild Is The Wind" (Elizabeth Fraser, Cocteau Twins: "This live version I've got is just… I don't know, I haven't got the vocabulary") and "I Put A Spell On You" (Peter Gabriel: "I can recall the emotional excitement of hearing something which was new, earthy, and gutsy"). "I'd been listening to Nina Simone," John Lennon told *Playboy*, "who did something like 'I love you!' in one of her songs and that made me think of the middle-eight for 'Michelle.'"

Aretha Franklin titled a 1972 album after Simone's most important song, "(To Be) Young, Gifted, And Black." But while that became an anthem for the civil rights movement in the United States, Simone grew disillusioned with her country and left in 1973. Time did not ease her feelings: "I do not believe in mixing of the races… " she told *Interview* in 1997. "Slavery has never been abolished from America's way of thinking. Desegregation is a joke."

Simone recorded sporadically in the 1970s, and became better known for her onstage truculence. Despite living mainly in Europe, she was hardly a fan of the continent. "Europe, I find, is like a graveyard," she declared in British newspaper *The Daily Telegraph*. "No one speaks, no one is friendly, no one talks, they ignore me completely."

LEFT Accepting homage onstage in Carnegie Hall, New York City.

By the 1980s, she had tired of fighting the establishment: "I'm not about protest songs anymore," she said. "I want to perform with symphony orchestras and choirs. I want to play concertos." Consequently *Let It Be Me* (1987) bore little trace of her activism, featuring instead songs by Bob Dylan, Janis Ian, and Randy Newman—and a reworking of "My Baby Just Cares For Me." In 1998 she guested at Nelson Mandela's 80th birthday celebration in Johannesburg, South Africa.

The 1990s saw her namechecked by Lauryn Hill on the Fugees' "Ready Or Not," and later years found her "Angel Of The Morning" sampled by Shaggy and "Black Is The Color Of My True Love's Hair" by AZ. Masters At Work and Coldcut were among remixers let loose on her material. Talib Kweli reworked her "Four Women," a groundbreaking portrait of black femininity ("My skin is brown, my manner is tough, I'll kill the first mother I see").

After a lengthy battle with cancer, Nina Simone died in her sleep on April 21, 2003, at the age of seventy. Her funeral began with a recording of Jacques Brel's "Ne Me Quitte Pas (Don't Leave Me)." To hundreds of mourners, South African singer Miriam Makeba described her as "not only a great artist, but also a freedom fighter." A wreath from Elton John, placed on the altar, read: "You were the greatest and I love you." The artist's daughter, Lisa Celeste Stroud, played piano. Simone's body was cremated at a private service in Marseille, France, and her ashes scattered across Africa—where, she said, "Everyone's friendly, everybody's warm and intuitive."

Appropriately, among the eulogies at her funeral was one from South Africa's government: "Nina Simone was a part of our history. She fought for the liberation of black people. It is with much pain that we received the news of her death."

WARREN ZEVON
(WARREN WILLIAM ZEVON)
LUNG CANCER

Born: January 24, 1947
Died: September 7, 2003

Tupac prophesied his own death, Johnny Cash and Ian Curtis created sonic epitaphs…but no one chronicled their own demise more meticulously than Warren Zevon—and got Springsteen, Dylan, and the Pixies to pay tribute.

Death shaped the singer-songwriter's discography from 1969's *Wanted Dead Or Alive* to *Life'll Kill Ya* (2000) and *My Ride's Here* (2002). If blackly comic lyrics provided insufficient clues, a skull with shades and a cigarette stared from many of his album sleeves.

Born in Chicago, Zevon was raised, he told *Rolling Stone*, "with a painting of an uncle, Warren, who looked just like me. He was a military man, a golden boy, an artist. He'd been killed in action… and I was brought up to follow in his footsteps. I guess that kind of background gave me the idea that destroying myself was the only way to live up to expectations." Accordingly, Zevon spent much of his career fueled by drink and drugs. He got clean in the mid-1980s, although a drunken jam with R.E.M. appeared as the *Hindu Love Gods* album in 1990.

After the failure of *Wanted Dead Or Alive*, Zevon began the 1970s as the Everly Brothers' musical director. His own career, kickstarted by friend Jackson Browne, peaked commercially with 1978's *Excitable Boy*, featuring the classic "Werewolves Of London." Other fine albums include 1981's live *Stand In The Fire* and 1982's flop *The Envoy*.

In August 2002, he was diagnosed with an inoperable form of lung cancer. "I might have made a tactical error in not going to a physician for twenty years," he told chat show host David Letterman. "It was one of those phobias that really didn't pay off."

Asked what he had learned, he said "I know how much you're supposed to enjoy every sandwich."

Given three months to live ("It'll be a drag if I don't make it to the next James Bond movie," he said), Zevon promptly fell off the wagon. "I said the one thing this guy should not do is die a cliché," admonished novelist and collaborator Carl Hiaasen.

"I guess destroying myself was the only way to live up to expectations."

With the help of friends, family, and stars like Springsteen, he channeled his remaining energy into *The Wind* (2003). Its recording was documented in VH1's *Keep Me In Your Heart*, during which producer Jorge Calderon suggested redoing a song when Zevon was feeling fresh. "I'm dying, Jorge," he replied, "I don't have no 'fresh.'"

"If you're lucky, people like something you do early and something you do just before you drop dead," said Zevon shortly after his diagnosis. After he died in his sleep, at home in L.A., *The Wind* won two Grammys. The star-studded tribute *Enjoy Every Sandwich* appeared in 2004. His ashes were scattered in the Pacific Ocean.

"What we're essentially dealing with is an existence that we don't understand," Zevon told *Songwriter* magazine. "That's why a lot of my work is about death…I don't consider it a subject to be avoided."

RIGHT "I'd like to meet his tailor…"— Zevon onstage, around 1980.

JOHNNY CASH
(J. R. CASH)
RESPIRATORY FAILURE

Born: February 26, 1932

Died: September 12, 2003

Over the course of half a century, Johnny Cash created some of the most enduring American popular music ever recorded. That his last recordings are regarded as some of his finest is testament to the depth of an outstanding talent.

His background was the humblest—the fourth of five children born into a country shack in Arkansas, with no electricity (he discovered country music via a battery-powered radio), though somehow his parents financed singing lessons for the boy. Recalled childhood friend Merline Hall, "It was not a false voice… when he sang, he meant every word he sang."

"[Wearing black] is still my symbol of rebellion... against people whose minds are closed."

Cash learned to play guitar while stationed with the Air Force in Germany. Discharged in 1954, he initially worked as a door-to-door salesman, but music drew him back. He formed country/gospel group The Tennessee Three, though after their steel guitarist dropped out, they turned rockabilly.

The band's stripped-down sound, and Cash's gritty, deep voice, impressed Sam Phillips (owner of the label Elvis recorded for, Sun Records). Starting in 1955 they scored a number of hits on Sun, including "Folsom Prison Blues" (inspired by a film Cash had seen in Germany, *Inside The Walls Of Folsom Prison*) and "I Walk The Line"—both slow, thoughtfully expressed numbers, soon to become

Cash classics. There was nothing showy or insincere about Johnny Cash—as demonstrated by his sober stage attire, which earned him the appellation "The Man in Black." "I wore black because I liked it. I still do, and wearing it still means something to me," he revealed in 1997. "It's still my symbol of rebellion—against a stagnant status quo, against our hypocritical houses of God, against people whose minds are closed to others' ideas."

After moving to Columbia Records in 1958, Cash embraced country music, becoming a regular on the Grand Ole Opry, and later enjoying hits with the mariachi-flavored "Ring Of Fire" and a cover of Bob Dylan's "It Ain't Me Babe." He had plenty of personal demons, though: "Back [in the early 1960s] he was so deeply into the amphetamines that he had lost an awful lot of weight," recalled country music writer Jack Hurst, "He looked like a wraith, but a powerful wraith." Cash was arrested for possession of amphetamines in 1965, and his addiction to the drug came close to destroying his health.

By the late 1960s, Cash's career was going from strength to strength, with an ABC TV show and country-pop hits such as "Daddy Sang Bass" (featuring future wife June Carter, of country royalty the Carter family) and the novelty "A Boy Named Sue," his bestseller. The latter was taken from his live album *At San Quentin* (1969), one of two renowned records recorded in prison (the other was at Folsom) that reinforced Cash's image as a down-to-earth man of the people—whether those people were locked up or not. ("He's as comfortable with the poor and prisoners as he is with presidents," Kris Kristofferson once remarked.)

RIGHT Cash onstage at the Hammersmith Odeon in London, 1966.

Cash rather lost his way during the 1970s and '80s, and it wasn't until the early 1990s that he experienced his artistic renaissance, with the help of Def Jam Records' Rick Rubin. Rubin had put out the first Beastie Boys album and produced the Red Hot Chili Peppers, but his work with Cash was the antithesis of those high-octane releases. Four albums in the "American Recordings" series were released during the last years of Cash's life, each featuring stripped-down covers of contemporary songs and reinterpretations of old-time standards. Cash's baritone was weaker now, and prone to cracking, but still arresting.

In the acclaimed video for Cash's moving take on Nine Inch Nails' "Hurt," June Carter Cash is visibly distressed at the sight of her ailing husband. Ironically, his wife passed away before Cash, in May 2003—a body blow from which he never recovered, though he resolutely pushed on with recording sessions.

Weakened by years of drug dependency, Cash had undergone double-heart-bypass surgery (in 1988) and suffered from diabetes; he was also diagnosed with the fatal neurological disease Shy-Drager syndrome in 1998 and was prescribed medication—but the diagnosis proved incorrect and he had to wean himself off the drugs. He claimed that a dentist had once broken his jaw during treatment but never fixed it, leaving him with the choice of having surgery (which might prevent him singing again) or a life on pain-killers. He stuck with the pain.

Johnny Cash was admitted to Nashville's Baptist Hospital in September 2003, following an attack of pancreatitis, and subsequently released, but three days later he died from respiratory failure, a result of complications arising from diabetes. His spirit remained undimmed to the last, though. In 2002, television talk show host Larry King asked Cash whether there was a cure for his illness. "No, I don't think so," came the reply. "But that's all right. There's no cure for life either."

RIGHT Cash onstage in New York in 1992.

ROBERT PALMER
(ROBERT ALLEN PALMER)
HEART ATTACK

Born: January 19, 1949

Died: September 26, 2003

By the time he hit commercial paydirt in the 1980s, Robert Palmer had paid his dues many times over. Born in England's Batley in Yorkshire, Palmer was raised in Malta (where his serviceman father was stationed), then returned to Yorkshire, joined his first band—the curiously monikered Mandrake Paddle Steamer—and studied graphic design. Moving to London in 1969, he sang with The Alan Bown Set, then blues-rockers Vinegar Joe.

Palmer's subsequent solo career reflected his love of blues and R&B. On debut *Sneakin' Sally Through The Alley* (1974), produced by Little Feat's Lowell George, he was backed by mighty New Orleans funksters The Meters. His sophisticated look (that of a slightly smug hairdresser to the stars) seemed somewhat at odds with his musical loves, though. "The media never really liked him, they didn't trust him," reflected future bandmate John Taylor. "He

was too good to be true…He was too smart, too cute, and dared to live abroad *in the Bahamas!*"

Success remained strictly modest until a 1985 collaboration with ex-Durannies and Chic-ers in supergroup Power Station, and the release of his own *Riptide* of the same year, which saw Palmer go platinum. The runaway success had much to do with the slickly sexy Terence Donovan-directed video for Grammy-winning single "Addicted To Love" (*Billboard* No. 1)—in which Palmer was backed by leggy lovelies in tight-fitting black dresses; like follow-up "I Didn't Mean To Turn You On," it sold a million copies. He'd come a long way from those gritty blues roots, to which he finally returned for 2003's *Drive*.

While visiting Paris with his partner, Mary Ambrose, Palmer died suddenly from a heart attack. He was buried in Lugano, the Swiss city that had become his home.

LEFT Palmer onstage performing "Addicted To Love."

ELLIOTT SMITH
(STEVEN PAUL SMITH)
SELF-INFLICTED STAB WOUNDS

Born: August 6, 1969

Died: October 21, 2003

Smith's earliest solo musical offerings— *Roman Candle* (1994) and *Elliott Smith* (1995)—were full of tales of the losers on life's margins, showcasing his gift for an impressionistic lyric and a haunting tune. He was concurrently a member of Portland-based punk troupe Heatmiser, but after their 1996 split, Smith poured his energies into his solo work; his next album, the Kierkegaard-inspired *Either/Or* (1997), may have been his best, a clutch of fragile but captivatingly melodic songs.

So far, so low key. After fellow Portlander Gus Van Sant used some of Smith's songs in his 1997 film *Good Will Hunting*, however, the indie singer-songwriter's profile expanded exponentially. "Elliott's music is literally the most important thing in *Good Will Hunting*," actress Minnie Driver noted later. "Elliott is like a character you can't see." Featured in Van Sant's film was the track "Miss Misery," which was nominated for an Oscar for Best Original Song. In atypical white jacket, Smith performed the track at the Academy Awards in 1998 (but the award went to Celine Dion).

Smith broadened this sound with a full band for *XO* (1998) and *Figure 8* (2000). The latter, which was recorded at the Abbey Road studios in north London, smacked distinctly of The Beatles' *White Album*. (His interest in the Fab Four ran deep; for the *American Beauty* soundtrack, he recorded a cover of their vocal *pièce de résistance* "Because," multitracking the complex harmonies himself.) The quality of his work was never in question, but commercial success continued to elude the troubled troubadour.

And he *was* troubled. Before the world had heard of him, Smith had undergone psychiatric treatment, and an uneasy melancholy purveyed much of his work; he'd developed a serious heroin habit (note the lyrics to "Bled White" from *XO*)—to which he added prescription pills and, later, crack. He argued with his record label, Dreamworks; the release date of his next album was postponed; and he was thrown in jail after a fight at a gig in L.A. Still, toward the end of 2003, he had nearly finished that record (the somber *From A Basement On The Hill*, released in 2004) and hopes were high that this one might take him over the top.

Smith had apparently become increasingly depressed in the final few months of his life, squabbling with his girlfriend, singer Jennifer Chiba; moreover, his perfectionism created a fractious relationship between Smith and her band, whom he was producing. Weary of Smith's suicide threats, Chiba had locked herself in the bathroom of their Los Angeles home on October 21, 2003, but flew out again when she heard a skin-crawling scream, to find the singer with a steak knife stuck in his chest.

An hour later, Smith was dead. Two chest wounds were apparently self-inflicted, but an air of uncertainty still pervades the case, not least because so few suicides choose to end it all by stabbing themselves through the heart. (In December 2003, an autopsy report floated the idea of homicide.) A hard core of Smith fans clearly had their suspicions, and directed them at Chiba in the form of accusations and threats.

Oh, and the name of Chiba's band? Happy Ending.

RIGHT Elliott Smith performing onstage in 1998.

RAY CHARLES
(RAY CHARLES PETERSON)
LIVER DISEASE

Born: September 23, 1930
Died: June 10, 2004

Ray Charles' achievements are astonishing enough in their own right; but then factor in the start he had in life…

Born into a poor family in Albany, Georgia, Charles became blind by the age of seven, due to glaucoma; if that weren't bad enough, as a child he saw his younger brother drown, and both his parents died while he was in his teens. Undeterred—driven all the more, if anything—he enrolled at Florida's St. Augustine School for the Deaf and the Blind, where he studied music and braille (which, in turn, helped him learn composition and arrangement).

"I met Ray when I was about fifteen and he was about eighteen," recalled legendary producer Quincy Jones, "and even then he was always so damn positive, like he could listen to a record of Billy Eckstine's 'Blowin' The Blues Away,' and he could tell you what everybody in the band was doing…It was Ray that taught me how to voice brass."

Having started out on the Florida club circuit as a singer and pianist with a laid-back, sophisticated sheen à la Nat "King" Cole, Charles drifted west to Seattle, making his first recordings in 1949. Atlantic Records picked him up in 1952, but he still hadn't found his voice on the R&B numbers he cut with them. That came after Charles worked with hell-for-leather bluesman Guitar Slim, who brought the fervor of gospel into secular song. Charles learned the lesson well, delivering an impassioned vocal on the driving "I Got A Woman" (1954, based on the hymn "Jesus Is All The World To Me"), soon covered by Charles fan Elvis Presley. He grafted more lyrics onto gospel songs to produce hits with "This Little Girl Of Mine" (1955, previously "This Little Light Of Mine"), and "Talkin' 'Bout You" (1957, hitherto "Talkin' 'Bout Jesus").

Unsurprisingly, many were shocked: "He's mixing the blues with the spirituals," Big Bill Broonzy carped. "I know that's wrong… he should be singing in a church." He dropped another stone-cold classic with 1959's "What'd I Say," an electric piano-driven stomper that nodded to rock 'n' roll, featuring call-and-response backing vocals (from The Raelettes) that derived from church meetings. (Rocker Eddie Cochran was another fan, and turned countless white audiences on to Charles by covering his "What'd I Say" and "Hallelujah I Love Her So.") Combining R&B rhythms with gospel passion, Ray Charles was laying the building blocks of soul music, though jazz was never far away (note the ballads and jazz-band arrangements of 1959 breakthrough *The Genius Of Ray Charles*).

He quit Atlantic for ABC in November 1959, with no immediate drop in quality. The warm mixture of weariness and love in his take on Hoagy Carmichael's "Georgia On My Mind" (1960) confirmed Charles as one of popular song's finest interpreters; he teamed up with ace arranger Quincy Jones and members of Count Basie's band to produce 1960's big-band bonanza *Genius + Soul = Jazz*; the comic, punchy "Hit The Road Jack" (1961) saw him play the part of a put-upon philanderer with gusto; and that same year he gave a performance of effortlessly charming innuendo on "Baby It's Cold Outside," a hit duet from 1961's *Ray Charles And Betty Carter*.

The singer was mixing and matching genres for fun now, but even for him his next move was a startling one. On *Modern Sounds In Country And Western* (1962, his only *Billboard* No. 1 album), he took inspiration from a genre that seemed utterly foreign to most

RIGHT Ray Charles in concert in 1966.

contemporary black artists, but the conviction and sensitivity of his vocals swiftly established the album as a milestone release, spawning a million-seller in the aching "I Can't Stop Loving You." The following year, Hank Williams' "Take These Chains From My Heart" provided another smash. In retrospect, of course, it made perfect sense: with its trademark tales of heartbreak, death, and hard-living, what was country music but white blues?

"I'm a musician, man," Charles told Q magazine in 1992. "I can play Beethoven, I can play Rachmaninov, I can play Chopin. Every now and then when I do dates with symphony orchestras, I play these things and I shock the hell out of people." Charles' eclectic approach to music making—being "in every camp," in Quincy Jones' words—frustrated fans, and spread the talent mighty thin. The early 1960s saw him consolidate his stature as one of popular music's giants, however, with a world tour in 1964, during which he sold out Paris' Olympia Theatre ten nights in a row—an unprecedented feat for any American artist.

During the first half of the decade, Charles was voted best singer five times by critics in *Down Beat* magazine, though by the mid-1960s much of the bite and edge had gone and he became an "easy listening" artist. In truth, he'd already packed several lifetimes' worth of innovation into barely a decade. Moreover, he had other priorities: busted in 1965, Charles spent the next year

kicking a long-term heroin addiction (to hide the tracks on his arms, he always wore long sleeves).

Between 1957 and 1971, Charles racked up thirty-two Top 40 hits (his 1966 cover of Buck Owens' "Crying Time" received two Grammys). He showed no signs of letting up in the 1970s, with regular tours, including trips to Japan, almost every year. As with any artist whose career spans several decades, Charles was capable of wild inconsistency and gargantuan misjudgements of taste; he produced more than his share of schlock and recorded highlights became fewer over time. But his talent never deserted him—note his impassioned take on Stevie Wonder's "Livin' For The City" from 1975's *Renaissance*. A sparkling performance in *The Blues Brothers* (1980) movie proved his gift for comedy was intact, while a few years later he provided strong vocal support on USA For Africa's "We Are The World."

Liver disease finally claimed Charles in 2004, but even death couldn't stop him: the posthumous *Genius Loves Company*—an easygoing collaboration with a host of admirers including Van Morrison, B. B. King, Willie Nelson, and Elton John—picked up eight Grammys. (He also left behind him two marriages, and twelve children by seven mothers.)

All in all, then, fully deserving of the epithet that Frank Sinatra bestowed upon him in the 1950s: genius.

RICK JAMES
(JAMES AMBROSE JOHNSON, JR.)
RESPIRATORY AND HEART FAILURE

Born: February 1, 1948

Died: August 6, 2004

As famed for bad behavior as *baaad* music, New Yorker James Ambrose Johnson, Jr. joined the navy at fifteen but promptly went AWOL. Fleeing to Canada, he cofounded the Mynah Birds with Neil Young (yes, *that* Neil Young) and rechristened himself Rick James.

Nephew of The Temptations' Melvin Franklin, James then joined Motown as a songwriter. He also developed his own cocktail of funk and rock. (George Clinton, who had already done just that, dubbed him "Trick James.")

"*Never mind who you thought I was—I'm Rick James, bitch!*"

James' career peaked with *Street Songs* (1981), thanks to "Super Freak," source of MC Hammer's "U Can't Touch This." He created much-sampled classics by the Mary Jane Girls ("All Night Long") and Teena Marie ("Square Biz"), and wrote hits for The Temptations and Eddie Murphy.

His cocaine-fueled lifestyle attracted the censure of jazz legend Dizzy Gillespie, who told James, "You remind me of Bird [Charlie Parker]. Boy, you better slow down." He was hospitalized several times between 1979 and 1984, convicted of assaults in 1991 and 1993 (though not the charge often associated with him of burning a woman with a crack pipe), and had a stroke in 1997.

He finally succumbed to heart and lung problems at home in California. The coroner found traces of nine drugs—including cocaine ("a helluva drug," according to James)—in his body. Stevie Wonder and Jermaine Jackson were among celebrities at his funeral.

"Never mind who you thought I was," he said in a phrase immortalized by American comedian Dave Chappelle, "I'm Rick James, bitch!"

ABOVE The punk-funker performs.

Behind the scenes

JOHN PEEL
(JOHN ROBERT PARKER RAVENSCROFT)
HEART ATTACK

Hippy princeling-turned-punk-iconoclast, DJ John Peel—born John Robert Parker Ravenscroft—found fame on the Fab Four's coattails. Having made his way to the United States in 1960, he was employed at Dallas radio station KLIF because his accent reminded Americans of The Beatles.

On his return to Europe, he joined Radio London, then moved to the BBC's Radio One. There he provided a perfumed blend of poetry and progressive rock, championing the likes of Pink Floyd and Tyrannosaurus Rex. His Radio One show gave rise to the Peel Sessions, a rite of passage for aspiring alternative acts. The Fall hold the record, appearing in twenty-four sessions.

In 1976, bored with a scene he had helped nurture, Peel embraced punk, playing the Ramones despite listeners' howling protests. This set the tone for the coming decades, in which Peel gave airplay to otherwise ignored acts, from the Bhundu Boys to Napalm Death. Forever straining for new sounds, he once abandoned traditional year-end countdown "The Festive 50" when his listeners' favorites proved too conservative.

In 2004, Peel succumbed to a heart attack while on holiday in Peru. Jarvis Cocker and Feargal Sharkey were among mourners at his funeral at St. Edmundsbury Cathedral in Suffolk. At his oft-stated request, "Teenage Kicks" by The Undertones pumped out of the 500-year-old church.

"If I drop dead tomorrow," he once said, "I'll have nothing to complain about—except that there'll be another Fall album out next year."

Born: August 30, 1939
Died: October 25, 2004

ABOVE The champion of alternative music in his prog-rocking early 1970s days.

OL' DIRTY BASTARD
(RUSSELL TYRONE JONES)
DRUG OVERDOSE

Born: November 15, 1968

Died: November 13, 2004

"He was one of my favorite rappers," said Kanye West. "I would have cut off a piece of my finger to have his voice."

Russell Jones, raised in the "Brooklyn Zoo" (providing subject matter for his later track of the same name), formed Wu-Tang Clan with his cousins Robert "RZA" Diggs and Gary "GZA" Grice in the early 1990s. The movie *Mad Mad Kung Fu* provided his pseudonym.

Dirty won over record company executives with a rendering of "Somewhere Over The Rainbow" but became better known for unhinged ranting. Gold teeth and dreads added to his cartoon psycho image, captured on 1995's *Return To The 36 Chambers: The Dirty Version*. An implausible cameo on Mariah Carey's "Fantasy" initiated a lasting friendship.

Success could not keep trouble at bay. In 1993, he was convicted of assault; in 1994, he was shot in the stomach. Publicity of 1997's *Wu-Tang Forever* was dominated by Dirty's derangement; *The Independent* spotted him "lolloping up and down the hall in a Versace shirt over a ketchup-and-Bailey's-spattered vest, merrily chanting 'Pussy, pussy, pussy!' to a tune existing only in his head." He claimed to be on Earth "only until I've finished building my spacecraft...I'm studying electromagnetic frequencies at the moment."

Father of thirteen kids, Dirty was arrested in 1997 for non-payment of child support. In 1998, he disrupted the Grammys to bemoan Wu-Tang going unrewarded. For the hit "Ghetto Superstar," he announced his new name: Big Baby Jesus. "I know y'all are nervous," he told his collaborators, "because

you've never heard the voice of God before." Dirty also rechristened himself Unique Ason, Dirt McGirt, and Osirus. "I just want to take it from one spot and move it to another spot like I'm fucking with the computer," he declared.

Despite hits with 1999's *Nigga Please* and "Got Your Money," arrests kept him in the headlines, notably for threatening security at a Des'ree concert. In 2000, Dirty spent a month on the run from rehab. He performed with Wu-Tang in New York, then was captured when crowds gathered to get his autograph in a Philadelphia parking lot.

In 2001, he was imprisoned—"in an unsafe place where the government is trying to kill me"—for cocaine possession. On his 2003 release, he signed to Roc-A-Fella, whose CEO Damon Dash cast him in the movie *State Property 2* as a nose-picking cook.

"I just wish I wasn't fucking with them drugs," Dirty said. "That's the biggest mistake of my life...That's what kills motherfuckers." In November 2004, at a Manhattan studio, he complained of chest pains. Shortly afterward, he died from an overdose of cocaine and painkillers.

Mariah Carey and Kurtis Blow were among mourners at Dirty's Brooklyn funeral. "To the public he was known as Ol' Dirty Bastard, but to me he was known as Rusty," said his mother. "The kindest, most generous soul on Earth." After the funeral, Dirty's body was cremated.

Fourteen months later, Wu-Tang returned to the road. "He'll be in our hearts," said GZA, "and he'll be in the hearts of the crowd."

LEFT Ol' Dirty Bastard with the Wu-Tang Clan onstage in New York, June 1, 1993.

231

DIMEBAG DARRELL
(DARRELL LANCE ABBOTT)
SHOT WHILE PERFORMING ONSTAGE

Born: August 20, 1966
Died: December 8, 2004

"If you're just trying to make it and get rich in this business, just go ahead and hang it up right now…" Dimebag Darrell advised in *Guitar World* in his final interview. "But if you want to do it because you fucking love it, then go for it."

Born in Dallas, Texas, Dime—aka "Diamond"—was converted to hard rock by Kiss (he had an image of guitarist Ace Frehley tattooed on his chest). In 1981, he and his brother, Vinnie Paul, formed Pantera, who evolved into crunching metal masters with the recruitment of vocalist Phil Anselmo. But after million-sellers like *Cowboys From Hell* (1990), *Vulgar Display of Power* (1992), and the *Billboard* chart-topping *Far Beyond Driven* (1994), the band acrimoniously splintered in 2003. Dime and Vinnie formed Damageplan, who unleashed *New Found Power* in 2004.

On December 8, 2004—the anniversary of John Lennon's death—Damageplan appeared at the Alrosa Villa club in Columbus, Ohio. Nathan Gale, a twenty-five-year-old with a history of mental illness, jumped a fence outside the club as the band began its first song, "Breathing New Life." He got onstage, pulled a handgun, and shot Dime in the head, then fired at people trying to intervene. A roadie, security guard, and fan were also fatally shot before a Columbus cop killed Gale as he held the gun to a band technician's head.

Gale's motive is unknown; theories that he was inflamed by Pantera's split, or the dispute between Dime and Phil Anselmo, have been discounted. "Alcohol should have killed Dime,"

fumed Black Sabbath's Geezer Butler, "Not a fuckin' piece of shit worthless fuck with a gun trying to re-create John Lennon's killing."

Eddie Van Halen was among thousands of mourners at a memorial service in Arlington, Texas. Dime is buried at the city's Moore Memorial Gardens.

Amid a slew of tributes from fellow metallers appeared an article entitled "Aesthetics of Hate: R.I.P. Dimebag Abbott, And Good Riddance" on the conservative Web site Iconoclast. "It basically said that Dime was untalented and that he reaped what he sowed," fumed Machine Head's Rob Flynn, who wrote the song "Aesthetics Of Hate" in response. "It's one thing to have an opinion about an artist, but…it then went on to cast this huge generalization over the metal community, calling us pathetic for mourning his death…I wanted to punch the fucking computer screen."

Six-String Masterpieces: The Darrell Abbott Art Tribute—featuring guitars custom-painted by artists from Marilyn Manson to Moby, and Kelly Clarkson to Kerry King of Slayer—was displayed at Ozzfest and other festivals in the United States. A bronze bust of Dime was unveiled on Hollywood's RockWalk in May 2007. Members of Pantera, Jane's Addiction, and Alice In Chains were among those at a subsequent show in his honor.

"All he wanted to do was make everyone happy," said Ozzy Osbourne's guitarist and Dime's friend Zakk Wylde. "He's sitting at God's tavern, having a cold one with Randy Rhoads and Hendrix."

RIGHT MTV2 Headbangers Ball Tour on April 1, 2004, at the Roseland Ballroom in New York city.

SYD BARRETT
(ROGER KEITH BARRETT)
PANCREATIC CANCER

Born: January 6, 1946

Died: July 7, 2006

"He was a visionary," said Roger Waters. "He was the key that unlocked the door to rock 'n' roll for me."

Roger Keith Barrett—nicknamed Syd after a drummer in his hometown Cambridge—was trained as a painter, but bewitched by The Beatles and Rolling Stones. "I was teaching him to play Stones riffs every lunchtime for a year at technical college," said David Gilmour. In 1965, Barrett joined Waters—another Cambridge pal—in London, and cofounded The Pink Floyd Sound.

Barrett's compact discography belies his importance. Pink Floyd's hits "Arnold Layne" and "See Emily Play," and *The Piper At The Gates Of Dawn* (1967) were largely his work. A couple of haunting cuts on *A Saucerful Of Secrets* (1968), 1970's scratchy solo albums *The Madcap Laughs* and *Barrett*, and outtakes and radio sessions complete his catalog.

Nonetheless, his influence extends from David Bowie ("His impact on my thinking was enormous") and Blur (whose "Far Out" is a nod to Barrett's "Astronomy Domine"), to R.E.M. (who covered "Dark Globe") and The Mars Volta (who performed "Interstellar Overdrive").

Pink Floyd—from whom he was ousted in 1968, his unreliability exacerbated by LSD—spent years in his shadow, to their irritation. "In the beginning the songs were all his and they were brilliant," Barrett's replacement Gilmour told *NME*, "but I don't think the actual sound of the whole band stems from Syd…Syd's thing was short songs."

Nonetheless, Barrett is referenced in Floyd's "Brain Damage" (*Dark Side Of The Moon*, 1973), "Nobody Home" (*The Wall*, 1979), and "Poles Apart (*The Division Bell*, 1994), and is the subject of "Shine On You Crazy Diamond," from 1975's *Wish You Were Here*—at the mixing of which he unexpectedly materialized in Abbey Road studios. Jerry Shirley, a friend of the band who drummed for Barrett in 1970, remembered: "This overweight Hare Krishna-looking chap…I asked him what he was doing lately. 'Oh, you know, not much…I get up, eat, go for a walk, sleep.'" Barrett's reported reaction to "Shine On": "Sounds a bit old."

"Syd's father's death affected him very heavily," explained Gilmour, "and his mother always pampered him—made him out to be a genius of sorts." Too fragile for stardom and damaged by drugs, he spent the rest of his life in London, then Cambridge—barely acknowledging his past. Waters, however, namechecked Barrett at Floyd's 2005 Live8 reunion, and appeared at a London tribute concert in May 2007, as did a Gilmour-led Floyd.

Although Barrett's death was initially attributed to complications from diabetes, he succumbed to pancreatic cancer in a Cambridge hospital. "So much of his life was boringly normal," his sister told *The Sunday Times*. Describing him as "a hopeless handyman," she said: "When Roger was working he liked to listen to jazz tapes. Thelonious Monk, Django Reinhardt, Charlie Parker and Miles Davis were his favourites…but apart from the early Rolling Stones, he'd lost interest in pop music a long time ago."

RIGHT The piper in his psychedelic, Floydian heyday, circa 1967.

ARTHUR LEE
(ARTHUR TAYLOR PORTER)
ACUTE MYELOID LEUKEMIA

Born: March 7, 1945

Died: August 3, 2006

Love was one of L.A.'s finest, their songs a combination of pop hooks, savage guitar, dextrous arrangements, and mesmeric lyrics. Their driving force was frontman Arthur Lee, who once stated—boldly but accurately—"Jimi Hendrix wasn't the first psychedelic black guitarist songwriter. I was."

The garage-folk sound on Love's 1966 eponymous debut album drew heavily on The Byrds, though their choppy, slightly sinister cover of Bacharach and David's "My Little Red Book" (*Billboard* No. 52) hinted at new directions. Lee was a prolifically gifted dandy who could produce infectiously catchy acid pop—such as "Stephanie Knows Who"—alongside the proto-punk "Seven And Seven Is" on sophomore album *Da Capo* (1967).

In common with fellow Los Angelinos The Doors and The Mothers Of Invention, Lee's Love never fully embraced 1967's Summer of Love. From the band's rented house—"The Castle," a Hollywood Hills mansion that had once belonged to Bela Lugosi—he could almost literally have looked down on the riots on Sunset Strip the previous year. Meanwhile, the Vietnam War was reaching its height. Lee's response was *Forever Changes* (1967), a timeless collection of dark—and darkly humorous—observations on the troubles of his times, set to hummable tunes and carefully crafted orchestration. Today acknowledged as a rock landmark, at the time the album bombed in the States, and the band dissolved.

Over the next few years, Lee took new Loves through three albums (*Four Sail* and *Out Here* in 1969; *False Start* in 1970), launched a solo career, and ultimately ran out of creative steam.

Commercial success remained elusive, partly because Lee always refused to tour widely; his appetite for drugs ("I took acid every day I could until 1972 or '73," he once claimed) didn't help. Jac Holzman, the boss of Love's label Elektra, later reflected, "As large as his talent…was his penchant for isolation and not doing what was necessary to bring his music to the audience."

Support from younger acts such as Shack, The High Lamas, and Baby Lemonade saw Lee return to live performances of Love material in the 1990s, though his erratic behavior damaged him again. In late 1996 he received a twelve-year prison sentence for illegally possessing and discharging a firearm (the charge was tacked on to two previous charges, hence the stiff sentence). Freed six years later, he took Baby Lemonade on the road, touring *Forever Changes* to great acclaim.

In April 2006, it was revealed that Lee was suffering from acute myeloid leukemia. Benefit gigs for medical bills followed, along with intensive bouts of chemotherapy and a bone marrow transplant from umbilical cord stem cells (he was the first person in Tennessee to receive such state-of-the-art treatment). It was all to no avail: Arthur Lee passed away in August 2006 at Methodist University Hospital in Memphis, Tennessee.

Wilful, then, but witty, too. Of his refusal to let Love play the 1967 Monterey Pop Festival, he once opined: "They said: 'Look at all the exposure you'll get.' Well, all the people that played there, Jimi Hendrix, Janis Joplin, Otis Redding, Al Wilson, Brian Jones, Mama Cass are all dead. Man, I don't need that kind of exposure."

LEFT Arthur Lee focusing on one of his stage performances in 1970.

JAMES BROWN
(JAMES JOSEPH BROWN)
HEART FAILURE

Born: May 3, 1933

Died: December 25, 2006

"The most exciting and thrilling R&B male performer of all time," said Aretha Franklin. "If you didn't have soul, he was going to give you some."

Soul Brother Number One, Mr. Dynamite, The Hardest Working Man in Show Business, Minister of the New New Super Heavy Funk…James Brown's influence stretches from the Stones (Mick Jagger: "He was a whirlwind of energy and precision") to Public Enemy (a career built on JB samples), and from Zeppelin (1973's pastiche "The Crunge") to Sinead O'Connor (one of hundreds who sampled "Funky Drummer").

Amid prostitution and gambling, Brown was raised in Augusta, Georgia. He was a promising boxer and baseball player, but went to jail from the age of sixteen to nineteen for car theft. At a baseball game against civilians, he encountered singer Bobby Byrd, with whom he united on being paroled. Brown hijacked Byrd's group to create the Famous Flames—who mixed gospel, jazz, and jive to

"If you're going to be big and popular, you're going to have to take the fall…"

electrifying effect. Little Richard was among their fans after seeing their supporting slot for one of his own gigs. "We opened up for him," remembered Brown. "He couldn't believe it. And he went back and told his manager, so in a way he discovered us."

"Please, Please, Please" (1956) became the first of fifty Top 10 R&B hits in the United States. "Night Train" upped the tempo, reflecting the performances that made Brown and his band a sensation. "When I saw him move, I was mesmerized," said Michael Jackson. "I knew that's what I wanted to do for the rest of my life, because of James Brown."

Fittingly, the work that brought the Famous Flames mainstream recognition was *Live At The Apollo* (1962). King Records boss Syd Nathan—who judged "Please, Please, Please" a "piece of shit"—was unconvinced by the prospect of a live album, obliging Brown to finance it himself. The result reached No. 2 in *Billboard* and remained on the chart for a year. "He didn't cross over," noted the Reverend Jesse Jackson, "Whites crossed over to him."

Ensuing hits found Brown and his band stretching R&B's limits to create funk. Beginning with 1965's playful "Papa's Got A Brand New Bag," they stripped it to the bone for 1967's "Cold Sweat." From the dance floor drama of R&B to the mechanical beats of electronica, its impact still reverberates today.

Brown utilized his success to become a powerful advocate of black equality. "For him to sing 'I'm Black And I'm Proud' at that time," said Jesse Jackson, "was an act of defiance that became part of our culture."

The revolution continued into the 1970s with—thanks to teenage prodigy Bootsy Collins—added bass. "Mr. Brown is the godfather of pure rhythm, who lived in a land of pure groove," said Bootsy,

RIGHT James Brown 1964 onstage at New York's Apollo Theater (Famous Flames on left: Johnny Terry, Bobby Byrd, and Bobby Bennett).

later a similarly pivotal influence with George Clinton. "I'm nobody but his son along with countless other musicians." Those musicians included Aerosmith, who covered 1969's "Mother Popcorn (You Got To Have A Mother For Me)," and *everyone* who heard 1970's "Get Up (I Feel Like Being A) Sex Machine."

Alongside Sly Stone and Curtis Mayfield, Brown used funk to express the energy and rage of Black America in the 1970s. Hits like "Get Up, Get Into It, Get Involved," "Soul Power," "King Heroin," "Talking Loud And Saying Nothing," and "Funky President (People It's Bad)," and albums like 1973's *Black Caesar* and 1974's *The Payback*, paved the way for hip hop. "He was not only the godfather of soul," said Ice Cube, "but the godfather of funk and rap."

ABOVE James Brown lying in repose during a public viewing at the Apollo Theater on December 28, 2006, in New York City.

LEFT James Brown onstage in London's Hyde Park on June 19, 2004, supporting the Red Hot Chili Peppers. A crowd of over 85,000 fans enjoyed the show.

In the mid-1970s, though, his position wavered. Overwhelmed by disco, dabbling with the drugs he had always warned against, and pursued by tax authorities, Brown had his last Top Ten hit for almost a decade with 1976's "Get Up Offa That Thing."

He remained a formidable live attraction, notorious for fining his band for anything from missed cues to badly shined shoes. In 1985, he returned to the Top 10 with "Living In America" and capitalized on the burgeoning hip hop scene with 1986's much-sampled "*In The Jungle Groove*."

Unfortunately, he became equally well known for drug-fueled skirmishes with the police and domestic strife, leading to further time behind bars. "If you're going to be big and popular," he conceded, "You're going to have to take the fall if there is a fall to be taken." These activities, coupled with unceasing touring, took their toll. "He hates doctors," said his manager after Brown confirmed he had diabetes. In 2002, he starred in the short film *Beat The Devil*, which saw Brown negotiating with the Devil (Gary Oldman) to beat the aging process.

Nonetheless, Brown refused to retire. "What would I do?" he asked after treatment for cancer. "I made my name as a person that is helping. I'm like the Moses in the music business." However, hospitalized for pneumonia in 2006, he succumbed to congestive heart failure on December 25. "James Brown's family and friends," said President Bush, "are in our thoughts and prayers this Christmas." Brown was seventy-three.

Driven from his Georgia home by activist Al Sharpton, Brown's body was brought to the Apollo Theater in Harlem—scene of his 1962 triumph—in a horse-drawn carriage. Thousands paid their respects, as they did at another service in Augusta. At the James Brown Arena, Michael Jackson paid tribute: "Words cannot adequately express the love and respect that I will always have for Mr. Brown. There has not been, and will never be, another like him." But family disputes kept him above ground in a gold casket for several months until he was finally laid to rest in South Carolina.

"I want to be remembered," he told *Rolling Stone* in 1998, "as a man that...loved people so hard, sometimes it looked like in the early days it was madness. It was just concern...If they're human beings, people will make mistakes. I've been there."

"He was a work of art," said Aretha Franklin. "He was as valuable and as rare as any Rembrandt or Picasso."

ROCK & ROLL

Heaven

LET'S END IT ALL...

...with a look at the lighter side of death. The acrid stench of the grave may seem to have no place in the pop charts, but we've found fifty odes to mortality—including a clutch of pop classics—that suggest otherwise. Next, we applaud those lucky rock 'n' rollers who have cheekily cheated the Grim Reaper just when his sickle was about to come down, or whose deaths were announced somewhat (ahem) prematurely. Finally, by way of a public health warning, we provide aspiring rockers with the lowdown on the most life-threatening positions in a band. Choose wisely, and you may make it to a second album.

ROCK & ROLL

Heaven

TOP 50 DEATH SONGS

1 **"St. James Infirmary Blues"** Louis Armstrong (1928)
Top version of much-covered lament. Man drops by morgue to see late girlfriend.

2 **"Gloomy Sunday"** Billie Holiday (1941)
Haunting song rumored to have inspired countless suicides. Ask Billy MacKenzie, who covered it in 1982. Oh, hang on…

3 **"Long Black Veil"** Lefty Frizzell (1956)
Deceased lover sings of illicit affair with best friend's wife. Moral: adultery is bad.

4 **"Stagger Lee"** Lloyd Price (1959)
American legend shoots innocent Billy in card game. Nick Cave's 1996 rereading ups body count considerably.

5 **"Tell Laura I Love Her"** Ray Peterson (1960)
Will he win the stock-car race and buy his baby a ring? Or will he crash and die? What do you think?

6 **"Johnny Remember Me"** John Leyton (1961)
He hears his lost lady love in the wind and the treetops. Produced by gifted-but-gaga Joe Meek.

7 **"Dead Man's Curve"** Jan and Dean (1964)
Daredevil teen racer exits road at notorious blind spot.

8 **"Terry"** Twinkle (1964)
Unfaithful girl only has herself to blame for boyfriend's motorbike crash. The UK's "Leader Of The Pack." Speaking of which…

9 "Leader Of The Pack" The Shangri-Las (1965)

Sweet girl tells biker boy it is over. He vrooms off. Tires screech. "Look out! Look out! Look out!" Melodrama *par excellence*.

10 "I Want My Baby Back" Jimmy Cross (1965)

Teen's girlfriend dies in car crash. They're reunited—when he digs her up…

11 "Hey Joe" Jimi Hendrix (1966)

Oft-covered murder ballad, though Hendrix's breakthrough hit is definitive. Man shoots unfaithful woman then hotfoots it to Mexico to avoid noose.

12 "Ode To Billy Joe" Bobbie Gentry (1967)

Her boy leaps to death from bridge. Quite why, no one knows. (Inspired a movie.)

13 "The End" The Doors (1967)

Song about killing dad and boffing mom graces *Apocalypse Now*. Die is cast.

14 "Honey" Bobby Goldsboro (1968)

Girl crashes car—but survives! Then, inconveniently, is abducted by angels.

15 "Midnight Rambler" The Rolling Stones (1969)

Boston Strangler: naughty boy.

16 "The Seventh Seal" Scott Walker (1969)

Knight is checkmated by Death. Inspired by 1957 film of same name.

17 "Suicide Is Painless/Theme From M*A*S*H" Johnny Mandel (1970)

Eerily matter-of-fact view of self-immolation.

18 "Lady D'Arbanville" Cat Stevens (1970)

Is she sleeping? Not exactly. Melancholy ode to grave-bound sweetheart.

19 "Ben" Michael Jackson (1972)

Tender tribute to pet rat. (See also Elvis Presley's "Old Shep.")

20 "I Love The Dead" Alice Cooper (1973)

Tender lament to blue-fleshed cadaver. (See also Cannibal Corpse.)

21 "The Great Gig In The Sky" Pink Floyd (1973)

Vocalist Clare Torry was paid £30 (U.S. $60) for warbling on what was originally titled "The Mortality Sequence."

22 "Psycho" Jack Kittel (1974)

Crazy killer lays waste to ex-wife, her paramour, puppy, and small girl. Songwriter Leon Payne committed suicide after composing song.

23 **"Rock 'N' Roll Heaven" The Righteous Brothers (1974)**
"If there's a rock and roll heaven, well you know they've got a hell of a band." Tribute to too-fast-to-live stars including Jimi, Janis, and Jim.

24 **"Seasons In The Sun" Terry Jacks (1974)**
Deathbed farewell to sundry loved ones, updating Jacques Brel's "Le Moribund" ("The Dying Man").

25 **"Emma" Hot Chocolate (1974)**
Atypical suicide song from 1970s popsters. Failed wannabe actress declares "I just can't keep on living on dreams no more" before exiting stage.

26 **"Detroit Rock City" Kiss (1976)**
Fan killed en route to show inspires band's best-loved song, complete with car-crash effects and a flamenco guitar solo.

27 **"(Don't Fear) The Reaper" Blue Öyster Cult (1976)**
Hairy rockers with tongues in bearded cheeks get Byrdsy on evergreen ode to the Great Beyond.

28 **"Hello, This Is Joanie (The Telephone Answering Machine Song)" Paul Evans (1978)**
Car crash claims narrator's girlfriend. How can he hear her again? Simple: call her answerphone…

29 **"Suicide Solution" Ozzy Osbourne (1980)**
Alcoholic ambiguity, inspired by AC/DC's Bon Scott and Ozzy himself. Cited in unsuccessful lawsuits by parents of troubled teens in United States.

30 **"One Hundred Years" The Cure (1982)**
Robert Smith's manifesto in nutshell: "It doesn't matter if we all die."

31 **"Hallowed Be Thy Name" Iron Maiden (1982)**
Postcard from Death Row.

32 **"Angel Of Death" Slayer (1986)**
Controversy-baiting anthem about Nazi lunatic Josef Mengele, memorably featured in *Gremlins 2* (the song, not Mengele).

33 **"Sometimes It Snows In April" Prince (1986)**
Misguided movie (*Under The Cherry Moon*) yields super soundtrack (*Parade*) and fine finale (this).

34 **"One Tree Hill" U2 (1987)**
For Bono's assistant, Greg Carroll, killed in motorbike accident. Named after volcanic island in Carroll's native New Zealand.

35 **"The Mercy Seat" Nick Cave And The Bad Seeds (1988)**
Last words from electric chair; not dead yet, but getting there.

36 **"Dead Homiez" Ice Cube (1990)**
Cube gets finger-waggingly stern. Four years later he records "Natural Born Killaz."

37 **"Then She Did" Jane's Addiction (1990)**

Dave Navarro and Perry Farrell's deceased mothers earn moving requiem.

38 **"Cop Killer" Body Count (1992)**

"If you believe that I'm a cop killer," grumbled Ice-T, "you believe that David Bowie is an astronaut."

39 **"Try Not To Breathe" R.E.M. (1992)**

Most of *Automatic For The People* is about death. Except the one about the snake.

40 **"Murder Was The Case" Snoop Dogg (1993)**

Trigger-happy rapper sells soul to Satan to allay doggy demise.

41 **"Disarm" Smashing Pumpkins (1993)**

"I never really had the guts to kill my parents," said Billy Corgan, "so I wrote a song about it instead."

42 **"I'll Be Missing You" Puff Daddy (1997)**

Police-sampling tribute to Notorious BIG from mogul pal.

43 **"Exit Music (For A Film)" Radiohead (1997)**

Written for Baz Luhrmann's *Romeo + Juliet*. Contributed "We hope that you choke" to *OK Computer*'s litany of cheer.

44 **"Mer Girl" Madonna (1998)**

Madge's spookiest ode to deceased mother.

45 **"Climbing To The Moon" Eels (1998)**

Heartbreaking highlight of *Electro-Shock Blues*, officially Best Death Album In The World… Ever.

46 **"Stan" Eminem (2000)**

Obsessed fan meets maker. Dido sample made her as big as Shady himself.

47 **"The Nobodies" Marilyn Manson (2000)**

Bitterest of Manson's reactions to 1999 Columbine High School massacre, for which he was fatuously blamed.

48 **"Jenny Was A Friend Of Mine" The Killers (2004)**

Jealous boyfriend murders girl; story continues in "Midnight Show" and unreleased "Leave The Bourbon On The Shelf."

49 **"The Cool" Lupe Fiasco (2006)**

Slain gangsta climbs out of grave, only to be robbed by his assassins.

50 **"Welcome To The Black Parade" My Chemical Romance (2006)**

Finest song about cancer patient to top UK chart.

ROCK & ROLL
Heaven

20 REAPER CHEATERS

As Tupac and Elvis prove, death is no obstacle to prosperity. But some have embarked on a tour beyond this mortal coil, only to find St. Peter turning them away from the Pearly Gates, while the deaths of others have been, as Mark Twain put it, exaggerated. We present some of rock 'n' roll's closest shaves—and greatest hoaxes…

1 JAN BERRY

Berry—of surf duo Jan and Dean—nearly performed the ultimate wipeout when his Corvette smashed into a truck in L.A. in 1966, presaged by Jan and Dean's "Dead Man's Curve" (which, at Berry's behest, concludes with a fatal car crash). Although brain damage affected his voice, he lived to perform again with Dean in the early 1970s. The Grim Reaper finally picked him up in 2004.

2 JERRY LEE LEWIS

They call him The Killer, but Jerry Lee Lewis nearly became The Killee in 1981, when his stomach (understandably) ruptured, the result of years of pill popping and booze sinking. Jerry Lee was hospitalized but survived, and remains the only major Sun star left alive (a fact reflected in the title of his latest album, *Last Man Standing*). And let's hear it for his bass player Butch Owens, too: during Lewis' forty-first birthday celebrations in 1976, the singer accidentally shot the bassist. Owens survived, so The Killer wasn't a killer after all…

3   JAMES MORRISON

Even polite singer-songwriter James Morrison gazed into the void. In 1984, the newborn Morrison suffered so severely from whooping cough that doctors suggested his mother turn off the life-support when he stopped breathing. "Technically," he remembered, "I died four times."

6   KURT COBAIN

After his coma-inducing suicide attempt in Rome in March 1994, Nirvana's figurehead was reported dead by CNN. But while that proved prophetic, other rock star deaths have proved—to quote Mark Twain—an exaggeration…

4   COREY TAYLOR

Slipknot's frontman, unsurprisingly, has a more colorful story. In 1989, a fifteen-year-old in an Iowa trailer park, Corey Taylor was, self-confessedly, "a total speed freak and really into coke. I remember waking up one morning in a dumpster. This is all conjecture on my part, because I lost a couple of days, but I think I OD'd at a party. And, instead of taking me to a hospital, [my friends] dumped me in a trash can, thinking I was dead."

7   ALICE COOPER

When an early 1970s edition of *Melody Maker* published a review in the form of an obituary, Alice Cooper was obliged to reassure fans, "I'm alive, and drunk as usual."

5   DAVE GAHAN

Depeche Mode's Dave Gahan graduated to heroin in time for a legendarily unhealthy 1993 tour. Shrouded in narcotic gloom, he slashed his wrist in 1995. In May 1996 in California's Sunset Marquis hotel, he packed a syringe with "the big speedball to heaven," shot up, and stopped his heart for two minutes. Rescued by paramedics, he was promptly arrested for cocaine possession and being under the influence of heroin.

8   TERRY JACKS

Prior to the release of single "Seasons In The Sun" (see "Top 50 Death Songs," page 244) in the United States, the publicity department at Terry Jacks' record label thoughtfully spread the rumor that the singer was dying from cancer. That cheery theme didn't stop the song from becoming a transatlantic No. 1, though. Ironically, the song's composer—Jacques Brel—did succumb to the disease four years later, in 1978.

9 IAN DURY

While DJ-ing at London's XFM station in 1998, Bob Geldof announced that a caller had just informed him of the death of Ian Dury. Geldof played "Reasons To Be Cheerful." (Nice programming, your Bobness!) Trouble was, he was two years too early. Possibly, one of the station's listeners, irate over XFM's takeover by the Capital Radio group—resulting in a more mainstream playlist—decided to spin him a fat one. The gaffe led *NME* to dub Geldof "the world's worst DJ," though Dury himself was reportedly tickled by the hoax.

10 DAVE SWARBRICK

In 1999, Fairport Convention folkie Dave Swarbrick was hospitalized with a chest infection, only to find his obituary in the *Daily Telegraph*. "It's not the first time I have died in Coventry," he quipped.

11 EMINEM

Did Eminem die in a car crash en route to a party in December 2000, blitzed off his face on a heady cocktail of drugs and booze? Most assuredly not, but that didn't stop bogus CNN and MTV sites flashing up reports to that effect. Neither did it prevent a crop of e-mails to AOL users entitled "Rapper Eminem Dies In Car Accident." That said, the notorious rapper did attempt suicide in 1997, via an overdose of painkillers, distraught after his partner Kim left him and banned him from seeing his daughter, Hailie.

12 BRITNEY SPEARS AND JUSTIN TIMBERLAKE

In 2001, two Dallas DJs thought they might "create a little commotion" by announcing Britney Spears and then-squeeze Justin Timberlake had died in a car crash. With JT and La Spears still in the land of the living, said DJs promptly found themselves in the land of the unemployed. Later that year, a hacker smuggled another report of Britney's death onto CNN's Web site.

13 LOU REED

Indeed, 2001 proved fruitful for fake fatalities. In May, an ersatz Reuter's e-mail, swallowed by U.S. radio, announced Lou Reed had overdosed on painkillers—despite persuasive evidence to the contrary (i.e., Reed being alive).

14 SHARON OSBOURNE

Meanwhile, in 2004, a technical error led to the ABC News Web site publishing an obituary for Sharon Osbourne.

15 DAVE GROHL

In May 2006, friends of Foo Fighters frontman Dave Grohl phoned up his wife to offer condolences over his unexpected demise. Said commiserations were, needless to say, premature. Just imagine Grohl's delight, when, the following year, he discovered that someone had added a death date—February 5, 2007—to his entry on www. wikipedia.org. It was all quite a surprise to the hale 'n' hearty "nicest man in rock," who later mused, philosophically, "I guess I've finally graduated to that status of being an Internet rumor."

16 MICHAEL JACKSON

Naturally, the biggest stars attract the biggest whoppers. When *The Onion* announced, tongue in cheek, "Coroners have officially pronounced Michael Jackson dead. From what we can tell, he died between eighteen and twenty years ago," in 2005, they were being satirical, and everyone knew it. In 2004, a London-based Web site announced Jackson had had a heart attack after overdosing on "more than two dozen sleeping pills." Not much there for satire fans.

17 PAUL McCARTNEY

Most famously, Paul McCartney was rumored to have perished in a 1966 car crash, and been replaced by a lookalike, Billy Shears. The funeral pyre was fueled in 1969, when a caller to a Detroit DJ also claimed Macca had died. *Abbey Road*'s cover provided a grab bag of death-related "giveaways." Furthermore, on the back of *Sgt. Pepper...* , McCartney is the only Beatle with his back to the camera.

18 PARIS HILTON

Heiress-socialite-accidental porn star-singer Paris Hilton swapped designer duds for a prison jumpsuit when she was incarcerated in 2007 for violating her probation. Tough, but not as tough as being knifed. In June 2007, a spoof CNN site announced: "Paris Hilton, who not more than four hours earlier was physically removed from a courtroom, has been stabbed multiple times." Contemporaneously, Hilton's suicide was falsely reported on a site mimicking Australia's ABC network site.

19 MARC ALMOND

Ex-Soft Cell singer Marc Almond nearly waved goodbye permanently in October 2004, after a motorbike crash in London. "My head was the size of a football," he recalled in January 2005. "I cracked all my ribs, collapsed a lung; there was a perforated ear drum and a broken shoulder. My arm is a dead weight—and the thing is that I am an arm performer. This is my drama arm!" Remarkably, and despite severe brain injuries that left him with a stutter, the one-time camp king of sleazy listening recovered to release a new album in 2007.

20 BOB DYLAN

In May 1997, the mighty Robert Zimmerman was hospitalized with a "potentially fatal" pericarditis. "I really thought I'd be seeing Elvis soon," joked rock's premier poet afterwards. He'd nearly come a cropper thirty years before, reportedly breaking his neck when he crashed his Triumph 500 motorcycle near his Woodstock home in July 1966. In fact, having rewritten the rock 'n' roll rule book with a run of stunning mid-60s albums, and nearly burned out during one of rock's greatest tours, Dylan's crash had an upside: it made him slow down.

ROCK & ROLL *Heaven*

DANGEROUS OCCUPATIONS

Does what you do in a band affect your chances
of succumbing to an early demise? Here are rock's
most perilous positions, in ascending order of risk.
Being a bassist is surprisingly safe—a large number
of the sub-group seem to have spent most of their
waking hours doing unimaginable quantities of drugs
(Nikki Sixx, Lemmy), yet still live to tell the tale.
There are, however, more cautionary stories. Take
out extra life insurance if you decide you want to be
one of the following:

1 DRUMMER

While a roll-call of the drummers we have omitted should suffice (including Karen Carpenter, Feeder's Jon Lee, Lush's Chris Acland, The Byrds' Michael Clarke, and metal journeyman Cozy Powell), drumming tops our chart thanks to just one man. Jeff Porcaro, cofounder of Toto and a sessioneer whose credits include Pink Floyd's *The Wall*, sprayed his yard with pesticide in 1992, only for an allergic reaction to trigger a fatal heart attack. The legacy of Spinal Tap—whose drummer John "Stumpy" Pepys died in a "bizarre gardening accident"—lives on.

2 SINGER (MALE)

Whether you are Darby Crash (fronted punk pioneers The Germs, died the day before John Lennon in 1980) or Falco (rocked Amadeus, but collided with a bus in 1998), you will buy the farm if you grab the mike. Bulking up is no defense, as Luther Vandross (stroke, 2005) and Barry White (kidney failure, 2003) demonstrate. The exception that proves the rule: Aerosmith's Steven Tyler. Oft found turning blue and vomiting blood in his narcotic heyday, Tyler's survival is even more remarkable because he began as a drummer.

3 GUITARIST

The fame! The fortune! The *Guitar World* obituary! Dimebag Darrell (see page 232), Stevie Ray Vaughan (see page 120), and Randy Rhoads (see page 91) illustrate that guitarists may not just die early, but die spectacularly. Even if you leave your car by a bridge and vanish, like Richey Edwards of Manic Street Preachers in 1995, history will judge you more dead than gone. Unless you have the unstoppable constitution of Keith Richards ("I was number one on the 'Who's Likely To Die' list for ten years").

4 KEYBOARD PLAYER FOR THE GRATEFUL DEAD

Ronald "Pigpen" McKernan cofounded the trippy behemoth. His drinking was more accomplished than his playing, and he died in 1973. Keith Godchaux expired in an automobile accident in 1980. Brent Mydland overdosed in 1990. Vince Welnick may or may not have cut his own throat, but was certainly dead by 2006. All five died in California. Bruce Hornsby, who filled in for a tour or two, is still alive and kicking, but was sampled on a Tupac record (so the omens are stacking up).

5 SINGER (FEMALE)

Janis Joplin (see page 32), Selena (see page 146), and Aaliyah (see page 194) are some of the songstresses that didn't even make it to thirty years old. Other premature deaths that didn't make it into the book include Eva Cassidy (killed by cancer at thirty-three years old in 1996), Ofra Haza (succumbed to mysteriously undisclosed illnesses in 2000 at forty-two years old), and Tammy Wynette (exhumed to settle a dispute about whether painkillers contributed to her 1998 demise—apparently, they didn't).

INDEX

Page numbers in bold refer to main illustrated references

Aaliyah **194–5**
AC/DC 52, 74
Ace, Johnny **12**
Adamson, Stuart **198**
Adler, Lou 156, 188
Aerosmith 62, 206, 241
Aguilera, Christina 23
Alice In Chains 118, 200, 201, 232
Allen, Rick 121
Allin, GG **131**
Allman, Duane 62
Allsup, Tommy 15
Ament, Jeff 118
Animals 151
Anka, Paul 15
Anselmo, Phil 232
Associates 157
Atkin, James 199
Austin, Mary 126, 128

B-52's 102
Back Street Crawler 52
Bad Company 52
Ballard, Florence **50–1**
The Band 106
Band Of Joy 78
Barrett, Syd 46, 86, **234–5**
Bators, Stiv **119**
Beach Boys 92, 94, 172, 173
Beale Streeters 12
Beatles 13, 19, 23, 56, 80, 114, 136, 196, 222
Beck, Jeff 54, 55, 151, 204
Beefheart, Captain 132, 143
Beers, Garry Gary 168
Bennett, Bobby 239
Bennett, Tony 10
Berry, Chuck 13, 114, 151
Berry, Jan 248
Bhundu Boys 229
Big Bopper 14, 15
Big Brother And The Holding Company 32
Big Country 198
Big Pun **182–3**
Black, Bill **20–1**, 56
Black Crowes 23
Blackmore, Ritchie 55, 158
Blackwell, Chris 88
Blake, William 34
Blind Melon 150
Blitz, Johnny 119
Blockheads 184, 185
Bolan, Marc **60–1**, 85, 210
Bolin, Tommy **55**
Bonham, John **78–9**, 121, 151
Bono 104, 164, 168, 171, 187
Bono, Sonny 186
Bonzo Dog Doo-Dah Band 143

Boone, Pat 49, 114
Bowie, David 38, 60, **84–7**, 120, 128, 140, 234
Boy George 128
Brilleaux, Lee **142**
Brown, James **238–41**
Brownson, Derry 199
Bryant, Elbridge **26–7**
Buckley, Jeff 49, 139, **164–5**, 213
Buckley, Tim **48–9**, 132, 164
Bunch, Carl 15
Burns, Bob 62
Burroughs, William 72, 102
Burton, Cliff **108–9**
Burton, James 58
Buzzcocks 122
Byrd, Bobby 238, 239
Byrds 24, 42, 124, 196, 237
Byrne, David 102, 146

Caballe, Montserrat 126
California, Randy **158**
Canned Heat 192
Carr, Eric **130**, 175
Carrie 199
Cartagena, Joseph 183
Carter, June 218, 220
Cash, Johnny 49, 114, 209, 216, **218–20**
Castillo, Randy 100, 101
Cave, Nick 171
Chambers, Martin 92
Chandler, Chas 28, 30
Chapman, Mark David 82
Charles, Ray 106, **224–7**
Chiba, Jennifer 222
Chicago (group) 64
Chicago Transit Authority 64
Clapton, Eric 8, 28, 52, 54, 67, 88, 120
Clark, Gene **124**
Clark, Michael 124
Clark, Steve **121**
Clash 40, 209
Cobain, Kurt 46, 86, **138–41**, 200, 249
Cobham, Billy 55
Cochran, Eddie 15, **16–17**, 36, 60, 114, 224
Cochran, Hank 16
Cochran Brothers 16
Cocker, Jarvis 13, 229
Collen, Phil 121
Colley, Dana 179
Collins, Allen 62, 62
Collins, Bootsy 238
Connolly, Brian **158–9**
Connor, Cecil "Coon dog" 42
Cook, Paul 104
Cooke, Dale 19
Cooke, Sam **18–19**, 97

Cooper, Alice 38, 132, 249
Costello, Elvis 13
Coxon, Graham 46
Cray, Robert 120
Crazy Horse 37, 37, 186
Cream 8, 28, 86, 125
Crickets 13, 15
Cromwell, Martha 68
Cropper, Steve 23
Crosby, Bing 85
Crosby, David 124
Crosby, Robbin 100, 101
Crumb, Robert 32
Curtis, Deborah 77
Curtis, Ian **76–7**, 216

Daltrey, Roger 67, 204
Damageplan 232
Danko, Rick 106, **178**
Davis, Bill "Sheriff Tex" 36
de Freitas, Pete **117**
Deacon, John 126
Dead Boys 119
Dean, James 60
Death Row 144, 154, 160, 203
death songs 244–7
Decloedt, Mark 199
Dee, Dave 16
Deep Purple 55
Def Leppard 121
Dempsey, Michael 157
Dench, Ian 199
Densmore, John 34
Denver, John **166–7**
Diana, Princess 86
Dicken, Bernard 77
Diddley, Bo 151
Diggs, Robert "RZA" 231
Dillard, Doug 124
Dingley, Nicholas "Razzle" 100
Dion and the Belmonts 15
Dodd, Dicky 72
Doherty, Denny 188
Dolenz, Mickey 136
Donovan, Terence 221
Doors 34, 125, 237
Double Trouble 120
Dr Feelgood 142
Drake, Nick **46–7**
Dre, Dr 144, 162, 206
Dury, Ian **184–5**, 250
Dylan, Bob 19, 53, 88, 106, 114, 116, 124, 178, 184, 196, 218, 251

E 13
Eazy-E **144–5**
Echo And The Bunnymen 117
Elliot, "Mama" Cass 32, **44–5**, 67, 237
Elliot, Missy 195

Elliot, Owen 45
Elliott, Joe 121, 158
EMF (Epsom Mad Funkers) 199
Eminem 250
Eno, Brian 38
Entwistle, John **204–5**
Epstein, Brian 82
Erasmus, Alan 122
Ethridge, Chris 42
Evans, Faith 154, 160, 162
Evans, Mal 82
Everly Brothers, The 114, 151

Fairweather, Bruce 118
The Fall 229
Famous Flames 238, 239
Farndon, Pete 92
Farriss brothers 168
Fat Joe 183
Fenton, Paul 210
Ferguson, Jay 156
Field, Tim 176
50 Cent 206
Finn, Mickey **210–11**
Five Wings 12
Flack, Roberta 68
Flowers of Romance 70
Flying Burrito Brothers 42
Foley, Zac **199**
Frampton, Peter 123
Frankenstein 119
Franklin, Aretha 23, 50, 163, 213, 238, 241
Franklin, Bertha 19
Franklin, Melvin 27, 228
Fraser, Andy 52
Fraser, Elizabeth 49, 213
Free 52, 52
Frehley, Ace 175
Frusciante, John 112
Fry, Stephen 143
Full Tilt Boogie Band 32
Fuller, Craig 72
Fuqua, Harvey 97, 98

Gabriel, Peter 23, 213
Gahan, Dave 249
Gaines, Cassie **62–3**
Gaines, Steve **62–3**
Garcia, Jerry **148–9**
Gaye, Marvin **96–9**
Geffen, David 163
Geldof, Bob 126, 168, 171, 184
Genshon, Russ 179
George, Lowell **72–3**, 221
Gilmore, Greg 118
Gilmour, David 86, 234
Ginsberg, Allen 125
Gods And Monsters 164
Gordy, Berry 50, 97, 98
Gossard, Stone 118
Graham, Bill **125**

Grant, Peter **151**
Grateful Dead 88, 125, 148, 149
Gray, John 63
Gretton, Rob 122
Grice, Gary "GZA" 231
Grohl, Dave 78, 102, 251
Grossman, Albert 32
Guercio, James 64
Guy, Buddy 120

Hammett, Kirk 108, 109
Hannett, Martin 77, **122**
Hanoi Rocks 40
Happy Mondays 122
Hardy, Françoise 46
Harman, David 16
Harris, Emmylou 42
Harrison, George 85, 88, 116, **196–7**
Harvey, Bill 12
Harvey, PJ 179
Hathaway, Donny **68–9**
Hawkins, Ronnie 106, 178
Hawks 106, 178
Heartbreakers 39
Helm, Levon 106, 178
Helms, Chet 32
Hendrix, Jimi 8, **28–31**, 32, 52, 55, 64, 125, 140, 156, 204, 237
Hetfield, James 108, 109
Highway QCs 19
Hillman, Chris 42, 124, 124
Hilton, Paris 251
Holly, Buddy **13–15**, 16, 114
Honeyman-Scott, James **92–3**
Hook, Peter 77
Hooker, John Lee 156, **192–3**
Hoon, Shannon **150**
Horrocks, Jane 184
House, Son 8
Houston, Whitney 203, 251
Hudson, Garth 106
Humble Pie 123
Hurt, Mississippi John 156
Hutchence, Michael **168–71**
Hynde, Chrissie 92, 93

Innes, Neil 143
International Submarine Band 42
INXS 168–71

Jabbers 131
Jacks, Terry 249
Jackson, Curtis 206
Jackson, Reverend Jesse 68, 154, 238
Jackson, Michael 27, 139, 241, 251

Jagger, Mick 24, 110, 120, 188
Jam Master Jay **206–7**
James, Rick **228**
James Gang 55
Jankel, Chaz 184
Jennings, Waylon 15
Jimmy James and the Blue Flames 28, 156
Johansen, David **38–41**
John's Children 60
Johnson, Brian 74
Johnson, Robert **8–9**, 10
Johnson, Wilko **142**
Jones, Brian 8, **24–5**, 28, 237
Jones, John Paul 78
Jones, Kenney 123
Jones, Mick 209
Jones, Quincey 224, 226
Jones, Steve 104
Jones, Terry 28
Joplin, Janis 8, **32–3**, 125, 140, 237
Journeymen 188
Joy Division 77, 122
Jungstrom, Larry 62

Kane, Arthur "Killer" **38–41**
Karven-Veres, Daniel 100, 101
Kath, Terry **64–5**
Kendricks, Eddie **26–7**
Kent, Nick 46
Kiedis, Anthony 112
Kilburn And The High Roads 184
Kilpatrick, Dean **62–3**
King, B.B. 12
King, Ed 63
Kirke, Simon 52
Kiss 40, 130, 175, 200, 232
Kleinow, "Sneaky" Pete 42
Knight, Curtis 28
Knight, Gladys 97, 195
Knight, Suge 144, 154, 160, 203
Koda, Michael 100, 101
Kossoff, Paul **52**
Kozmic Blues Band 32
Kreuzman, Bill 148
Krieger, Robby 34
Kristofferson, Kris 32, 218
Krokus 109

Laine, Frankie 10
Lane, Ronnie 123
Led Zeppelin 8, 78, 125, 151
Lee, Arthur **236–7**
Lee, Tommy 100
Legend, Bill 210
Lemmy 28

Lennon, John 12, 13, 16, 67, **80–3**, 85, 114, 132, 136, 196, 213
Lesh, Phil 148
Levy, Doug 131
Lewis, Jerry Lee 10, 103, 248
Lillywhite, Steve 187
Little Feat 72, 73
Little Richard 28, 114, 238
Livingston, Bunny 88, 110
Lobban, Dennis "Leppo" 110
Lopes, Lisa "Left Eye" **202–3**
Lopez, Jennifer 146, 183
Love (band) 237
Love, Courtney 139, 140
Love, Darlene 186
Love, Mike 172, 173
Lucas, Gary 164
Lydon, John 70
Lynne, Jeff 116
Lynott, Phil **104–5**
Lynyrd Skynyrd **62–3**

McCartney, Paul 13, 16, 28, 67, 80, 136, 173, 196, 251
MacColl, Kirsty 184, **187**
McCulloch, Ian 117
McDaniels, Daryl "DMC" 206, 207
MacGowan, Shane 187, 209
McGuinn, Roger 124, 196
Mackenzie, Billy **157**
McLaren, Malcolm 39, 70
McLean, Don 15, 116
Malfunkshun 118
The Mamas And The Papas 56, 188
Mandrake Paddle Steamer 221
Manson, Charles 94, 173
Manuel, Richard **106–7**
Manzarek, Ray 34
Marks, David 172
Marley, Bob **88–90**, 110, 180
Marquees 97
Marriott, Steve **123**
Mars, Mick 100
Marvin, Hank B. 13
Mason, Dave 45
Mastrangelo, Carlo 15
May, Brian 126, 128, 158, 209
Mayfield, Curtis **180–1**, 241
Mercury, Freddie 86, **126–9**, 158
Metallica 108, 109

Milli Vanilli 174
Mitchell, Mitch 28
Mizrahi, Sil "Sylvain, Sylvain" 38, 39
Molina, Ralph 37
Monkees 30, 136, 188
Moon, Keith **66–7**, 143, 204
Moore, Gary 104
Moore, Scotty 20, 56
Moore, Will 192
Morris, Stephen 77
Morrison, James 249
Morrison, Jim 8, **34–5**, 36, 140
Morrison, Van 125, 164
Morrissey 39, 187
Morton, George "Shadow" 39
Morvan, Fabrice 174
Mother Love Bone 118
Mothers Of Invention 72, 125, 132, 133, 237
Mötley Crüe **100–1**, 158
Motörhead 175
Motown 26, 50
Murcia, Billy **38–41**
Murray, Frank 104
My Backyard 62
Mynah Birds 228

Napalm Death 229
Napier-Bell, Simon 60
Nash, Johnny 88
Navarro, Dave 112
Neil, Skylar 100, 101
Neil, Vince 100
Nelson, Ricky **103**
Nesmith, Mike 30
New Order 77, 122
New Yardbirds 78, 151
New York Dolls **38–41**
Nico **113**
Niggaz with Attitude 144
Nilsson, Harry 67, **136–7**
Nirvana 86, 139–40, 140
Nitzsche, Jack 37, **186**
Noble Five 62
Nolan, Jerry **38–41**
Notorious BIG, The 153, 154, **160–2**, 183
Nyro, Laura **163**

O'Brien, Dion 176
occupations, dangerous 252–3
Ochs, Phil **53**
Ol' Dirty Bastard **230–1**
Oldfield, Mike 143
One Percent 62
Ono, Yoko 80, 81, 82, 136, 199
Orbison, Roy **114–16**, 135, 196
Osbourne, Ozzy 45, 91, 131

Osbourne, Sharon 91, 250
Outcasts 123

Page, Jimmy 54, 72, 78, 151, 204
Palmer, Robert **221**
Pantera 232
Parker, Colonel Tom 20, 56
Parsons, Gram **42–3**
Patton, Charlie 8, 192
Payne, Rufe "Tee-Tot" 10
Pearl Jam 118, 119, 139, 200
Pebbles 203
Peel, John 16, 143, **229**
Pengilly, Kirk 168
Peregrine-Took, Steve 60
Perry, Lee "Scratch" 88
Peter, Paul and Mary 166
Peterson, Roger 15
Petty, Tom 116, 116
Phillips, Dewey 22, 56
Phillips, John **188–9**
Phillips, Mackenzie 188
Phillips, Michelle 45, 188
Phillips, Sam 20, 22, 56, 218
Pierson, Kate 102
Pilatus, Rob **174**
Pink Floyd 72, 229, 234
Pixies 179
Plant, Robert 78, 151, 151, 164
Plasmatics 175
Pogues 187, 209
Poindexter, Buster 39
Pop, Iggy 77, 85, 86, 119, 184, 209
Powell, Billy 63
Power Station 221
Presley, Elvis 10, 13, 16, 20, 22, 23, 36, 55, **56–9**, 114, 151, 218, 224
Pretenders 92, 93
Pretty Things 24
Priest, Steve 158
Primes 50
Primettes 50
Prince 139, 180
Puff Daddy 153, 160, 183, 195

Quarrymen 16
Queen 126, 128

Ramones 186, **190–1**, 229
Rankine, Alan 157
RCA 19, 22, 36, 56, 166
Red Hot Chili Peppers 112, 220
Redding, Noel 28, 30
Redding, Otis **23**, 237
Relf, Keith **54**
Reprise 43

Rhoads, Randy **91**
Ric Powell Trio 68
Richards, Keith 24, 38, 42, 74, 110, 139, 140, 188
Roberston, Robbie 106
Robinson, Smokey 19, 26, 97
Rocket From The Tombs 119
Rockets 37
Rodgers, Paul 52, 128
Rolling Stones 13, 23, 24, 52, 54, 72, 88, 125, 187, 196
Ronson, Mick 85–6
Ross, Diana 51, 97
Rossington, Gary 62
Rothschild, Paul 32
Rotten, Johnny 70
Rovers 12
Rubin, Rick 220
Ruffin, David **26–7**
Russian roulette 12

Saldivar, Yolanda 146
Salvage, Rick 121
Sandman, Mark **179**
Santana 125
Sardo, Frankie 15
Schneider, Fred 102
Scott, Andy 158
Scott, Bon **74–5**
Selena **146–7**
Sex Pistols 39, 40, 70, 79, 85
Shakur, Tupac **152–5**, 160, 162, 216
Shangri-Las 39
Sharkey, Feargal 229
Sheeley, Sharon 16, 17
Simmons, Gene 130, 175
Simmons, Joseph "Run" 206, 207
Simone, Nina **212–15**
Simonon, Paul 209
Sinatra, Frank 163, 196
Singing Children 19
Siouxsie And The Banshees 70
Sixx, Nikki 100–1, 158
Sixx Pakk 101
Slade 60
Slovak, Hillel 45, **112**
Sly And The Family Stone 88
Small Faces 123
Smile (band) 126
Smith, Connie "Guybo" 16
Smith, Elliott **222–3**
Snider, Dee 166
Sons of Satan 62
Soul Stirrers 19
Spears, Britney 250
Spector, Phil 186, 186

Spirit 156
Springfield, Dusty **176–7**
Springsteen, Bruce 139, 209
Spungen, Nancy 70, 71
Staley, Layne **200–1**
Stanley, Paul 130, 175
Stanshall, Viv **143**
Staple Singers 125
Starr, Ringo 67, 128, 178, 196, 204
Stewart, Rod 38, 123
Stone Roses 122
Stone, Sly 49, 241
Stotts, Richie 175
Streisand, Barbra 45, 163
Strickland, Keith 102
Stroud, Lisa Celeste 214
Strummer, Joe **208–9**
Sugarman , Danny 34
Sumner, Bernard 79
Supremes 51
Sutcliffe, Stuart 82
Swarbrick, Dave 250
Sweet 158
Sweetshop 158

T-Rex 60, 61, 210
Talking Heads 23, 187
Taylor, Corey 249
Taylor, John 221
Taylor, Phil 92
Taylor, Roger 126, 128
Taylor, Vince 84–5
Temptations **26–7**, 50
Terrell, Tammi 97
Terry, John 239
Thin Lizzy 104
13th Floor Elevators 32
This Mortal Coil 49
Thomas, Rozonda "Chili" 203
Thornton, Big Mama 12
Thunders, Johnny **38–41**, 92, 119
Timbaland 195
Timberlake, Justin 68, 250
Tlbot, Billy 37
TLC 203
Took, Steve "Peregrine" 210
Tosh, Peter 88, **110–11**, 180
Townshend, Pete 67, 143, 204, 209
Traveling Wilburys 116, 196
Trippe, Matthew 101
Tucker, Bob 20
Tucker, Mick 158
Turner, Ike and Tina 186
Tyler, Toby 60
Tyrannosaurus Rex 60, 210, 228

U2 77, 122, 128, 168, 187
Ulrich, Lars 108, 109

Vai, Steve 132
Valens, Richie 14–15
Van Zant, Ronnie **62–3**
Vandross, Luther 86
Varese, Edgar 132, 135
Vaughan, Jimmie **120**
Vaughan, Stevie Ray 85, 120
Vedder, Eddie 118
Velvet Underground 38, 113
Vicious, Sid 39, **70–1**, 85
Vincent, Gene 16, **36**, 114, 184

Wailers 88, 90, 110, 180
Walden, Snuffy 52
Watkins, Tionne T-Boz 203
Weir, Bob 148
White, Clarence 42
White Stripes 45
Whitfield, Norman 26
Whitten, Danny **37**
The Who 66, 67, 125, 184, 204
Wildcats 62
Wilkeson, Leon 63
Williams, Hank **10–11**, 49, 114
Williams, Otis **26–7**
Williams, Paul **26–7**
Williams, Wendy O. **175**
Willis, Pete 121w
Wilson, Brian 94, 172, 173
Wilson, Carl 95, **172–3**
Wilson, Cindy 102
Wilson, Dennis **94–5**, 172, 173
Wilson, Mary 50, 51
Wilson, Ricky **102**
Wilson Phillips 188
Wonder, Stevie 50, 180, 228
Wood, Andrew **118**, 200
Wood, Natalie 22
Wood, Ron 123
Wu-Tang Clan 230, 231
Wynette, Tammy 175

Yaffa, Sami 40
Yardbirds 54, 151
Yates, Paula 168, 171
Young, Angus 52, 74, 91
Young, Neil 37, 62, 140, 186, 228

Zappa, Frank 72, 102, 125, **132–5**, 166
Zevon, Warren **216–17**
Zimmerman, Ike &

CREDITS AND ACKNOWLEDGMENTS

Corbis: p39 (Katy Winn), p41 (Bettmann), p118 (t) (Karen Mason Blair), p118 (b) (Karen Mason Blair), p130 (t) (Lynn Goldsmith), p135 (Lynn Goldsmith), p138 (S.I.N.), p148 (Roger Ressmeyer), p150 (t) (Karen Mason Blair), p150 (b) (Henry Diltz), p160 (Mitchell Gerber), p161 (S.I.N.), p162 (Peter Morgan), p164 (DEAN RICHARD), p165 (S.I.N.), p166 (John Atashian), p174 (t) (Lynn Goldsmith), p175 (t) (Lynn Goldsmith), p179 (t) (Tim Mosenfelder), p179 (b) (S.I.N.), p185 (Denis O'Regan), p193 (Derick A. Thomas), p196 (Bettmann), p199 (b) (S.I.N.), p207 (Lynn Goldsmith), p208 (Neal Preston), p221 (b) (Lynn Goldsmith).

Getty Images: p11 (Getty Images/Handout), p12 (Frank Driggs Collection/Contributor), p13 (t) (Hulton Archive/Stringer), p13 (b) (CBS Photo Archive/Contributo), p14 (r) (Hulton Archive/Staff), p15 (Hulton Archive/Staff), p18 (CBS Photo Archive/Contributor), p20 (Michael Ochs Archives/Stringer), p21 (Michael Ochs Archives/Stringer), p23 (Michael Ochs Archives/Stringer), p26 (Hulton Archive/Staff), p27 (Robin Platzer/Contributor), p28 (Lipnitzki/Contributor), p34 (CBS Photo Archive/Contributor), p37 (b) (Michael Ochs Archives/Stringer), p44 (CBS Photo Archive/Contributor), p49 (Jack Robinson/Contributor), p50 (Archive Photos/Stringer), p52 (b) (Debi Doss/Contributor), p53 (b) (David Fenton/Contributor), p57 (Charles Trainor/Contributor), p59 (Hulton Archive/Stringer), p68 (Michael Ochs Archives/Stringer), p71 (Hulton Archive/Stringer), p81 (Central Press/Stringer), p82-83 (New York Times Co./Contributor), p92 (George Rose/Contributor), p93 (George Rose/Contributor), p95 (Robin Platzer/Contributor), p96 (Doug McKenzie/Contributor), p99 (Evening Standard/Stringer), p101 (Michael Ochs Archives/Stringer), p110 (Hulton Archive/Stringer), p114 (Hulton Archive/Stringer), p120 (t) (Tim Mosenfelder/Contributor), p121 (b) (Hulton Archive/Stringer), p126 (Dave Hogan/Staff), p130 (b) (Michael Ochs Archives/Stringer), p132 (Nancy R. Schiff/Contributor), p133 (Tom Copi/Contributor), p134 (Evening Standard/Stringer), p137 (Julian Wasser/Contributor), p139 (Frank Micelotta/Stringer), p141 (Charles J. Peterson/Contributor), p143 (b) (Keystone Features/Stringer), p144 (Al Pereira/Contributor), p145 (diverseimages/Contributor), p147 (Barbara Laing/Contributor), p149 (b) (Evan Agostini/Contributor), p153 (diverseimages/Contributor), p154 (Malcolm Payne/Contributor), p155 (Kimberly Butler/Contributor), p159 (Anwar Hussein/Contributor), p163 (b) (Terrence Spencer/Contributor), p167 (Rick Browne/Contributor), p172 (Michael Ochs Archives/Handout), p173 (Michael Ochs Archives/Stringer), p174 (b) (Time Life Pictures/Stringer), p175 (b) (Hulton Archive/Staff), p176 (Michael Ochs Archives/Stringer), p177 (Michael Ochs Archives/Stringer), p178 (t) (Dion Ogust/Image Works/Contributor), p180 (Michael Ochs Archives/Stringer), p181 (Michael Ochs Archives/Stringer), p184 (Steve Pyke/Contributor), p190 (Michael Ochs Archives/Stringer), p191 (Michael Ochs Archives/Stringer), p192 (Michael Ochs Archives/Stringer), p194 (Tim Mosenfelder/Contributor), p195 (Evan Agostini/Contributor), p198 (b) (Dave Hogan/Staff), p201 (Frank Micelotta/Stringer), p202 (Frank Micelotta/Stringer), p203 (Marion Curtis/Contributor), p212 (Bernard Gotfryd) p213, (Michael Ochs Archives/Stringer), p214 ((Bernard Gotfryd), p215 (Tom Copi/Contributor), p216 (Michael Ochs Archives/Stringer), p217 (Waring Abbott/Contributor), p225 (Bill Ray/Stringer), p227 (Scott Harrison/Contributor), p229 (Kevin Winter/Staff), p230 (diverseimages/Contributor), p231 (diverseimages/Contributor), p232 (Scott Harrison/Contributor), p233 (Scott Gries/Staff), p236 (Michael Ochs Archives/Stringer), p237 (Michael Ochs Archives/Stringer), p238 (RDA/Contributor), p239 (Michael Ochs Archives/Stringer), p240 (Jo Hale/Stringer), p241 (Bryan Bedder/Staff).

Merle Allin: p131 (t) (Merle Allin), p131 (b) (Merle Allin).

Redferns Music Library: p2 (Robert Knight), p7 (Ron Howard), p8 (Deltahaze Corporation), p9 (Deltahaze Corporation), p16 (Gems), p19 (RB), p24 (Ivan Keeman), p25 (John Hopkins), p31 (Robert Knight), p32 (Gems), p33 (Donna Santisi), p36 (t) (Rick Richards), p36 (b) (David Redfern), p37 (t) (Gems), p38 (David Warner Ellis Photography), p40 (Ian Dickson)), p42 (GAB Archives), p43 (Gems), p45 (RB), p46 (Keith Morris), p47 (Keith Morris), p51 (RB), p52 (t) (Gems), p54 (t) (Harry Goodwin), p54 (b) (Chris Morphet), p55 (Fin Costello), p58 (Steve Morley), p61 (David Warner Ellis Photography), p63 (Gems), p65 (David Redfern), p69 (RB), p72 (Fin Costello), p73 (Fin Costello), p74 (Dick Barnatt), p76 (Jon Super), p77 (Chris Mills), p78 (Robert Knight), p79 (Jorgen Angel), p80 (Steve Morley), p84 (Mick Hutson), p85 (Nicky J. Sims), p87 (Mick Hutson), p88 (Graham Wiltshire), p89 (Graham Wiltshire), p90 (Gai Terrell), p91 (t) (Fin Costello), p91 (b) (Fin Costello), p97 (t) (David Redfern), p100 (Ebet Roberts), p102 (t) (Ebet Roberts), p102 (b) (Donna Santisi), p103 (t) (Ebet Roberts), p103 (b) (Ebet Roberts), p104 (Jorgen Angel), p105 (Erica Echenberg), p106 (Mick Gold), p107 (Elliott Landy), p108 (Fin Costello), p109 (Krasner/Trebitz), p111 (Fin Costello), p112 (t) (Ebet Roberts), p112 (b) (Ebet Roberts), p113 (t) (Ebet Roberts), p117 (Ebet Roberts), p120 (b) (Clayton Call), p123 (t) (Lorne Resnick), p123 (b) (David Redfern), p124 (t) (Jorgen Angel), p124 (b) (Cyrus Andrews), p127 (Bob King), p128 (Erica Echenberg), p136 (Gems), p142 (t) (David Redfern), p142 (b) (David Redfern), p143 (t) David Redfern, p146 (GAB Archives), p157 (b) (George Chin), p158 (Harry Goodwin), p163 (t) (Ebet Roberts), p186 (Ray Avery), p187 (t) (Kerstin Rodgers), p188 (GAB Archives), p198 (t) (GAB Archives), p199 (t) (Mick Hutson), p200 (Mick Hutson), p204 (Ebet Roberts), p205 (Chris Morphet), p219 (Jan Olofsson), p220 (Ebet Roberts), p221 (t) (Ebet Roberts), p222 (Trevor O'Shana), p223 (Carey Brandon), p228 (t) (GAB Archives), p228 (b) (GAB Archives), p234 (Harry Goodwin), p235 (Andrew Whittuck).

Rex Features: p10 (Everett Collection), p17 (, p22 (Everett Collection), p35 (Globe Photos Inc), p48 (Globe Photos Inc), p53 (t) (Ray Stevenson), p56 (Sipa Press), p60 (Roger Bamber), p64 (Andre Csillag), p66 (David Thorpe), p75 (Philip Morris), p94 (Lynn McAfee), p97 (b) (Sipa Press), p113 (b) (Sipa Press), p115 (Dezo Hoffmann), p117 (b) (Andre Csillag), p119 (t) (Geoffrey Swaine), p119 (b) (Ray Stevenson), p121 (t) (Andre Csillag), p125 (c.Tavin/Everett), p129 (Ilpo Musto), p140 (Sipa Press). p152 (Sipa Press), p156 (t) (Brian Rasic), p156 (b) (Fotos International), p157 (t) (Stills Press Agency), p168 (Geoffrey Swaine), p169, p170 (Brian Rasic), p171 (Austral International), p178 (b) (Lynn McAfee), p187 (b) (Brian Rasic), p189 (Linda Matlow), p206 (Peter Brooker), p209 (Photoreporters Inc.), p210 (Harry Goodwin), p211 (Dezo Hoffmann),,p218 (c.20thC.Fox/Everett), p224 (Mephisto), p226 (MB Pictures).

The authors would like to thank the following for their part in helping to put this book together:

Andrew Greenaway and idiotbastard.bravehost.com
Mark Bennett
Louise Sugrue
findadeath.com
findagrave.com
rocksbackpages.com
sleazeroxx.com
MOJO magazine

Uncut magazine
Last Train To Memphis: The Rise of Elvis Presley (Peter Guralnick)
  Abacus, 1995.
Careless Love: The Unmaking of Elvis Presley (Peter Guralnick)
  Little, Brown, 1995
Knocking on Heaven's Door (Nick Talevski) Omnibus, 2006
Number One in Heaven: The Heroes who Died for Rock 'n' Roll (Jeremy Simmonds)
  Penguin, 2006.